I0750744

Chas. A. Sumner

POEMS:

BY

SAMUEL B. SUMNER

AND

CHARLES A. SUMNER.

NEW YORK:
THE AUTHORS' PUBLISHING COMPANY.
1877.

DEDICATION.

TO THE MEMORY OF OUR MOTHER,

PLUMA AMELIA BARSTOW SUMNER,

LONG SINCE DEAD, FROM WHOSE CULTURED LIPS WE LEARNED OUR FIRST AND BEST LESSONS, THIS VOLUME IS AFFECTIONATELY INSCRIBED.

PREFACE.

THE following verses and rhymes, written at different periods of our lives, and alternating from grave to gay, will not lack variety at least ; and will afford some entertainment, we trust, to all classes of our readers. Several pieces may be deemed lacking in dignity or poetic art, many are juvenile compositions, and many are of special local interest ; but for reasons which will be obvious, and by advice of those whose judgment we value, we insert them in this collection. Not without timidity, but relying upon the public indulgence, we launch this little venture on the uncertain sea.

CONTENTS.

PAGE.

POEMS.

THE TRUE LIFE;

A RHYMED SERMON,

DELIVERED ON SEVERAL OCCASIONS.

In earlier days, before life's troubled sea
Had oped the vortex of its cares for me;
When, to my youthful and enraptured glance,
Stretched out afar its beautiful expanse,
Luring the voyager, by the charming scene,
To launch forth, hopeful, on its breast serene;
When youth was fresh, and boyhood could descry
No cloud of threat'ning in the distant sky;
When, unencumbered with the toils of life,
Its whirl of business, and incessant strife,
The hours sped on, with grateful leisure fraught,
With scope for fancy and untrammeled thought;
Freedom to stroll through Academus' shades,
To con the classics, and to woo the maids;
Each wingéd pleasure in its flight to seize,
And idly wanton in the lap of ease;
Ah, then, my muse! in many a rhythmic line,
Gave I my offerings at thy sacred shrine!

In many a sonnet, fashioned by thine aid,
Some new Dulcinea saw her charms portrayed;
O'er many a pun, in sportive numbers drest,
My list'ning chum applauded with a zest;
To many a crude conception of the brain,
Provoking mirthful, or satiric strain,
Reserved from Fancy's evanescent throng—
Thou gav'st a being, and a garb, in song.

Remorseless years! amid whose length'ning train,
O'er the broad waste of time's extended plain,
Close on your footsteps, in a concourse vast,
Stalk the weird spectres of the fading Past;
Mark ye, how yonder, in despairing gloom,
What splendid hopes have found their early tomb!
See in those forms, with cypress wreaths entwined,
What tearful mem'ries ye have left behind!
See, fallen prostrate with insensate clods,
The crumbled relics of those household gods!
See brave resolves, begot in pomp and state,
Consigned in silence to an early fate;
See grand beginnings vanish into air,—
The things that were, and not the things that wear—
See even Genius veil its sacred fire,
Its flame, uncherished, suffered to expire;

See many a wild, yet beautiful idea,—
Too transcendental for our mundane sphere,—
Nipped at its budding, in a soul intent
On notions coupled with their—ten per cent.!

To deal with facts;—to banish earlier dreams;
To clutch the baubles which the world esteems;
To grasp the work-day, "practical" ideas,
We enslave the thought, and dedicate the years!
In sharp pursuit of worldly fame, or pelf,
Our first is bartered for our second self.
Unlike, dissentient, when we join the two,
Our life entire is monstrous to the view.
No graceful outline, no symmetric whole
Attests the healthful progress of the soul.
No pleasing fitness of the parts combined,
Shows the true culture of th' immortal mind.
So oft we note, in our maturer years,
How faint a semblance of our youth appears.
We cheat our nature of its first estate;
Some powers we fetter; some we stimulate.
Some tastes we stifle, which the soul prefers,
To please our clients, or our customers.
Some light, mayhap, which we were born to shed,
We cloak and smother, for the sake of bread;

While some lone talent,—singled out, perchance,
The veriest creature of a circumstance,—
We task and torture to our being's end,
Because, forsooth, it yields—a dividend!

Not so, the great, eternal Source of mind,
Its education and its growth designed.
To use not one, but all His gifts to man,
Is to fulfill the wise creative plan.
No vain appendage—no superfluous taste,
No talent given for neglect or waste,
Came from His hand, who graciously imbued
Man with His essence, and pronounced him good.

The dearest homage which the soul can show
To its great Author, is, itself to know.
Itself to cherish and develop here,
As ripening only for a higher sphere.
As but rehearsing on the stage of time,
For that grand Drama—awful and sublime—
When the vast Drop-scene shall be rolled away,
The glorious Hereafter to display!
When Heaven's full orchestra their strain begin,
And the Forever shall be ushered in!

The sure philosophy of life to learn,
And then to practice, is our chief concern.

The wisest, happiest method to pursue;
To shun the false—tô cultivate the true.
Not all alike, in power, and skill, and grace,
Hath the great God endowed the human race;—
Some, life's abstruser mysteries may sound,
And tread the caverns of the deep profound;
Others, on Fancy's airy wing may fly
To scenes unwitnessed by the vulgar eye.
Some, 'neath the lordly portals of the brain,
Their royal visitants may entertain;
Guests, that from far ideal realms have come,
To find with mortals a congenial home.
Not all, alike, in goodly shape, and fair,
The tabernacle of the Soul prepare,
Profuse with decoration—fitly wrought
To wait th' indwelling of the new-born thought;
Yet 'tis no partial Hand that first outpours
Upon our race these intellectual stores;
Nor hath thy fellow reason to avow
Himself more blest, more fortunate, than thou.
Each, in his own unique, peculiar plan,
Hath the beginnings of a perfect man.
Nay, e'en the basest brother of our kind,
In the recesses of his dormant mind,
Some germs—all undeveloped—may behold,
Which might have reproduced an hundred fold.

Blame thou not Nature, but thy froward will,
Who fail'st a glorious mission to fulfill.
To thine own self, and Nature's laws be true;
Keep life's great purpose in thy constant view;
Live less for Time, nor set such priceless store
By paltry pebbles on the barren shore,
But lift thy gaze, O mortal! to descry
The boundless ocean and the starry sky.
Learn well the mysteries of thy first degree;
Conform what is, to that which is to be;
So, when thy brief apprenticeship shall end,
From corner-stone and base thou may'st ascend;
In grand proportions may thy structure rise—
Its lofty towers upreared against the skies—
Till, master-builder, lastly thou shalt come
To crown thy life-work with its lordly dome!

In the great reck'ning at the final day,
When the recording angel shall display
The grand sum-total; and our life appears
By thoughts computed—not by length of years—
That life the truest and the best may seem,
Which mortals scoffed at, as an idle dream.
Perchance the dreamer, disenthralled, shall stand
Preferred disciple, at his Lord's right hand;
While hover 'neath the empyrean skies,
Souls of the thrifty, and the worldly-wise!

Thrice blest the pilgrim on Life's thorny road,
Which leads him onward to his long abode,
Who, while he fails not duly to bestow
A just attention to affairs below,
Regards these only at their real worth,
Nor barters heaven for a patch of earth.
Who ne'er forgets, amid his round of toil,
How unsubstantial is this mortal coil.
With ready will, to earn his bread attends,
But ne'er confounds life's means with life's great ends.
Who deems it not man's paramount pursuit
To build a factory, or to make a boot;
Nor thinks his duty hath been wholly done,
Who leaves a fortune to his darling son.
Who loves to search within his storied mind,
Some sparkling jewel of a thought to find.
Who keeps some inner chamber of the heart
From life's concerns and cankering ills apart,
Where, oft withdrawing, weary and depressed,
His spirit finds a solace, and a rest.
Who glads the ear with music, and the eye
With forms of beauty loves to gratify.
Who walks with sages that have gone before,
And treads a measure with the bards of yore.
Who loves at times in cheerful way to spend
A social evening with a pleasant friend.

Who prizes books, and sedulously heeds
The word of truth he garners as he reads.
Loves a bright hearth, with happy faces round;
A family board, with wholesome plenty crowned;
Loves to do alms; promotes each noble cause;
Communes with nature, and reveres her laws;
Free from the touch of time's corroding tooth,
Learns the choice secret of eternal youth;
Learns to subdue each rebel passion's rage,
And glides from manhood to serene old age.
In fine, who lives a life of generous aim;
Lives not alone for power, or wealth, or fame;
Lives to develop as a perfect whole
The various traits that constitute the soul;
So, at the harvest-time, himself to yield
A sheaf, well ripened, in the Master's field.

I know, the world, time-servient, disagrees
With vain ideas and heresies like these;
I know full well what sages will dissent
From such a strain of idle sentiment;
I know the proverbs of the worldly-wise,
What plans of thought and action they advise;
How small the orbit, how confined the groove,
Within whose limits they exhort to move;
But I believe, the two extremes between,
Our better sense may find the golden mean.

That while avoiding a contracted sphere,
Which quite absorbs us in its one idea;
And while, with like disfavor, we disown
The jack-at-all-trades, or the lazy drone;
A liberal course our steps may still pursue,
To human kind, and human nature, true.

Poor slave of Mammon! though thy sordid brain
Be steeped with lust of pleasure or of gain;
Within thy bosom thou may'st yet behold
A wealth more precious than thy heaps of gold.
A gem so brilliant, it can far outshine
The choicest product of Golconda's mine.
A vital spark from the celestial flame,
Which now and ever must exist the same.
It is thy soul; to slavish bondage doomed—
Nay, 'tis thyself, O man! thou has entombed!
See with what layers of avarice and of guilt,
Thine own dark sepulchre thyself hast built!
See how thy purer hopes and joys have fled
To habitations of the early dead!
See life's sweet graces, its emotions kind,
The holy ties that love and friendship bind;
Th' inspiring glories of creation,—all
Shut out and banished from thy prison wall!

See, one by one, the harsh obstructions roll
Before the windows of thy buried soul!
One opening still admits its ghostly light,
To show the ruin, to appal the sight;—
Ah! 'tis thy faithful memory! would'st thou gaze
Out from thy dungeon at those earlier days?
One glance, remorseful, sorrowing, wouldst thou cast
Along the mournful vista of the past?
See then thy childhood, with its sports beguiled;
By selfish care and avarice undefiled;
Its golden moments, pure and unalloyed,
In guileless thoughts and gentle deeds employed.
See thy bark launched on youth's enticing stream,
Whose ripples glisten 'neath the morning beam;
See the glad banks in vernal freshness bloom,
And flowers that breathe a ravishing perfume;
While Hope—the siren—to the voyager sings,
And beck'ning onward, waves her shining wings.

Well might thy vision seek to linger there,
Amid a scene so bright, so passing fair!
Fain wouldst thou deem the picture all complete,—
No mortal life could hail a dawn more sweet,—
But look! how soon the swelling stream runs high,
The storm-king threatens in the angry sky;

The troubled waves their cheerless banks divide,
While the sad Hours stand up on either side,
To tell the number of thy past misdeeds,
Like hooded friars, counting o'er their beads!

Could we unlock their chambers, and disclose
In human hearts, their multitude of woes;
Could we but half the agonies reveal,
Which placid brows and studied smiles conceal;
Our souls would own the picture strangely true,
The faithful Muse would offer to the view.
Alas! how many a wreck in human mould,
Consumed with passion or the lust of gold,
Lives only to pervert creative plan,
And dies, the shameful counterfeit of man!
Our educations, and the vicious rules,
Which so obtain in Fashion's latest schools;
The standards of our modern excellence,
The praise accorded unto base pretence;
The sycophantic homage often shown
Toward foppish idiots for the wealth they own;
The estimate of man by what is his;
By what he has, and not by what he is;
That "aristocracy," which seeks to find
The wealth of purse, and not the wealth of mind;

Which greets plain worth with supercilious laugh,
But fawns obsequious round a golden calf;
That eager thirst for gold, which scruples not
At means unworthy, so it may be got;
Which buries all else in a common grave,
And grudges time to grasp, and hoard, and save;
These, with their kindred causes, serve to bind
And dwarf the nobler impulses of mind.
These make our life a disproportioned whole,
And thwart the expectations of the soul.
Yet he who rashly ventures to assail
The social wrongs and vices which prevail,
Is deemed a mad fanatic, or a fool,
Whose verdant notions should be sent to school.
'Tis little sympathy the world bestows
On him who seeks its follies to expose;
And that enthusiast, who with ardor warm,
Plants, in his dreams, the standard of reform;
Who fondly thinks to part the clouds away,
And hail the dawn of the millennial day,
May well take heed, lest he erelong shall be
At Mammon's shrine, himself a votary.
For so the world, with its mysterious charms,
Our earlier impulse and intent disarms,
That he who first with brave assurance vows
Mankind's amelioration to espouse,

Or, less combative, hopes to keep aloof,
And shun the rabble 'neath a quiet roof,
Little by little, yields him to the tide,
And downward floats, the motley crew beside.
Thus, in his progress, proves the adage true,—
"Dwellers at Rome must do as Romans do!"
So fares the world;—so, none of Adam's seed;—
No rank, profession, school, position, creed,
Escapes from Mammon's avaricious clutch,
Or shuns his all-contaminating touch.
Thus, in one scale, untrue, but still obeyed,
Actions and motives everywhere are weighed.
By one false test, incessantly applied,
Man's daily conduct is discussed and tried.

All-potent Mammon! like a monarch throned,
O'er the broad earth thy sovereign power is owned!
And—strange to tell—where freedom vaunteth most,
And counts her empire a peculiar boast—
There Mammon holds his most distinguished court,
Where willing subjects faithfully resort.
There, abject mortals, servient 'neath his nod,
Acknowledge him their ruler and their god.
There, too, he finds, to guard his regal state,
On every hand a zealous advocate.

As some rich rogue, his knaveries to hide,
Keeps able counsel ever at his side,
Retained, their skill and eloquence to lend,
Their client's fame and fortune to defend;
To blink the point, and make "His Honor" see
Vast odds 'twixt tweedle-dum and tweedle-dee;—
So Mammon lacks not, in these latter days,
A host of minions who can chant his praise,
Extol his glories, magnify his fame,
And fling the cloak of custom o'er his shame.

And so the Press, whose once united tone
Might drive each despot from his lawless throne;
Whose voice, concordant for the truth and right,
The world might rescue from its moral blight—
Perverts its power; and busily repeats
The idle talk and jabber of the streets.
Panders to passion, and to morbid taste;
Observes the current, and with eager haste
Adopts the tenets of the winning side,
And floats conspicuous with the rushing tide.
Confined by ties of party, or of sect,
The general weal it cares not to effect;
Of demagogues and knaves the pliant tool,
And selfish interest its guiding rule,

It aims the public ear to tickle well,
And make the paper, or the volume, sell.

Nay, e'en the Pulpit—such is Mammon's power—
Shapes oft its tenets to the passing hour;
Its doctrine moulds to suit the hearers' views,
And, like a mirror, must reflect the pews.
Here, where we look for Truth's peculiar source—
Where thought from time should hold its brief divorce;
Whither approaching, with a reverent awe,
To hear God's word, and learn his sacred law,
The world's concerns and cares should ne'er intrude,
But hearts should flow with love and gratitude;
Where all should meet—high, humble, rich and poor,
And leave their false distinctions at the door;—
As worms, alike predestined, and for whom
The same great Leveler opens wide the tomb;—
See, even here, with patronizing smile,
How Mammon, proud and pompous, treads the aisle!
And sits quiescent, with a slumberous eye,
While Reverend Cream Cheese hums a lullaby.
Here Fashion's votaries, in a vast array,
Convene to hold their weekly gala-day;
And while the sinners for forgiveness sue,
Their hats and flounces pass in sharp review!

Go search through Christendom where'er we may,
We witness Mammon's universal sway.
In each department of our social state,
He stamps his impress with a crushing weight;
And leads his subjects passively along,
A blinded duped, infatuated throng!
Ah! when will mortals from their follies turn,
The simple theory of life to learn?
With faithful vision see and own a truth,
Which nature shows us in our early youth;
Regard life only for its nobler ends,
And live as brothers, and as generous friends;
As fellow-travelers toward that common bourne,
From whose mysterious confines none return.

My hope is slender—but I can conceive
How man his social errors might retrieve;
Pursue a course by selfish care unvexed,
And so spend this life as t' insure the next.
I can conceive a social state, wherein
The strifes, the bickerings, the discordant din,
Insane excitements, mutual distrusts,
Unholy passions and unbridled lusts,—
Might all be banished from our midst away,
And Reason hold her kind and gentle sway.
"There is no joy but calm, the spirit sings,
Why should we toil, the roof and crown of things!"

Could we our possibilities but see,
How near a Heaven this earth of ours might be!
Behold its glories, lavishly outspread
Around us, and beneath, and overhead!
Mark how, as myriad eyes, whose glance is love,
The stars smile down upon us from above;
And softly close their eyelids, one by one,
As through the startled ether soars the sun;
His coursers guiding o'er the vast highway,
That spans from East to West, the realms of Day!
See, o'er the face of this terrestrial ball,—
In hill, and vale, and lake, and waterfall;
In fountain, river, rill and ocean wave;
In mountain-dome, and hoary cliff and cave;
In tree and shrub,—in foliage and in flower;
In shady grove, and in sequestered bower;
In rolling prairies, and in grassy glades,
What wondrous beauty everything pervades!
Then see, responsive to a moderate toil,
How Plenty leaps out from the teeming soil!
How Earth from out her rich, exhaustless stores,
Yields up her minerals and her shining ores;—
Her varied products, neither sparse nor few,
Enough for comfort and for luxury too.
Kind Nature meant not that a single one
Of all her children, 'neath her generous sun,

Should starve; or suffer from the galling chain,
Which Want imposes in its cruel reign;
While some proud neighbor, with a wealth untold,
Should hoard his treasures of superfluous gold—
The fruit of speculation, out of which
He woke some morning to be labeled "rich"—
'Twas never meant that some should pampered be,
While others feel the pinch of poverty;
That mother Earth, upon her fruitful breast,
Should surfeit half her babes, and starve the rest!

Methinks some strange perversion hath been wrought
From that original creative Thought,
Which turned to shape in Earth, and gave control
To Man, as lord and ruler of the whole.
A strange perversion, which, increasing through
The lapse of ages since the world was new,
Hath come to make of this our social life,
A scene of jealous and discordant strife;
To make our race to false restraints conform,
And one worm lord it o'er his fellow-worm.
This man, to-day, exults in pride and power,
Pet child of fate, and hero of the hour.
With cool disdain he treats the humble poor,
Who turn, awe-stricken, from the rich man's door.

But mark how Fortune with its fickle glow,
Loves to dispense alternate weal and woe.
Another generation turns the scale ;
The poor grow rich ; the wealthy bankers fail ;
And they, whose fathers, only yesterday,
With golden sceptre held a potent sway,
Now in their turn pursue the walks of toil,
While beggars' offspring occupy the soil.
Our life's a see-saw, marked with ups and downs ;
A curious mixture, both of smiles and frowns ;
A treacherous sea, whose surface, calm to-day,
Yawns wide to-morrow to engulph its prey.
And yet, strange man! unschooled through all the years,
Along whose course life's vanity appears,
The will-o'-wisp of fortune still pursues,
The self same chase persistently renews.
Lives, not to gather that substantial good,
Which shall go with him o'er the Stygian flood;
Not those possessions, which shall last sublime,
Beyond the empire and the waste of time :
Not that ripe soul, which, rising o'er the sod,
In full perfection shall ascend to God ;
But such mere baubles as the hour affords,
With tireless zeal and industry, he hoards;

Pursues each worthless phantom as it flies;
And so toils on, till that last enterprise
Of getting buried, claims the shrinking thought,
And one word tells his simple record—"Nought!"

If half the hours we toil were set apart
For generous culture of the mind and heart;
If, while sojourning on time's transient shore,
We trifled less, and thought and felt the more;
If all united with an equal zeal
In temporal duties for the common weal;
And not as now, one labored to excess,
While his rich brother lolled in idleness;
If all reserved, from daily cares aside,
An ample leisure, wisely occupied;
The world, methinks, would still move on apace,
And healthier progress would attend the race.
Our art, and science, and inventive skill;
The loom, the sledge, the plow-share and the mill,
The calls of industry on land and main,
Would still invoke their patrons not in vain.
Then most, I ween, of progress we should find
In the rich growth and onward march of mind;
In the rare studies which so well impart
The choicest graces to the human heart;

In the sweet social pleasures, kindly given
As earthly foretastes of the joys of Heaven.
A life more real, earnest, manly, free,
This life ideal we should find to be.
Peace, like a river, through our midst would flow,
And earth become a paradise below.
The same great Power that overruleth all;
Fashions the orbs, and notes the sparrow's fall;
That bids us for the morrow take no thought,
But seize the boon the present hour hath brought;
For man's necessities would still dispense
The boundless favors of Omnipotence.
And if, perchance, each temporal estate
Should yield its increase at a slower rate;
If unto each, with competence content,
His capital should yield a less per cent;
If sea and continent should greet our eyes
With fewer fruits of worldly enterprise:
Yet if, instead, to bless the human race,
More thought, more love, and charity had place;
If all within this mighty brotherhood
Preferred the lasting to the transient good;
Such would be wisdom's part; and we might then
Have poorer fabrics, but have better men.

There is who hath not, yet hath wealth untold—
Better than rubies, or than shining gold.
There is who hath, and yet so poor is he,
No words can show his depth of poverty.
There is a solid wealth, which hath no end,
Which pays its dividends though banks suspend;
And whose possessor, though a peasant's son,
Consorts with nobles, and himself is one.
Give me this wealth, and though in humble sphere
I keep my calling while I sojourn here;
Yet not the gold of Ophir, nor the gems
From India's cave, nor royal diadems
Can buy the passport I shall bear with me,
To earth's and heaven's "best society."
There is a sweet refreshment in the thought
Of dignity too precious to be bought.
There is a badge of manhood, whoso owns,
May scorn distinctions, and look down on thrones;
Despise conventional decrees and rules,
And bear complacently the sneers of fools.
The man who entertains within his breast
A ducal Soul, as an abiding guest,
Accounts no honor paramount to that:
He is your only true aristocrat.

All things are his ; his park is the whole land ;*
His bath the sea, his walk the ocean strand ;
The forests and the rivers he shall own ;
The mountain summit is his lofty throne ;
He shall possess, where, in their little day,
Others as tenants, and as boarders, stay.
He shall be lord of land, and sea, and air ;
Where e'er snow falls, or water flows, or where
The birds take joyous wing the dawn to greet ;
Where day and night in sombre twilight meet ;
Where e'er the heaven is hung with cloudy forms,
Or sown with stars, or terrible with storms ;
Where e'er are outlets into space above ;
Where e'er is danger, wonder, awe, or love ;
There sheddeth beauty, plenteous as the rain,
For him, proud monarch of the vast domain.
Each voice, for him, shall have a meaning sound ;
And though he walk the spacious earth around ;
He shall discover in each proffered boon,
Nothing ignoble, or inopportune.

Cease now, my muse, thy unaccustomed strain,
And seek thine old retirement once again.

---

* This, and the following nineteen lines, are a paraphrase of an extract from R. W. Emerson's Essay, "The Poet."

If thou has uttered but one earnest word,
These list'ning friends have treasured as they heard;
If one true sentiment thou hast expressed,
Which finds an answering echo in each breast;
Then well hast thou performed the pleasing task,
And vouchsafed all thy humble bard could ask.

S. B. S.

MUSIC.

THERE'S music in the winds :
Whether they whisper gently thro' the trees,
Or sweep tempestuous across the seas,
Or waft sweet perfumes in the evening breeze ;
There's music in the winds.

There's music in the streams :
That break their waters down the craggy steep,
Or o'er the shining pebbles gaily leap,
Or seaward roll, in channels broad and deep ;—
There's music in the streams.

There's music in the fields :
The verdant meads that stretch across the plain,
The sloping hill-side, orchard, pasture, lane,
The crops of yellow corn and waving grain ;
There's music in the fields.

There's music in the woods :
The wildernesses where the fleet hind roves,
The sighing pine-cliffs and the vocal groves,
Where bird-choirs hymn their praises, plaints, and loves ;—
There's music in the woods.

There's music in the sea :
The diapason of old Ocean's roar,
Whose wild waves in perpetual encore
Rehearse their glad Te Deum evermore ;—
There's music in the sea.

There's music in the storms :
That run their courses over heaven's highway,
And turn the day to night—the night to day ;
Whose thunders rattle, and whose lightnings play ;—
There's music in the storms.

There's music in the stars :
That fair Astarte's queenly robes adorn ;
That sang together at creation's morn,
When, at Jehovah's mandate, Earth was born ;—
There's music in the stars.

There's music through the whole
Of Nature's realm ; around, beneath, above ;
Where e'er our eyes we turn—where e'er we rove ;—
But sweetest of all music far, is Love :
The music of the soul !

S. B. S.

THE IRRETRIEVABLE.

THE sun is falling in the west;
His last beams cut the billow's crest,
Snow-white with the glistening foam;
For the choicest waters are filtered up
To the rolling brim of old Neptune's cup,
As the sea-bird's welcome home;
And the Fleet-Wing's sails are gaily drest
With the rainbow tints, so fondly prest
On the gracefully swelling dome.

The grand old clouds drawn closely round,
Present the Day-king, enthroned and crowned,
In his fullest glory dying;
And to travel that beautiful silver road
To the golden gate of my Lord's abode,
The spirit is sorrowfully sighing!

* * * *

The sun is set; his work is done;
And the timid moon has just begun
To cast her shadows, thin and pale,
As I take my watch on the gallant deck,
To descry the distant loom or speck,
That betokens land or sail.

Now the sea runs high, and the sweeping blast
With its angry stroke sways the mizzen-mast;
  Every timber crackles sharp;
And hark! on the quivering shroud and stay,
Old Boreas' icy fingers play
In mournful numbers, and numbers gay;
O list to the sailor's harp!

I welcome the hour, so fit for thought
On what the past with its woes has wrought;
I mark—with what grief!—how awfully fraught
  Was the simplest word and deed;
Ay, the crisis acts of my life are known
From the lowliest impulse and hope to have grown—
In a heedless hour was widely strown
  The poisonous, blasting seed.

But no! this night I will banish care,—
The heavens above are transcendently fair,—
My soul, like the orbs that are glittering there
  Above the troublous waves,
That once and now against me beat,
Shall rise, and gaze, but only greet
The pleasant sea, the temperate sheet;
Alone the forms and faces meet
Which in old times did seem so sweet,
That now I scarcely dare repeat,—

"Some sleep! I know the vacant seat!
I've seen the grass-grown graves!"

From earliest hours my life I trace;
And halting memory's rapid pace,—
I linger round each cherished place;
I kiss each bending, tearful face;—
Low, soothing, deep-breathed peace.
I mind me of the gladsome child
On whom a tender mother smiled;
A boy by purest sports beguiled;
Whose heart, uncankered, undefiled,
From Faith knew no release.

I wake. "O Heaven!" I almost scream—
"Prolong this soul-enrapturing dream!
What I have been, but let me seem!
At the first fountains of Time's stream,
To catch a single passing beam
Of Innocency, let me lie!"
Like a half-drownéd wretch I rise,
And far beyond the gathering skies,
A cruel fiend returns my cries;
My God the cravéd boon denies;
I gasp with downcast, tearful eyes,
"Would God that I could die!"

I never more shall dare contrast
The present woe with the lovely past.
My doom is sealed; the die is cast;
I cannot differ from the last.
For hark! Hear the heavy death-bells toll!
And look! How the dead possibilities roll
In a long dark line to the Judgment goal!
This day, this hour with judgments is foal;
But the joys of my youth shed the gloom of my soul!

C. A. S.

FLEETWING, at Sea, off Cape Horn, September 6, 1856.

A VALENTINE.

Lady, 'twas on this day,
As old traditions say,
    That Love was born.
It was a gladsome birth,
Fit cause for joy and mirth
Among the sons of Earth—
    A race forlorn.

On this, his natal day,
Young Cupid—blithe and gay—
    His pastime takes.
The cause of Love he fights;
Fond hearts in bliss unites;
The torch of Hymen lights;
    Its flame awakes.

His well-directed dart
Has pierced me; and my heart
    Beats tremulous.
O, Lady, may thine own
Beat in sweet unison,
And Love's pure flame alone
    Be born in us!

S. B. S.

VALENTINE—TO L——.

I wish that I could say to you
The words that would convey to you
    The measure of my love;
But language isn't strong enough,
Nor are our meetings long enough,
Nor are there strains of song enough
    Its height and depth to prove.

'Tis that which causeth pain for me;
'Tis so entirely vain for me
    To utter all I feel;
And I am conscious all the while,
As we the charming hours beguile,
How somewhat doubtingly you smile
    At what I can't reveal.

O, I am sure, that if you knew,
And read my inmost feelings through,
    You could but yield return
Of love for love; which, come what will,
Through all the future can but thrill
This heart; and on its altars still,
    Forevermore shall burn!

S. B. S.

ONE VALENTINE'S NIGHT.

WHAT long ago I might have read—
  Had fortified myself to know—
So long the waiting deadened dread,
  And friendship's hopes began to grow—

But yesternight, while conning o'er
  A journal from the dear old place,
I saw—what I had skipped before—
  The grieving tidings, face to face!

I'd held the paper as a screen
  Against the blazing on the hearth;
But when I saw what was between—
  Two aged deaths and one small birth—

My hands dropped with a nerveless grasp;
  I stared into the very flame;
Then wonder if my crimson cheeks
  Were scorched with fire or flushed with shame.

The desert winds blow in a moan!
  The good flag's halliards whip the staff;—
The one—the music of a groan,—
  And one, the mocking of a laugh.

Let the derisive sounds concert
  Suggestive, tantalizing chants;
In pauses we may introvert,
  And spring a strength from Nature's taunts.

Out of a sadness may we bring
  A nameless sweetness, which belongs
To olden times, and takes the sting
  From sighs and semblances of wrongs.

Though much has passed to leave regret,
  Some cherished memories remain;
The woe I brave or can forget:
  Blow, dreary winds, across the plain!

C. A. S.

Fort Churchill, Nev. Ter.,
February 14, 1864.

AFTER A LOVER'S QUARREL.

On her brow, clouds of anger were blended,
While sorrow sat heavy on mine;
In a mad moment I had offended,
And she bade me depart from her shrine;—
A shrine I so fondly had knelt at,
And decked with my darlingest flowers;
A shrine I in rapture had dwelt at,
In my life's most enrapturing hours.

And so I go forth, sad and lonely,—
Tormenting regret in my soul;—
Sweet fruit turned to ashes; and only
A wretchedness passing control.
And so all my path seems o'ershaded,
And the saddest of lessons I learn;
And I mourn with a conscience upbraided,
Lost joys that may never return.

One hope I shall timidly cherish;—
It is in her bosom to find
A heart, which, though love itself perish,
Can never be other than kind:
A heart so forgiving and tender,
No hate can endure there long while.
O, Heaven, from all ill defend her!
O God! change her frown to a smile!—S. B. S.

ODE;

SUNG AT FOURTH OF JULY CELEBRATION, GREAT BARRINGTON, MASS., JULY 4TH, 1850.

(AIR:—"America.")

WITH joy we celebrate
This day, from which we date
Our Nation's birth;
Day when that patriot band
For freedom took their stand,
And made Columbia's land
The pride of earth.

This day, let East and West,
With equal favors blest,
Sing freedom's song;
Let North and South, to-day,
Cast all their strife away,
And, joined in glad array,
The strain prolong.

Stayed be the impious hands
That seek to hurl the brands
Of discord round;
Still let our rallying cry
Of "Union" rise on high,

Till regions far and nigh
    Shall catch the sound.

God ! 'neath whose watchful eye,
All things in earth and sky
    Fulfill their end ;
Guide Thou our Ship of State
Secure through Peril's strait ;
Still grant propitious fate,
    And still defend !

So shall its towering form,
Unscathed through wind and storm
    Ride on its way ;
Our favored land shall be
The home of liberty ;
Her sons shall worship Thee,
    And Thee obey.

S. B. S.

WHY I WEEP.

I WEEP as I look on thee, obdurate fair one,
So lavish of smiles, and so charming to view;
So ready in meshes of love to ensnare one,
And leave him heart-broken, to find thee untrue.

I weep as I think the bright dreams of to-day
Must give place to regretful awak'ning to-morrow;
That these pleasure-wing'd moments so soon must away,
And the sunshine of love be o'erclouded with sorrow.

I weep as I think that the heart I so prize
Is reserved for some other, more favored, more blest;
That some other shall bask in the light of those eyes,
Of those heavenly smiles for a lifetime possessed.

So, whenever henceforth thou beholdest me weeping,
O think of the heart that implores to be thine;
Of the tender affections consigned to thy keeping,
And the pure vows I fain would present at thy shrine.

And, whenever thy 'kerchief to mine waves reply,
And thine eyes beam upon me like beams of the sun,
I will shed one more tear, I will heave one more sigh,
For I feel thou art jesting, and only in fun.

S. B. S.

VALENTINE.

CRUEL one! it's hardly fair
Thus to steal one's heart, I say!
'Tis a treasure quite too rare
To be wrested thus away.
Have some mercy, pr'ythee, do!
And the stolen heart restore.
Henceforth, then, I promise you,
I'll expose myself no more.

Or, if you should think it best,
In return to give me thine;
So we'll let the matter rest,
I'll take yours, and you keep mine.
Or, (I'm not disposed to falter,
Since this mischief is begun.)
Drawing near to Hymen's altar,
Let us join them both in one!

S. B. S.

A SONG FOR THE BOYS.

HURRA boys! Life's conflict is opening before us;
With many a foe to be valiantly met;
Let our banner be raised, let it proudly wave
o'er us;
With firm hearts and true, we'll be conquerors
yet!

Press on without fear,—all forebodings dispelled,
By doubts undismayed, nor by menaces awed;—
Press on, nor let action, nor struggle be quelled,
While Error and Vice are seen stalking abroad.

High stations of honor are waiting us now;
Proud triumphs, and lasting rewards may be
ours;
And anon, shall adorn each victorious brow
The evergreen wreath, decked with Fame's fairest
flowers.

Our fathers before us fought nobly and well;
Be it ours to continue what they have begun;
So that history's page alike proudly may tell
Of the patriot sire, and the patriot son.

Then let's on to the strife, boys! our banners unfurled,—
Our weapons unsheathed, and our bright armor on;
Let our watch-word be truth; let our field be the world,
In the triumph of right be the victory won!

S. B. S.

IRELAND'S OPPORTUNITY.

A YANKEE'S ADDRESS TO THE FENIANS.

HOW LONG have ye cherished for Erin, in vain,
The hope to behold her a nation again?
How long on her neck is the Britisher's heel?
How long has his mocking returned her appeal?

Lo! now is the day-spring, ye pris'ners of Hope!
The strength of your arms with the tyrants may cope;
For the vows of our land with this promise are thrilled:
The woe-time of Erin is nearly fulfilled.

When the tocsin of war from our brothers went forth,
And the patriots poured from their homes in the North;
'Mong the first in the line, with their Banner of Green,
Were the boys who *court-martialed* the son of a Queen.

And on the first field that our soldiers contest—
Undisciplined, though of the bravest and best—

Waving far in the van, lone in triumph was seen,
By the Flag of our Country, that banner of
Green!

From Hatteras Inlet to Lexington's streams,
The Ensign of Erin exultingly gleams;
At Vicksburg and Hudson 'tis dauntless unfurled,
Up the cloud-circled mountain resistlessly hurled!

In Sherman's grand marching it heads a brigade;
In skirmish or battle, manœuvre or raid;
From Generals commanding, to privates in file,
You may number the sons of the Emerald Isle!

Shall we fail to remember, now Peace has re-
turned,
Their fame in our vict'ries so valiantly earned?
Shall we fail to remember "Neutrality's Queen,"
By supporting the yeomen now "wearing the
green?"

Oh, no! Speed the time when the Briton must
yield
To Fenian and Yankee the freedom-lit field!
When his plunder our Nation will make him dis-
gorge,
Or tear from his bunting the cross of St. George!

And when from our Navy each ocean shall be
To the commerce of England a bottomless sea:
As our Flag from the spankers of frigates are seen,
While the mast flies the Harp-blazoned Banner of
Green!

C. A. S.

VIRGINIA CITY, NOV. 23. 1865.

TO HELEN.

Now pr'ythee, dear Nell,
Don't affect such a swell,
Nor take on in such terrible fashion :
I've told you before,
That it vexes me sore,
When I see a sweet face in a passion.

I think it's too bad,
You should go and get mad,
And that, too, in despite of my coaxing—
I really supposed,
When at first you disclosed
So much anger, you only were hoaxing.

But be this as it may :
If it be as you say—
And I certainly hav'n't a doubt of it—
I mean to hold fast
To the fun that is past,
And I know that you can't cheat me out of it.

Until life's sun is set,
I shall never forget
How with love we were, both of us, dying :

How I vowed to be true,
And, sweet rogue, so did you,
And we knew all the time each was ——!!!

So, Nelly, good-bye!
Do not squander a sigh,
Nor in sad melancholy grow thinner:
For how shameful 'twould be,
If you did so for me,
Such a vile, irreclaimable sinner!

Now, don't fling away
A poor "minstrel's last lay,"
But remember to what cause you owe it;
But for this fuss alone,
You might never have known
That your "dearest of friends" was a poet.

S. B. S.

THE FALL OF THE YEAR.

THE blighted flower, the rustling leaf,
The mournful winds that round us sigh,
Are tokens all of Nature's grief,
That summer's past, and winter nigh.

The King of Day, so bright erewhile,
From his high station looking down,
Seems hardly to vouchsafe a smile,
But sends aslant a sullen frown.

To kindlier climes the timid bird
Hies with his fond and gentle mate;
No longer is their warbling heard,
But all is drear and desolate!

So dies the year! its death how sad!
But 'tis not sadness of despair;
For spring again the earth shall glad,
Nature her robes of green shall wear.

So, though our life must pass away,
While time speeds on with restless wing;
Our souls shall hail a brighter day,
And flourish in eternal spring.

S. B. S.

HOPE.

Where does he live who cries "No lack;"
  Who lives not lacking all?
Who sends his faithful memory searching back,
  And ferrets out a hope that he may call
In very truth, one fully met?
  A yearning with a trust,
Chaste, dignified, high set,—
  Else 'twere no hope, but lust.

We never have our true desires;
  We hardly search aright;
Too soon appreciative sense expires;
  The circumstance is tardier than the right.
We have no answers, but in darkness grope.
  Life may be, should be, but a single hope;
For who but God of Heaven can furnish scope?

C. A. S.

LINES WRITTEN IN AN ALBUM.

There's a strange, unwonted feeling, thoughts of olden time revealing,
O'er my spirit softly stealing, like a magic-woven spell;
'Tis a feeling half of gladness, tho' 'tis deeply tinged with sadness,—
With a melancholy sadness, as I speak the word "farewell,"
And thy voice is heard to echo back the thrilling word "farewell!"

Thy remembrance I shall treasure with a sentiment of pleasure,
With an unbeclouded pleasure, until time with me shall end;
For, embalmed in recollection, there will be the sweet reflection,
That in undisguised affection, thou hast ever been a friend;
In my joy and in my sorrow, thou hast ever been a friend.

Fare thee well! tho' fate may sever, friendship's flame shall last forever,

Burning on and burning ever, while its incense rises high;
Till at last, when life is ending, angel voices sweetly blending,—
All harmoniously blending,—thou art welcomed to the sky,
And thou hast thy home forever—aye, forever—in the sky!

S. B. S.

TO A LADY

ON RECEIVING A BOUQUET OF FLOWERS.

LAST eve, as I strayed, to my wondering view
A fairy appeared, as at times fairies do:
From some bright world afar, to this dark one of
ours,
She had trippingly come, with a handful of flowers,
As fair as could blossom in valley or grove,
All speaking one language—the language of love;
And while I stood rapt, such a vision to see,
She blushingly smiled, and she gave them to me.

There were red and white roses, in bud and in
bloom,
Which vied in exhaling their choicest perfume;
And a sweet little pink showed its face here and
there,
As it breathed out its life on the soft evening air.
All these lent their fragrance, and others beside,
And the whole in a bunch with blue ribbon were
tied,
And I thought, as I gazed on their beauties com-
bined,
Such beauty, world over, I hardly could find.

All this of the flowers; but how shall I portray
The bright looks of her, so much fairer than they—
The beautiful giver; beneath whose sweet smile,
No wonder the flowers bloomed so richly the while.
Ah! well may my sullen, but sensible muse,
To attempt such a task of description refuse;
For grace so transcendent, the muse must confess,
No tongue can portray, and no language express.

But while memory lasts, and I ponder them o'er,
The bygones of youth and the blest days of yore,
Thine image, fair maiden, where'er thou shalt be,
Oft-times in sweet visions will come back to me.
These flowers I would cherish, must droop and decay—
Their ephemeral beauty must soon pass away;
But the maid who bestowed them—her radiant face—
In my happy remembrance shall still have a place.

S. B. S.

A COMBAT.

ORIGINALLY PUBLISHED IN THE SAN FRANCISCO HERALD.

One of the most determined and sanguinary canine conflicts anywhere recorded in history occurred in front of our sanctum, yesterday, between a couple of ordinary looking curs, with some interesting skirmishing by a gang of infuriated phists—(wonder if that is the correct orthography?)—and a general movement in the direction of the stampede by the animals of a half dozen butcher carts. For fifteen minutes the street was in an agonizing uproar, and excited men deliberately walked over each other in attempting to catch glimpses of the belligerent brutes, as the tide of battle carried them from one side of the thoroughfare to the other, against the heels of kicking horses and under the wheels of moving vehicles. They—— we can't begin to portray the scene in prose. Let us invoke the Muses, and measure off the picture in pentameter:

One was a cur of famed combative strain—
The English bull, with terrier intermixed—
Skin smooth and white, broad-breasted, ears erect,
Tail brief, eyes red, protruding under-jaw,

And all those points which men, versed in the art
Of canine conflict, view with favoring eyes.
A butcher owned him, and he strode the earth
Like one that deemed the better part his own.
The other was a shaggy, homely brute,
With coat unkemped, and drooping tail and ears,
And aspect mild, and deprecating mien.
His restless eye, and gaunt, ungainly shape,
Told that he lived neglected, and had earned,
By toilsome march for many a month gone by,
A bare subsistence of unwholesome food
Through desperate forays into kitchen yards,
And feats of reckless plunder everywhere.
He chanced, in passing by the butcher's stall,
To cast upon the fat and savory joints
A look of longing, yet with no intent
Of open seizure or of felony.
'Tis true, his hollow stomach tempted sore
The little virtue left by pinching want;
Still he resisted, and with measured trot
Was journeying onward, when the butcher's cur
Insolent with plenty, and with angry jaws
Still red with recent revels, upward sprang,
And after the retreating stranger sent
A growl of scorn. The latter stopped and turned—
The jeer and insult grated to the quick;

And with the fire of noble fathers dead
And turned to sausage, and with bristling back,
He boldly faced the scorner of the poor.
No word was uttered; each the other eyed,
And showed his teeth with sanguinary growl,
Hurling defiance and undying hate,
And courting combat in its direst form.
Around they walked, stiff-legged and menacing,
In circle, to survey the 'vantage ground;
Then with a howl of pent-up, smothered rage,
They sprang together, and the silent street
Roared with the tumult of the struggling dogs.
The fur flew. Then a score or less of curs
Mingled their voices with the general din.
Upreared they fought, and lying down they *fit*,
And through the street they rolled in noisy strife,
While plunging horses and excited men
Gave zest and glory to the combatants.
Approached the dogs unto the northern curb,
When——

But the character of an epic poem—in which category of literature we humbly class the above—will not permit us to give the result of the encounter in verse. It would render the production entirely too didactic. The *Iliad* leaves the fall of Troy to the historian, after burying its defender; we will, therefore, mention here that, after a prolonged struggle against the 'northern curb' alluded to in the poem, the dog of the butcher beat a yelping and cowardly retreat, leaving his plebeian foe master of the field. The return of the victor to the southern portion of the city will probably be made the basis of an 'Odyssey.'"

C. A. S.

BARNUM'S BABY SHOW.—1855.

WHO says the world moves not apace, in this our happy age,
When "Young America" so soon comes bouncing on the stage;
When e'en the babies, yet untaught to lisp a mother's name,
Forsake their cradles to compete for favor and for fame.

When Gotham holds her lofty seat, queen city of the nation,
Proud patroness of enterprise throughout the whole creation;
Whose voice from press and business mart, rolls out its potent thunders,
And last, not least, whose Barnum keeps the world agape with wonders!

Come one, come all, both old and young, and mingle in these scenes.
Come spinsters of uncertain age, and misses in your teens.

Ye rusty, crusty bachelors! shake off your false
alarms,
And boldly face our new recruits—our infantry in
arms!

Lo! from the four extremities of famous Yankee land,
Come juvenile competitors—a happy, hopeful band;
Babes fat and fair; triplets; ah me! a dozen pairs
of twins!
Thus some poor mortals suffer two-fold penance for
their sins!

Alas, that in this novel strife its prizes should be won,
At sacrifice of here and there some mother's darling
son;
Some bright one midst the family group, who reigns
without a peer,
Lured from his little realm to find a hundred rivals
here!

But surely, each maternal lip in triumph will declare
Her's was the loveliest offering; the fairest of the
fair;
The sweet delusion nature gave, still reigns within
her breast,
Each partial eye *its* jewel sees, the brightest and the
best!

Kind matrons! * on whose nod depend the fortunes of the hour,
Whose taste shall choose from out the wreath, the rarest, sweetest flower;
Forget not, how in olden time that naughty apple came
Among those rival goddesses, to wake the envious flame.

When Paris—inconsiderate youth, Hecuba's ill-starred son,—
Presumed among the matchless three, to name the peerless one;
And so, upon his foolish head, Minerva's hate came down,
While Juno lowered upon his race with her revengeful frown.

My song should cease; but still the muse would linger to propose
A health to Barnum—wondrous man! the friend of baby-shows;
In all the fields of enterprise a champion shrewd and bold,
Beneath whose magic hand, whate'er it touches turns to gold!

---

* The lady judges.

Years hence, perchance, some hale old man—his grandchild on his knee—
Will oft recount the bygone times, when young and blithe was he;
When bright and lustrous was the eye, now weak with age, and dim,
And boast about that early prize that Barnum gave to him!

Now to each little cherub face a double health is here—
May time add yet another charm with each succeeding year;
Till life's meridian sun, in all its richness shall unfold
The blossom, fair and beauteous, as the infant bud foretold.

S. B. S.

MEMORY AND HOPE.

THE night was clear, the air was keen,
The ground was covered thick with snow,
And far above, the glittering sheen
Of Heaven's bright orbs would come and go.

I felt old Boreas' stinging bite,
As shrieking through the sash he came,
And saucily addressed my light,
As if she were an olden flame.

Half drunk with fun, the jolly god
Bore the light snow-flakes from their bed,
And rushing up the narrow road,
Whirled fiercely round the traveler's head,

Who, just returned from Congress Hall,
Was quite unable well to shift,—
While striving Buncombe's speech to call,
He could not, somehow, see the drift.

Ha! how the laughing stars, so mild,
Watch the mad frolic from on high;
They seem to say: A favorite child
Is privileged to tease and cry.

I dropt the curtain on the scene,
 And back within my chamber turned;
When burst the doors that stood between
 My callous heart and brain that burned

With recollections of the past—
 Aroused, enkindled from their sleep;
The sweetest breeze, the harshest blast,
 The day to sing, the night to weep.

Allotted by the mighty King—
 All pass before my shrinking eye;
Nor first the sorrows bear a sting,
 While every joy upheaves a sigh.

As hooded monk and mail-clad knight,
 Upon their patron's natal eve,
With gorgeous pomp and solemn rite
 Th' illuminated castle leave;

Commanding all the numerous train
 That forms the lordly retinue,
They file upon the darkened plain,
 From whence in silence they may view

The vestal, silver lamps that shine
 Depended from the casements high;

Nor is there movement in the line,
  Until they flicker, leap and die ;

So, from the portal of my mind
  Leads covered hope and steeled despair,
Innumerable host, that wind
  Beneath the gateway-torches' glare.

The arsenal of thoughts and deeds
  At last forsaken—all apart,
Each nature on the other feeds—
  Heart looks on mind, mind searches heart.

" Ha ! good Rodolpho, didst thou mark ?
  Some cursèd menial yet remains ;
I see her 'mid the light—nay hark !
  Hear'st thou her desecrating strains ?

" Haste ! good Rodolpho ; give thy steed
  The freest rein, and to me bring
The audacious wretch ; with greatest speed
  Her carcase to the dogs we'll fling."

" Stay, my good knight," old Lubin cries,
  "I'm sure my lord his word withdraws ;
Yon form and voice is from the skies,
  Our Lady smiles upon the cause."

Why did I fail the form and voice
  Of childhood's innocence and peace
To recognize? But now rejoice!
  Hope argues from them, doubtings cease.

Blest Heaven, we see, that ere the soul
  Is quite divorced from Faith and Truth,
Before remembrances are whole,
  An angel trims the lamp of youth.

With cruel throbbing pulsed my head,
  My brain with thousand vagaries teemed,
As, worn and weary, on my bed,
  I threw my panting self and dreamed.

Amid my native hills I roam,
  I hear the brooks, I taste the breeze;
Disposed at once to joy and gloom,
  I mark each scene of childhood's glees.

Mysterious presence by my side!
  And stranger still in that I know
It is my love, and joy, and pride,
  That close attends where'er I go.

Full recognition with the morn,
  My longing, anxious spirit had;
'Twas then I knew that face and form—
  I know it now, and—— I am sad!—C. A. S.

LINES READ AT A SUPPER

OF COMPANY C, FIRST BATTALION INFANTRY, MASS. VOL. MILITIA, GREAT BARRINGTON, 1855.

ONCE on a time Lieutenant C., upon my reveries stole,
His right hand held his last cigar; his left, my button-hole;
"We're going to have a supper, Sam, next Saturday," said he,
"Here goes your name; don't say me 'nay'—you must be there to tea!

"The clergy are invited guests; the yeomen near and far,
The lawyers, and a host beside who practice at the bar;
The Captain, and his soldiers all, with tinsel, fife and drum;
I tell you," said Lieutenant C., "this military's some!

And furthermore, this brief advice you'll find is haply timed;
Come not, equipped and armed alone, but duly cocked and primed;

For when the cloth is cleared, we trust you fellows
 of the law
Will undertake to satisfy our intellectual maw.

Give us a speech, or sentiment, or both, if you
 prefer;
Or, should your Muse prove tractable, just coax a
 smile from her;
Come on at least with ready will, and only do your
 best,
And I—your most admiring friend—will answer for
 the rest."

Thus spake the First Lieutenant, and in quest of
 other prey,
Left me, his latest victim, to ponder on my way;
To cogitate some shirking scheme, or supplicate the
 muse,
Who rarely suffers a default when an attorney sues.

'Tis hard, methought; 'tis passing hard, such pres-
 sing friends to meet,
While walking very quietly along the village street;
To have them chalk you for a speech, and pledge
 you to fulfill;
But harder yet to shake them off, unless you say
 you will.

So hither to our feast I bring, for better or for
worse,
An honest toast, though plainly clad in unambitious
verse;
Forget the garb that clothes the thought, uncomely
though it be,
But to the naked sentiment, drink heartily with
me!

The Boys of Berkshire! skilled alike in arts of peace
and war;
Proud owners of this fair estate their fathers battled
for;
With hands to do, and nerve to dare, in Freedom's
sacred cause,—
Defenders of their country's rights; upholders of
her laws;

A health to these, the worthy sons of brave, immortal sires!
Forever may their bosoms glow with patriotic
fires!
No hireling troops are our defence; but Freedom
proudly rears
Her flag, and hopefully regards our Berkshire Volunteers!

A health, a double health to these; should Freedom e'er invoke
Her sons to rally and resist the rash invaders' stroke;
Not last, not least; but first and best, where thickest fight appears,
Look ye to find our noble boys; our Berkshire Volunteers!

S. B. S.

FEMALE EQUESTRIANSHIP.

PREFACE TO REPORT OF COMMITTEE AT EXHIBITION OF HOUSATONIC AGRICULTURAL SOCIETY, 1855.

In this our age so fraught with startling things,
When each nine days some new-fledged wonder brings;
When good old grand-dames rub their pious eyes,
And heave by turns their Partingtonian sighs;
When each young stripling, ere he learns to read,
Aspires to manage his two-forty steed;
Forsakes his primer, and, as best he can,
Displays the pony and the fast young man;
When beardless boys with martial headgear crowned,
Scare all the horses in the country round;
Defy the foeman with prodigious might,
Though well assured there's none at hand to fight;
When innovations such as these begin,
Ought not our ladies to be "counted in?"
Aye! burst the barriers that have kept her fast,
And give to woman all her "rights" at last!
May she not speak, though blest with healthful lungs,
And doubly favored with the gift of tongues?
While man his seeming precedence attains,
May she not sometimes drive, and hold the reins?

On this our annual Farmer's holiday,
Hath she no charms and graces to display?
While man pursues his schemes for fame or pelf,
May she not seek some market for herself?
In sooth she may; nor let one cynic dare
To chide this feature of our Berkshire Fair!
Come then, and in these festive sports engage!
Come spinsters all of problematic age,
Come on, fair matrons, and ye laughing girls,
With raven tresses or with auburn curls;
Come one, come all to ply those nameless arts,
Which make such havoc with our tender hearts.
Who knows how many an unrecorded prize
Lurks now within some bashful lover's eyes;
How many a swain beholds but to adore
Some favorite lass he almost loved before!
Ah! who can tell, from such a scene as this,
What hopes may follow, or what nuptial bliss;
What life-long pleasures, 'neath the smiles of fate,
Upon the issue of these moments wait!

Health to the daughters of our worthy dames!
The brightest jewels which old Berkshire claims.
Despising not the duties of their sphere,
Behold the trophies of their labor here!

See the rich products of the dairy-room ;
The tasteful fabrics of the housewife's loom ;
The laces, silks, and works of finer art ;—
Say, hath not woman well sustained her part ?
And last, not least ; hath she not shown her skill
To guide the steed, and curb him at her will ?
O may our boys prove no ungrateful churls,
Who own such soil and court such lovely girls !
Be it their pride to cherish and defend
These best of treasures Heaven to man could lend !

S. B. S.

LINES FOR ST. JOHN'S DAY.

Another festal day's return :
  Thrice uttered be the greeting,
As round those lights that brightest burn,
  The Brotherhood are meeting.

No anniversary of Time
  Our Order's records centre—
When first she ope'd her gates sublime
  And bade the pilgrim enter.

Who have not passed by Mount Moriah,
  Nor learned the sealed Ionic,
May deem the widow's son of Tyre
  Possessed no word Masonic.

But let rejected skeptics cry,
  Her ancient dates are fiction;
Few will presume to her deny
  John's Saintly benediction.

And, lo! the bond in Art confessed,
  When skilled with square and gavel,
Through Europe's courts, from East to West
  The Masters freely travel.

When round Cologne encamped the Craft—
  Those wonderful adapters,—
Who crowned the simple Doric shaft
  With Corinth's beauteous chapters;

When he, whose architecture wove
  In stone the hymn and psalter,
Upreared the Pantheon far above
  St. Peter's gorgeous altar;

When rectitude of heavenly law,
  Once symboled by the plummet,
Was typified to heights of awe
  In Strasbourg's piercing summit;

Or when Milan's cathedral choirs
  First sang the strains of Starble—
As burst into a spray of spires
  That soaring wave of marble.

Albeit the operative tools
  Of true Masonic labor,
Now yield the Order's nobler rules,
  Toward God, and self, and neighbor.

We bring not from the distant Past
  A legendary story—
The grandest living structures cast
  Her monumental glory.

Thanks to the Architect Supreme!
  Who by the TEMPLE's building,
By every joinéd block and beam,
  By splendid wealth of gilding,

By column and by vestibule,
  And by the place vail-hidden,
Presented Wisdom's perfect school,
  To which our lives are bidden.

No more the Pantheistic thought,
  Life is a plant's expansion:
MAN BUILDS A HOUSE; his deeds are wrought
  In texture of a mansion.

The pavement of a ground-floor shows
  A handiwork indented;
The walls which faithfulness enclose,
  By justice are cemented.

O, bond of Truth! O, mystic tie!
  That binds our heart-strings human,
In brotherhood that passeth by
  The vaunted love of woman!

Where, in the wide world's mighty scope,
  Are found the homes not wanting
Thy blessed power for Faith and Hope,
  'Gainst hollow cheer and canting!

The Ark whose capitals we greet—
  Which holds the workmen's wages—
Has safely reached the Master's seat;
  Borne down the Lodge of Ages.

So shall it move, majestic, grand,
  Through Time's prescribéd cycle,
'Till on the sea and on the land
  Shall stand the angel Michael!

C. A. S.

CHRISTMAS LINES,

SENT WITH A PACKAGE TO THREE BOARDING-SCHOOL MISSES, CHRISTMAS DAY, 1853.

I SAW them at the window,
So like the Graces Three;
The loveliest and fairest
The eye could wish to see;
And from those merry voices,
Melodious and clear;
The welcome, "Merry Christmas!"
Came floating to my ear.

There stood the charming Annie,
I always loved so well;
And Lou, for whom my fondness
I hardly dare to tell;
And lastly, tho' not leastly
Of all the Merry Three,
There stood the merry Julia—
Oh what a witch is she!

And so I just bethought me,—
All bashfulness aside;—
To send this bunch of sweetness,
(*My love solidified!*)

And now, adieu, sweet maidens!
And always think of me,
When you recall the Christmas
Of Eighteen Fifty Three!

S. B. S.

A POEM,

DELIVERED AT BOYS AND GIRLS' FESTIVAL, JULY 4, 1856, AT GREAT BARRINGTON.

As WEARY traveler, panting for repose,
Halts on his journey, where some streamlet flows;
Seeks out some grassy couch beneath the trees,
And shuts his eyes, and calmly takes his ease;
So comes our Goddess, with a gladsome mien,
Lured by the aspect of this joyous scene.
Sated with glory and the deafening noise
Of crackers, guns, and patriotic boys;
Crazed with the medley—both of sounds and
sights,—
The crowds, the din, the independent fights;—
The very music all at once she scorns,
Intoxicated with so many horns;—
Weary of these, we bid her welcome here,
This nice old lady, in her eightieth year.
Hearty, and hale, and fair she is, as when
Her earliest presence cheered the soul-tried men.
Her waist grows ampler, and her arms, 'tis true,
Have kept on stretching all her lifetime through.
For many a year, perplexed with want and toil,
With meddling neighbors and some family broil,

In fair proportions her estate has grown,
By thrift and tact she more than holds her own.
Her buxom form, for aught that now appears,
Bids fair to last another four-score years—
For well she knows, whatever may befall,
Her CONSTITUTION can survive it all.

Fain would the muse, with voice attuned to praise,
Repeat the story of her earlier days;
Recount the strange adventures of her youth—
A tale of romance, but of treasured truth—
How she and Jonathan conspired to wed,
And when it was, and what the neighbors said;
How, ever since the nuptial knot was tied,
Flocks, acres, children, all have multiplied.
How, from the thirteen patrimonial farms,
Hard earned at first, and kept by force and arms,
The bounds have widened toward the setting sun,
Till Jonathan is lord of thirty-one!
How, vexed and jealous at the rare success,
Britannia sought her daughter to distress;
How Johnny Taurus came from o'er the sea,
To put in force the tax upon his tea;
Fought eight long years, a strong and vigorous pull,
And earned right well his name of Johnny Bull.

How, once again, he strove the boys to *lick*,
And tough "Old Hickory" caused him to "cut stick."
In later times, how, on a foreign field,
Old "Rough and Ready" quite forgot to yield;
How, from the first, through each successive year,
On land, on sea, in every noble sphere,
In science, arts, and legislative skill,
With sword and plow-share, and the gray goose-quill,
With wind and water, earth, and fire, and steam,
And lightning harnessed like a docile team;
In every branch of commerce and of trade,
Where man's proud impress ever yet was made;
Columbia's Sons, with ready zeal addressed,
Have proved themselves the foremost and the best;
All this at length, the Muse would fain rehearse,
In faithful numbers and befitting verse;
But, closely scanning the assembled throng,
Forbears discreetly to protract her song.

Columbia's goddess once again beholds her natal day,
Her gallant sons and daughters fair are joined in glad array—

From hill and dale, from north and south, from east
to western shore,
Sound praises and thanksgivings for the patriot men
of yore.

Fair Liberty beholds the scene with just maternal
pride,
She gazes at her rich domain, extending far and
wide,—
Her noble lakes, her busy streams, her prairies and
savannahs,
While from them all, in unison, ascend the glad ho-
sannas.

"Alas!" she cries, "that in my name, one recreant
traitor should,
With impious hand, essay to part this glorious sister-
hood!
That midway o'er so fair expanse, should stretch
that odious line—
My sons! guard well the heritage, 'tis yours—all
yours—and mine!"

* * * * * *

All sated with glory and swelling with pride,
From the "noise and confusion" now turning aside,
The goddess of Liberty hitherward strays,
On the fresh face of youth and of beauty to gaze.

"Ah! these are my jewels!" with rapture she cries,
As she pauses to wonder, while feasting her eyes—
"No regal display with its semblance of bliss,
Can present such a heart-cheering picture as this!"

With a radiant smile are her features o'erspread;
Every trace of disquiet has vanished and fled;
Not a shadow there lingers of doubt or of care,
For she looks at her jewels, and cannot despair.

Here she spies a bright youth, who in progress of years,
At the far west shall live with the brave pioneers;
And that ruby-lipped lass, as a Southerner's bride,
O'er a cotton plantation shall one day preside.

All this picturesque group shall be scattered afar,
As old time rushes on with his clattering car;
But no absence or distance can wither or chill
That remembrance of youth, that shall cling to us still.

And our goddess well knows, that as each rolling year
Shall bring round in its circuit this birthday so dear;
Every eye shall be bright, and by every tongue,
From old ocean to ocean her praise shall be sung.

No new State in its birth shall embarrass her cause,
For no traitorous subject shall question her laws;
But the new State each Sovereign honestly craves,
Is where Hymen presides, and the lords are the slaves.

Lo! her chariot waits, and the goddess is in it;
She has got an appointment in Texas next minute—
She is donning her robe—'tis of red white and blue—
Now she waves us her hand—and she bids us adieu!

S. B. S.

OLD SCENES.

My boyhood home is fresh to view;
  The gladdening spring has dressed
The landscape with her foliage new,
  And all the earth seems blest.

The fine old street once more is paved
  With shadows from the elms,
Whose branches have for centuries waved
  In clear, ethereal realms;

And interclasped their wrinkled hands,
  With bridal verdure clothed,
As though in earth they heard their bans;—
  By Driad Priests betrothed.

The hills and mountains are replete
  With glory as they stand:
The one, soft sloping to our feet,
  The other sharp and grand.

And close below the rugged steep,
  The Housatonic flows;
Like moat before a fortress keep,
  Defiant to its foes.

And dotting all the valley plain,
  Are mansions of the proud,
Who leave the city's strife for gain
  In summer's sultry cloud,

In quiet haunts like these to find
  From care a sweet release,
And gather for a burdened mind
  The recompense of Peace.

This day above an hundred, seems
  Enriched by Nature's rule ;
The sun is temperate in his beams ;
  The winds are low and cool.

Now, while the morning hours remain,
  I'll seek some favorite place,
Where I can wake an olden strain,
  Some childhood lines retrace.

And first my thoughts are westward turned,
  Beyond the pine-clad hill.
Alas ! I'm told the grove is burned ;
  In ruin lies the mill.

The woods destroyed, the marble bed
  Untouched by workmen, save
When at a summons from the dead,
  To decorate a grave.

So that to click of bar or spade
  Within our burying grounds,
The muffled drill alone is made
  To give responsive sounds.

That ravished and deserted spot
  I cannot wish to see;
For what it was, and now is not,
  Would mournful speak to me.

Across the river, 'neath a spring,
  Near to the mountain's crest,
A rock of reddish hue juts forth,
  As from a mother's breast.

Nor treble labor of ascent,
  Nor lack of picture grace
From yonder rock, do now prevent
  My visit to its base.

But I remember, vivid, when
  I last stood there at dawn
With one I shall not see again—
  For George has long since gone.

Two names upon the southern side,
  Were rudely carved by him;
But, I am told, before he died,
  The marks had grown quite dim.

O, friend, beloved! No sculptured stone
  Affords my heart relief;
I see in that rough rock alone
  My monument of grief.

Forgive me, then, if I refuse
  To walk where oft with thee,
Those paths—in pleasure others choose—
  They're sacred now to me.

Then what direction shall I take,
  Where I in ease may look?
Will memories jarring discord make
  Along the Roaring Brook?

Would any thing of recent change
  Unpleasant feelings bring,
Should I decide to visit now
  The "Evanescent Spring?"

The morning hours are fully passed;
  The sun rolls down his zenith wave;
As with a fancy, pleased at last,
  I turn my steps toward Belcher's Cave.

A hard and patient search revealed
  The cavern's mouth to me again;
For nature cunningly concealed
  The entrance to the forger's den.

Well I remember, venturous Dave
  Would lead us creeping through the porch;
Then suddenly illume the nave
  With flashes from his birchen torch.

And when we boys would, proud, declare
  Dave's cool contempt for snakes and ghouls;
Droll Tom would say: "He's oft been there,
  In search of Belcher's forging tools."

Ah, me! when on far distant shore,
  I stood beside each lowly grave;
I did not think I should once more
  Repeat their names in Belcher's Cave.

Here history and tradition both
  Rehearse of charities and crimes;
The one, recorded under oath,
  The other, tales of grandame's times.

A lad who sought his father's ewe,
One day, descried a curious smoke;
The bank soon up the chimney flew,
  And this illegal broker broke.

What days were "celebrated" here!
  Here there were scenes of wildest mirth;
The grandest frolics of the year
  Were held around this spacious hearth.

* * * * * *

I want the pictures of the early morn ;
  Not the cold thinking of the mind mature ;
With harsh demands of duty these are born ;—
  The former only in our hearts endure.

Awake, ye echoes of the joyous past !
  I summon now a happy youthful throng.
Come all, as when we here assembled last,
  With jest, and trick, and anecdote, and song.

Fond recollections crowd a swift-winged hour,
  By turns provoking me to laugh and weep ;
'Till they, and my emotions, lose their power,
  And gladly (wearied) I recline and sleep.

And as I slept, Lo ! I was in a trance ;
  A fairy troop surround my flinty bed ;
With pantomimic gesturing they dance ;
  Then, close approaching, the Titania said* :—

* * * * * *

Again the fairy waved her golden wand—
  A lovely form descended from the clouds !
Madonna-like, her look was sweet and fond ;
  A nameless grace her noble brow enshrouds.

---

* What Titania said, is of too personal a nature to be here inserted.

She sat before me on a silver throne!
  Her chastened beauty warmed upon my heart;
Methought another, higher sphere was known,—
  Of which earth-scenes some blessed hints impart.

Again the sceptre waves! The spell is broke;
  The dear illusion can no longer please:
For O! how full of agony I woke,
  And found that I was weeping on my knees!

An impulse, irresistible and strange,
  Prompts me to climb the craggy ledge above;
From whence I view the glorious set of sun,
  And learn the meaning of the dream of love.

Through the thick covering of the village trees,
  A pleasant cottage meets my roaming eye;
Instant, as though borne to me on the breeze,
  Sweet thrills of recognition force a sigh!

C. A. S.

VALENTINE.

The Lady Helen is strangely fair,
Endowed with charms and graces rare;
With lustrous eyes, whose glance is rapture,
And beautiful masses of golden hair.

A rich bloom, like the summer rose,
Upon her soft cheek courts repose,
And o'er her features, when she smileth,
A gleam as of sunlight comes and goes.

Her brow is placid and serene;
Her form the proudest e'er was seen;
And, like the classic Grecian Helen,
She seems by nature pronounced a queen.

Her very presence hath a spell,
Within whose light I've loved to dwell; —
To sit, and gaze, and only listen,
To catch her syllables as they fell.

Her heart, they say, hath boundless worth,
Her beauty scarce can symbol forth;
In her, a spirit meet for Heaven,
Its gentle influence sheds on earth.

Unmarked amid the passing throng,
These eyes have gazed enraptured long;
This heart hath throbbed with wild emotion,
That fain would break and outpour in song!

I could a tale of love unfold;
But the truth were just as well untold;—
'Tis precious little for me she careth,—
A rusty bachelor forty years old!!

But with thy leave, Saint Valentine,
This wreath of poesy I'll twine;
But whence it comes, and who's the author,
The Lady Helen could never divine.

S. B. S.

TO ADA ——.

THOU hast the wealth of beauty ; thou art fair,—
  As oft thy faithful mirror must have told thee ;—
Endowed with charms and comely grace so rare,
  That all must pay thee homage who behold thee.

Thou hast the wealth of mind ; to quest of lore,
  Classic and modern, thou hast given thy youth ;
And—glorious thing in woman—hast in store
  Treasures of thought, of wisdom, and of truth.

Thou hast the wealth of soul ; that nobler part,
  In all its depth and plenitude is thine,
Which gives the richest graces to the heart,
  And makes us kindred of a race divine.

Thus, thrice-endowed with wealth, I may not doubt
  That whosoe'er thyself and thine shall win ;
Will find a temple, beautiful without,
  And ornamented gorgeously within.

S. B. S.

TOUCHES AND HINTS.

POEM DELIVERED AT ZETA PSI BANQUET, CALIFORNIA.

It seems as if the gracious Will
  That hollowed out the bay,
And smote the outer, rock-ribbed hill,
  To ope a golden way

For sea and ship, for home and hope;
  Was equal in behest
That man should plant on yonder slope
  The College of the West.

The long, low beach of sedge and vines;
  The slow-retreating plain;
The emerald upland, which reclines
  Against the mountain chain,—

Whose steep ascent and swelling girth
  Lend dignifying powers
To that choice spot of all the earth
  For academic towers!

O, beauteous scene for brain and heart,
  Our students' life beguiles;
The sleeping vale, the teeming mart,
  The ocean and the isles!

With ever-varied shifting phase
  Of motion and repose;
With morn's impenetrable haze,
  With evening's gorgeous close!

With shimmering noon, and glittering night,
  Of such translucent beam,
As on the meditative sight
  Revives the Berkeleyan dream!

Where wintry snows are never known,
  Nor enervating heat;
Within the isothermal zone,
  A sure and perfect seat.

Where nature for the site supplies
  The Oracles of Fate,
A bounteous wisdom justifies
  The Nation and the State.

And, thanks to many a noble friend,
  Of unsectarian aim,
Whose large endowments here descend
  With honor to his name.

And, thanks for toil in leading chairs,
  By men of cultured skill,
Who, 'mid a thousand teasing cares,
  Have kept an even will.

Auspicious history! From this page
  We lift a trustful gaze;
Though weightiest issues mark the Age,
  And anarchies amaze.

Strong Fort of Faith! Assaults are vain;
  Thy banners never furled!
While Time may last, thou shalt retain
  The Outlook of a world!

Fair priestess! who shall yet indite
  Ten thousand glorious names;
With reverent sentiments to-night,
  We dare invoke thy flames!

"Room for Reformers! with their sovereign plan
To heal or mitigate the woes of man."
The cry is ancient as our Nation's time,
Yet born anew in every tapster's rhyme.
The field has widened at each fresh demand,
Till desk and forum ope on every hand.

GIVE HEED, O PEOPLE! is the prophet shout,
Of those whose theory is the "Latest out."
Nor less potential is the summons borne
To found a sect, or lift a race forlorn;
Or force a city corner upon corn.

Alike their dignity,—the crowd to back ;—
The long-eared medium, and the short-haired quack.

The simple truths our patriot Fathers saw,
Sketched in resolve and molded into Law ;
By which in perils unsurpassed they stood—
Built with their bones, cemented with their blood :
Are all too narrow for the modern seer,
Whose wondrous License strikes the popular ear !
Whose published writ is, Readiness for "fame,"
Won through a bloodless martyrdom of shame.

Pretending now a scientific lore,
And now a message from the 'other shore ;'
In either case prepared to tell, in terms,
The grandest compound and the primal germs ;
Rehearsing nonsense in exultant tone,
As if the lectures made creation groan ;
In any case, prepared to scoff and sneer
At every custom decency holds dear ;—
Seducing ignorance with lascivious charms,
And healthy conscience stinging with alarms.

Such are Outriders, on the secular coasts,
For less unselfish, less courageous hosts ;
Who now disclaim, and afterwards suggest
The "Progress" programme may be for the best ?

With cunning glance, to note in every move
The points debauched communities approve;
Lest they should fail to pander, just in time,
To some new doctrine, vicious but "sublime!"

See worthy subjects for the prison lock,
Unblushing labor with the corporate stock,
To cover up the robbery of a ring,
Or fast enthrone some great monopoly king;
Until the people, rising in a storm,
Announce their temper for a real reform.
When Lo! the foremost, with the loudest cheer,
These rear-guard veterans suddenly appear!
Their functions now a double game of cheat:
Shape voted verdicts to a flat defeat;
The while they make their own promotion sure,
And preach a flattering gospel to the poor;
Then in some office, lucrative and warm,
They whisper sadly of a lost Reform!

Behold the highest council in the land!
What men dishonored! and what rogues command!
The jovial scoundrel (or the lucky fool),
Rich from his ventures in a gambler's pool,
For bigger tricks, or personal regard,
Concludes to take the senatorial card.

Instant proclaims, in condescending tone,
His champion platform, as the "Laborers' own!"
Secures his organs by a brand new "dress,"
A monthly stipend, and a mammoth press.
Pensions electors and the hovering scribes
Who write his speeches and discount his bribes.
Assumes the toga with an easy air,
And flings, off-hand, the talks his friends prepare.
(Reminding cronies—in their private chat,—
"Though wit had prestige, we've reformed all that.")

Who shall these workings and these powers abate?
Inform the masses and preserve the State!
Where will you find the valorous strength and will
To push these creatures from the seats they fill?
Who shall come forward and combine to raise
The social standard of our earlier days;
When thieves, by purchasing official place,
Could not obtain an honest household's grace;
When those whose name no stamp of honor bore,
Would not presume to cross the good man's door?

Behold the masters of the daily "Press"!
Whose broadening power is almost measureless.
How few perceive, confess, and trembling bear
The moral burdens in the realm they share.

How many to such high position bring
The view and purpose of a sordid thing.
Perhaps buy out, and run with vengeful cast,
Some well-born journal with an honored past.
Breed typhoid-tumults o'er a clerkship wrong ;
Misquote large markets, and old "jobs" prolong.
Inlay their columns with the tales that smirch,
And pass the platter in the wealthiest church.
Spurn trifling offers from the babbling trade,
And keep their virtue on a dress parade ;
Maintain their cipher at the thousandth score,—
And shed contempt on every dollar store.
Let others falter with a timid qualm,—
Their voice, we know, is always for Reform.

A tearful pity touches the distress
Of those compelled to read our neutral Press.
Where circumstantial suppositions surge,
In reckless grammar, to the very verge
Of dire conclusions on the mooted head,
Of what was once surmised to have been said.

Who can presume to adequately greet
The fervid, candid, superficial sheet?
Where every flabby "Reformation" scheme,—
Creed of fanatic, and the sick man's dream,—

Is treated gently,—in a *savant* style,
Proudly repressive of the reader's smile.
Where, every day, in paragraph and lines,
The special hobby of the tripod shines ;—
In tireless iteration making known
A Balance Regulator, all his own !
A short, infallible, perspicuous code,
Which sets each subject his appropriate load.
The very rich shall all the taxes pay ;
The very poor need only vote and play.
The prentice builders shall their wages rate,
And draw an extra tribute from the State ;
While those who mark the trestle-board and chart,
Must take their income in a love of Art.

Who shall expose the communistic scamps ?
Combat agrarians, and the lecturing tramps ?
To real complaints appropriately reply ;
To borrowed doubts return the reasons why ?
With pleasing humor dissipate their chaff,
And send their problems to the idiot's laugh ?
Incline the people for the public weal,
To crush their counsels with contemptuous heel ;
The mighty gulfs resistlessly present,
'Twixt just ambition and vile discontent ;

Illume anew the pathway and the scope
Of careful judgment and a healthy Hope?

For such a service—welcomed in the van—
Expect the College-educated man!
To some, a special and a noble call:
A sphere of duty, more or less, to all.

What though uncounted thousands never own
The debt in such essential service grown?
What though a legion cannot understand
That any dangers shadow o'er the land?
And, least of all, suspect explosive force
From such a shallow, freedom-prating source?
Though every warning is decried and hissed,
The threats portentious and the debt exist.

And O, the grateful tribute, on this score,
Due the *alumni* who have gone before!

Enough of surface thinking in the land.
Sufficient privilege at each youth's command.
More than enough of Proverb lore extant,—
Oft wreathed in context of revolting cant.
As well predict a harvest-field of grain
On arid hill-side or Sahara plain,
From equinoctials and the lunar heat;
As with the tribes of ignorant conceit

Rely alone for fructifying powers
On wealth's rewards and moral saw-dust showers.
The need momentous is the souls combined
With quick, electric, cultivated mind;
At whose decree economies shall rest
Beneath profound, inexorable test.

With no detraction of the highest force
We speak emphatic for the College course.
Since history's pages, at each calm review,
Approve the framers, "wiser than they knew."
The fostered relish for established fact,—
The root of structure and the sum exact.
The mental habits which the schools have shown,
Wed to the nerves and bred into the bone.
The days appointed and the tasks assigned
To try the vigor of the pupil's mind,
Before a bench of criticizing friends,
Whose cheering counsel with their censure blends.
The builded will to check the Fancy's haste,
And make it wait on judgment and on taste.
The fine attrition in the class retreat,
'Mid growths of friendship,—never more so sweet!
The duress for self-introspection keen;
The hard, remorseless wearing of the green.
The glorious sovereignty which this drill implies
To summon, portion, point, and focalize;

Till given topics at the chosen hours
Feel the white burning of harmonious powers;
With not a faculty allowed to roam
Till law and contrast drive the statement home.

Vast opportunities denote,
  The deepening want for men,
Whose discipline shall antidote
  The shams of speech and pen.

Whose quenchless passion for the truth
  Shall find a scholar's art,
As from the fresh, brave soul of youth
  The fit suggestions start.

Here grandest fruits of sound review
  In physics and in thought,
With all the lights of Science new,
  Instructingly are brought.

Here for Life Tournaments we bid,
  With Learning and with Love;
Where Logic's iron hand is hid
  Within the knightly glove.

Priestess of Wisdom! In whose torch
  The lights of satire play:
Grant its imparted fires may scorch
  The falsehoods of the day.

Priestess of Wisdom! Genial glow
The censers by thy side!
Inspire the God-sons thou shalt know
With warmth of manly pride;

And guard the children of thy heart,
Linked in a mystic grace,
As from thy altars they depart,
To take their waiting place.

No vaunt of spirit or of mein,
No over-zeal for strife;
But ready for each earnest scene
That consecrates a life.

LINES,

READ AT ST. JOHN'S CELEBRATION, F. AND A. M., GREAT BARRINGTON, 1858.

In ancient times, when Israel's king that famous
fabric reared,
In which his glory and his wealth so manifest appeared;
He, in his wisdom, first gave heed to Heaven's great
law to man,
And ORDER, beauteous and sublime, through all the
process ran.

No sound of axe or metal tool, through all the time
was heard;
No craftsman broke the harmony by one contentious
word;
For so the work was portioned out by Solomon the
wise,
From corner-stone to capital, no discord could arise.

Eleven hundred men, thrice told, as Master Masons
wrought,
And eighty thousand Fellow-Crafts the quarried marble sought;

While Entered as Apprentices were seventy thousand more,
Who, through the progress of the work, the heavy burdens bore.

A vast Fraternity they were—a labor vast to share,
Who always on the Level met, and parted on the Square;
And three Grand Masters gave the rules by which the work was done;—
The King of Israel, King of Tyre, and He—the widow's son.

The columns and pilasters were of Parian marble wrought;
The timbers from the famous groves of Lebanon were brought;
Of cedar, fir, and olive wood, the stately walls were made;
And all within, and all without, with gold was overlaid.

Thus, two great structures had a birth; the one, of wood and stone,
The other, framed and fashioned of Fraternal Love alone;

The one was joined in all its parts by cunning work
of art;
The other, by the ligaments that fasten heart to
heart.

The one stood out in bold relief against the vaulted
sky;
The other raised no towering front to greet the vulgar eye;
The one was all resplendent with its ornaments of
gold;
The other's beauty lay concealed beneath its mystic
fold.

Age after age hath rolled away with time's unceas-
ing tide,
And generations have been born, have flourished
and have died,
Since wrought our ancient brethren on that Temple's
massive walls,
And thronged its lofty colonnades and walked its
spacious halls.

The Temple, with its wondrous strength, hath yielded unto Time.
The Brotherhood that flourished there, still lives
and lasts sublime.

The one, a mere material thing, hath long since
passed away ;
The other holds its vigorous life, untouched by
Time's decay.

Long may it live, through coming years its excellence to prove,
And Masons ever find delight in offices of love ;
Till summoned hence, the glory of that Upper Lodge
to see,
When the GRAND MASTER shall confer on each, his
last degree.

S. B. S.

VERSES,

READ AT ST. JOHN'S CELEBRATION, PITTSFIELD, JUNE, 1860.

THE muse who is courted scarce once in a year,
Is apt to grow shy, when you wish she'd draw near.
Like most other divinities, she too prefers
To grant wishes of those who pay some heed to hers.

So I found yester eve, as I made invocation
For aid in a forthcoming tight situation;
For all my advances she met with a slight,
And said, "Poets, like Masons, had better keep
bright."

To compromise matters I promised a sonnet,
Or some sensation theme, like the new style of bon-
net,—
The one lately over from Paris, you know,
With the vast, overhanging, immense portico!

Then the smiles and the frowns o'er her countenance
passed;
But 'twas plain to be seen which would triumph at
last;
So she hastily twined this rude garland of song,
And bestowed it on me—and I brought it along.

* * * * *

As over life's thoroughfares jostling we go,
Toward the same fated goal where the dark waters
flow,
It is well by the wayside to pause now and then,
To recall that we're brothers and feel that we're
men.

All along on our march, if we will but behold—
Life's sunny oases their beauties unfold;
We may linger to rest and refresh, if we will,
Like the Craftsman of old, at the brow of the hill.

We honor the Order, whose festival day
Brings the brotherhood hither in gladsome array,
To join in this ancient, fraternal communion,
This cordial, old-fashioned Masonic re-union.

We honor the Order, whose principles dear
Make each man with his fellow a recognized peer;
And whose language of emblem and signal are
one,
'Neath a boreal sky and a tropical sun.

Whose ritual, solemn, antique and sublime;—
Outliving its history—lasting as time—
Still charms and controls with its mystical sway,
As in Solomon's reign and Zerubbabel's day.

We honor its tenets, which gladly bestow
Equal favors on all—on the lofty and low;
High as heaven, broad as earth, deep as nethermost
 sea,—
Even such should a true Mason's charity be!

We ope not our portals at wealth's proud behest,
Nor to fame with her plume and heraldical crest;
But to him, high or humble, who honestly brings
The warm, throbbing heart from which Masonry
 springs!

That heart, whether hid 'neath the vesture of toil,—
'Neath the garb of the peasant who tilleth the soil,
Or the fabric in which one worm dresseth another,
We hail it the same as the badge of a brother.

'Neath the mariner's jacket, afar on the deep,
You shall test it, and find it is never asleep;
'Neath the rude savage breast, when no mortal is
 nigh,
It is visible still to the All-seeing Eye.

Its presence is heeded in every zone;
By priest on the altar, by prince on his throne;
Wheresoever the tribes and the races belong,
Lo! Masonry's vast multitudinous throng!

And Masonry's mission: 'tis simply to prove
'Mid the discords of life, how potential is Love:
To revere what is sacred, to feel what is human,
To show good will to man and true honor to woman.

Be it ours in our day to preserve it alive.
In Faith, Hope and Charity, long may it thrive;
Till mankind, in the light of its deeds shall agree
That the whole world one Grand Lodge of Masons
should be!

S. B. S.

LINES,

READ AT ST. JOHN'S CELEBRATION, OF EVENING STAR LODGE, LEE, MASS., JUNE, 1859.

(WRITTEN DURING THE EXERCISES.)

THERE'S one thing stands exceeding clear,—
And much as I expected,—
It comes from West, and South, and East;
"My boy, you're just elected!
So make a speech, or sing a song!
(They say that Cincinnatus
Presents a chap, who's troubled, too,*
With—very slight—*afflatus!*")

This morn, as Sol rose in the East,
To call his craft to labor;
"Come, come!" said he,—"it's time for you
To stir yourself, my neighbor!
You know you're of the '*Lesser Lights,*'
My adolescent brother!"
Said I—"Don't call me that again;
If I'm one, you're another!

---

* Another poem was read on the same occasion by F. O. Sayles, Esq., of Berkshire Lodge, South Adams.

Don't think because you closed your Lodge
So gloriously last even;
And left us striving to peer through
That golden gate to Heaven;
And cheered sweet Orient with a smile,
And, like a gallant lover,
Dispelled the gloom, and placed instead
That Royal Arch above her;

Don't think," said I,—" to rise at morn,
Behind that mask up yonder;
And chase our pleasant dreams away
By muttering so like thunder!
And don't—I beg you—don't repeat
Those tricks in—hydrostatics;
Which make poor Luna hide her face,
And give me such rheumatics!

We meant to have a holiday;
A feast of love and reason—
And celebrate, with right good will,
This rare old festive season;
But how am I to keep the step,
Or swing a dext'rous gavel,
With all these twinges at the joints,
To plague me while I travel!"

"Come, come!" the Day-king gave response,
  "Don't fret in such a manner;
The time is up, and brothers now
  Are rallying 'neath your banner.
Old Cincinnatus left his plow
  To serve his fellows, gladly;
You know the rest—so don't desert
  Your colors quite so badly!"

So here I come—all out of breath—
  But if you would "see Sam;"
Or ask if he's among this throng,
  I beg to state—"I am!"
I'm always there, in soul or flesh,
  In spite of adverse weather,
Where, in the bonds that bind true hearts,
  True men are met together.

And very pleasant 'tis to gaze
  On scenes like these, my friends;
Where brothers meet in glad embrace,
  And wit with wisdom blends;
Where beauty smiles to crown the feast,
  And music breathes her strain;—
Where youth exults with high impulse,
  And age—is youth again!

O, what are all the baubles worth
  We strive to win and save,
While scrambling, as we blindly do,
  From cradle on, to grave!
We go shell-gathering all our days,
  As babes, as boys, as men;
While still the solemn question comes,
  "What then!"—ah, yes! what then!

The time is up;—chop off the string!
  Now, join, each grateful brother!
And mark, kind friends, who're not of us,
  How Masons *toast* each other!
OUR GENEROUS HOSTS! all hail to you—
  Ye men of high endeavor;
And thou—bright EVENING STAR—shine on,
  Forever—and forever.

S. B. S.

TO BELLE.

SOMETHING WAS AND IS NOT.

I TAKE the old familiar walk
  To the brow of the pleasant hill,
From whence we've watched the evening sun
  Its parting rays distil.
I stand upon the oaken bridge,
  And mark the waters glide,
The same as I have seen them, dear,
  When seated at your side.
    And O! my heart, it will go back,—
      I cannot keep it still,—
    I cannot change its tortuous track
      By virtue of my will.
        And I wonder sadly, strangely,
          If there yet a heart may be,
        Whose memories of olden time
          Are somehow linked with me!

There's not a bush, or briar, or tree,
  I see no wayside flower,
But what suggests some thought of thee,
  As of a long-flown hour.

Kind nature tunes her various voice
  To suit my listening ear;—
The breezes do not now rejoice,
  No laughing stream I hear;
    But a soft and plaintive song is borne
      From the circling mountain slopes;
    And the murmuring river seems to mourn
      The dirges of my hopes:—
        As I wonder sadly, strangely,
          If there yet a heart may be,
        Whose pleasant memories of old
          Are somehow linked with me!

No hot and feverish state of brain
  Induces me to find
In yon half-burned and ruined mill
  A picture of my mind.
Its fallen timbers, charred and black,
  Its flood-gates swept away,—
Appropriate types they well may seem
  Of my premature decay.
    Through the swollen dam, unceasingly,
      The swollen torrents roll;
    So pour the streams of inner life
      O'er the embers of my soul.

And I wonder sadly, strangely,
  If there yet a heart might be,
Whose memories of olden time
  Are somehow linked with me!

If e'er thy feet retrace the paths
  In the meadows and the glade,
Where oft, in love's communion sweet,
  Together we have strayed;
And the thought of an olden time rise up,—
  Thy soul's unbidden guest,—
Think of me at my best, dearest,
  Think of me at my best.
    For I ne'er shall view the evening sun,
      From the brow of the pleasant hill,
    Or stand upon the oaken bridge,
      Above the ruined mill,
        But I shall wonder, O how sadly!
          If one noble heart there be,
        Whose tender dreams of bygone scenes
          Are somehow linked with me!

C. A. S.

ATLANTIC CABLE POEM.

READ AT RECEPTION OF CYRUS W. FIELD, AT STOCKBRIDGE, MASS., AUGUST, 1858.

HUZZA! the magic cable's laid; and now, across the main,
Britannia hails her daughter fair, who answers back again:
With lightning flash, through watery depths that roll and surge between,
Columbia's President responds to Britain's smiling Queen.

Rejoice, ye sons of men, rejoice! the wondrous deed is done!
The hemispheres, like Siam's Twins, at last are joined in one!
One little iron ligament unites each mighty part,
Through which the swift pulsations throb, as beats the planet's heart.

Now, hand in hand, in warm embrace, the Old World and the New,
As bridegroom and as bride, rejoice in wedlock firm and true;

The sea-wave stoops its lofty crest, and kissing either shore,
Consents, the sacred tie shall last till Time shall be no more.

"For ages past,"—the sea exclaims,—"I've all the while been fighting
With might and main, to keep this pair their marriage vows from plighting;
I've tossed and foamed, and roared between, and made an awful pother,
But all for nought;—e'en now the rogues are whispering to each other!

Hail, mighty Science! once again we note thy conquering tread,
And praise thee for this last and greatest blessing thou hast shed;
For who may count, or comprehend the vast, unmeasured good,
That hence shall flow to benefit the world's great brotherhood!

And thanks,—our heartfelt thanks to them,—the men of tireless zeal,—
Who ventured all, and battled all, t' advance the human weal;

Who hoped, and dared, and bravely wrought, 'gainst
wind, and wave, and storm,
The grand achievement of the age, in triumph to
perform.

The Cyrus of the olden time, for deeds of valor
done,
A deathless name emblazoned on the page of
Xenophon;
And school boys now, in solemn quest of ancient
Grecian lore,
Peruse his dying speech; and wish—he'd died an
hour before!

No haughty, steel-clad foeman hath our modern
Cyrus slain;
No thousands of the enemy lie stretched upon the
plain;
A nobler victory by far, our Berkshire boy shall
claim;
A loftier niche is hewn for him within the halls of
Fame!

Old Neptune is the vanquished foe; and he whose
praise we sing,
The hero of a bloodless fight, hath conquered
Ocean's King!

Let old Eolus blow his gales, and Neptune nurse
his ire;
Our thought shall still dart through the deep, in
words of living fire!

Now, to the mighty Lord of Hosts, all praise and
glory be,
Who giveth man to hold enchained, the everlasting
sea;
To tame the lightnings, rule the winds, the continent
to span;
Glory to God on high; and on earth, peace; good
will to man!

One parting cheer;—one joyous cheer;—let all the
welkin ring!
Let all with one accord lift up the voice to praise
and sing.
Old Berkshire greets the nations all, the islands far
awa'—
Three cheers for FIELD, her gallant son! Huzza!
Huzza!! Huzza!!!*

S. B. S.

---

* At the delivery of this poem, the assembly all rose and joined in the cheer at the conclusion, with splendid effect.

TWO WEEKS.

Two WEEKS ago, my dearest dear,—
It seems as 'twere full many a year!
Before, time was a shallow stream;—
It deepened in love's radiant beam.
Before, I felt earth's cares alone,
Now, sweetest joys and hopes are known.
Ah! what experience can it be
That fires this finer life in me?
Something from out my heart is given—
Something has filled my soul with Heaven.
The world's best praise, its slanderous sneer,
I neither covet now, nor fear.
O! what has wrought this mighty change,—
To me inexplicably strange?
Tell me, my dear, for you must know,
What's passed since two short weeks ago.

C. A. S.

LINES,

RECITED AT DEDICATION OF ALUMNI HALL, WILLIAMS COLLEGE, AUGUST, 1859.

I MUST confess to something like that same old perturbation,
Which, very oddly, used to come before the recitation;
When called to give some lucid guess about the orbs celestial,
With notions quickened by the gaze of certain orbs terrestrial.

You see, that sanguine autocrat,* (and slightly sanguinary),
Who, thinks, no doubt, the feast is best when most the dishes vary—
Makes game of me; and brings me here—a sort of scapegrace son—
Along with Colt's artillery † to fire this mi-nute gun!

Hard by the spot, where, years ago, Fort Massachusetts stood,
To keep at bay the savage foe,—the red men of the wood,—

---

* Rev. Dr. Durfee, who invited the author to deliver a poem on the occasion.

† Allusion to Hon. J. D. Colt's speech, same occasion.

Another fortress stands to-day, its beacon light to shed,
And better read men supersede the red men long since fled.

Thanks to the Colonel! generous soul, who shelled his substance here;
Beheld his comrades' patient toil, and gave them words of cheer;
Who caught, in hope and faith, some glimpse of this refulgent light;
Whose hope is now fruition; whose courageous faith, our sight!

'Tis strange how Fortune oft-times lures her very darlings on,
And makes them sufferers while they live, but heroes when they're gone!
The jealous dame but dealeth right, and history ceaseth never
To show how self decays *with* self, but good deeds live forever.

That generous gift bestowed in faith, in fortune's darker hour;—
Th' assuring voice which faltered not amid the tempest's power;—

I tell you, these shall live for aye, embalmed in grateful story,
And Ephraim Williams! thy name blended,—*semper sit in flore!*

A hundred years and more have sped since he, our founder, died.
He fell as falls the robust oak—in fulness of his pride;
Ere life's expanding bud had fairly opened into bloom,
His soul—swift-summoned—found its God; his mortal part, its tomb.

He could not know, he could not see, in all his fondest dreams,
How far abroad that little torch should send its kindly beams;
Nor how, through all the centuries, its life-imparting rays
Should help illumine isles afar, and set the earth ablaze!

Behold the lesson, how complete; the moral, how sublime;
Behold what simple acts outlive the wasting force of Time!

The grandest awe invests our life; and conscience
bids us heed
What wondrous possibilities attend each thought
and deed.

Come now, my brothers, leap with me the gulf of
years between,
And pause a moment to survey the beauty of the
scene.
Let Memory, smiling through her tears, her garner-
ed treasures bring,
And o'er us, let her sister, Hope, her radiant halo
fling.

These peerless mountain-monarchs stand, defiant as
of yore,—
(The rock-ribbed fogies still insist that tunnels are
a bore.)
The sky o'erhead appears to hold its primitive condition,
And Green and Hoosic flow as erst, in faithful coali-
tion.

But Green and Hoosic float no more the Sachem's
light canoe;
The engine shrieks where once was heard the In-
dian's wild halloo;

And e'en that sage old cheese, the moon—tho' strange may seem the story—
Comes, tempted by the midnight glass, to our observatory.

And still, here stands Fort Williams;—aye! I vastly like the name;—
Our Alma Mater seems a sort of Anglo-Spartan dame;
Behold her sit with jewelled robes, and many crowns upon her,
To welcome home her gallant sons, and note their scars of honor!

And hence, upon each natal day, our best of nursing mothers
With hearty benediction sends a class of learnéd brothers;
And bids them go where duty calls, wherever that may be,
Throughout our country's broad domain, or far beyond the sea.

And hither, on each natal day, come fresh men by the scores,
To fill the void, and, in their turn, to tread these classic floors;

O, happy youths who thus begin, each with his new-found peers,
To gather the experiences of these bright college years!

And hither, also, we have come, to hold our brief re-union;
To meet once more beneath these shades in sweet but sad communion.
Our mother's waist has ampler grown; more numerous rise her towers;
Her sunshine bringeth sure return in ceaseless golden showers.

But, Alma Mater! as we stand around the family tree,
Thou dost not show us, after all, what most we long to see.
Thy very words of welcome do but send our thoughts astray,
If, haply, we might catch one glimpse of that sweet yesterday!

The very forms that now respond to names of "auld lang syne,"
Bear marks of life's approaching noon, or afternoon's decline;

And others—dear, departed friends!—old men, and
youths as well—
For such the death-star speaks the truth we need
not words to tell.

But this we know, who linger yet, our feelings are
not colder,—
And Alma Mater more than holds her own, as she
grows older.
Upon her brow we find no trace of anxious doubt or
care;
Her means of influence multiply, and how can she
despair?

And now to FORTRESS WILLIAMS, a parting toast is
here;
And Alma Mater; may she live till Time's remotest
year;
And long as earth and sea endure, may her renown
increase;
"Her ways be ways of pleasantness, and all her paths
be peace!"

S. B. S.

HELENA.

I CANNOT praise thine eye, thy form ;
I cannot tell the faith I place :
Within thy heart—so kind and warm—
I could not number every grace.

My tongue refuses to declare
The fascinations which I feel ;
Nay, while the blissful bond we share,
Why search the figures on the seal ?

Our full communion, strong in health,
No selfish reckoning abides ;
Open and free we hold our wealth,—
Not as the miser counts and hides.

Yet, not in passion's fevered school
Have we attained our mutual thought ;
The worthiest judgment bore the rule,
And into love wise sanction wrought.

Hours that are past, how close in peace !
May years to come our hopes sustain ;
'Till time's swift river finds release
Within the unencircled main.

C. A. S.

VERSES,

READ AT CELEBRATION, 4TH JULY, 1861, AT GREAT BARRINGTON, MASS.

I THOUGHT it would be so! 'Twas only this morning
A young man approached me and uttered his warning;
Said he; "My dear fellow, mind what you're about;
If you call round to dine, you'll be surely called out!"

"Called out!" I exclaimed, with perceptible choler—
"Pray, what do you mean? Don't I hand out my dollar?
May n't I mingle, forsooth, in these festival scenes,
And punish my share of the sweet peas and greens?

I never fight duels;—I ne'er was put through
The diet of pistols and coffee for two;—
So I tell you, my friend, with an emphasis stout,
I'll be shot if I stand it:—I won't be called out!"

"Not so fast!" said the youth;—"there's no malice prepense,—
Take my words in a mild and Pickwickian sense;

Do not torture your nerves in such terrible shape—
I'm trying to help you get out of a scrape.

You see, years ago,—it's no business of mine—
But you flirted, they say, with the musical Nine;
And gossips still whisper, that if the truth's known,
You cherished a passion you haven't outgrown.

And to-day, after dinner, when stomachs are full,
And people grow heavy, and jokes become dull;
Just as likely as not, some sly fellow will shout,—
'There's a bird that can sing—let us whistle him out!'"

"My stars!" I soliloquized;—"what shall I do?
I can't make a speech after dinner, that's true;
And as for a song—well, it might have been worse;
As the least of two evils I'll stick to the verse!"

So, a national toast, very hastily drest
In a homespun apparel, and coarse at the best,
I bid you be drinking: fill up the glass then,
And with lips that are loyal shout forth your Amen.

The Star Spangled Banner! though traitors would rend it,
With firm hearts and true we will ever defend it;

Still proudly upheld, it shall float on the gale,
Nor one orb in its bright constellation shall pale!

While burn in the breasts of their children the fires
That kindled aforetime the zeal of our sires;
We swear that forever, on land and on sea,
It shall still wave triumphant, the Flag of the free!

When the untempered passions that govern the hour,
Have spent their wild rage and exhausted their power;
Far aloft, never doubt, up in heaven's free air,
We shall gaze and thank God that our Flag is still there!

O ever undimmed may those colors unfold;
The red, white and blue, and the spangles of gold;—
Still proudly, still firm to the breezes unfurled,
The hope of the nations; the joy of the world!

S. B. S.

MEMORIES.

A POEM DELIVERED BEFORE THE ALUMNI OF WILLIAMS COLLEGE, AT THE COMMENCEMENT OF 1861.

Capricious Muse! about whose temples throng
Adepts and bunglers in the art of song;
Before whose shrine in loyal homage bent,
Unnumbered bards their votive gifts present;
Behold; another suppliant stands aloof,
Impatient, noting each severe reproof
To hapless mortals, as they venture near,
"Begone, impostors! pray—how came ye here?"

But list, coy mistress of that wondrous art,
Which holds such empire o'er the human heart;
Before thy smile its magic spell withdraws,
I plead like Brutus—"hear me for my cause!"

In bygone days, ere yet with reverent awe
I dared approach the sages of the law:
Ere yet from day-dreams of my youth I woke,
To grapple Blackstone, and contend with Coke;
To drudge and labor for litigious men,
"And scrawl strange jargon with the barbarous pen;"
When hours were golden, and when life was new,
And all its scenery wore a roseate hue;

Oh, then, thou know'st, I sought, nor quite in vain,
To weave pet fancies in poetic strain.
Dame "Technia" might relate, did she but choose,
What court I paid thee, now reluctant muse;
So might her sons, who bid me now essay
To catch some glimpses of that earlier day;
And, home returning, having wandered long,
To deck these altars with a wreath of song.
O, then! in memory of the days lang syne,
Once more attune this slighted harp of mine;
Touch with thy sceptre its neglected strings,
Shape these rude numbers as thy suppliant sings;
Glad with thy presence and auspicious mien
This rare occasion, this inspiring scene.

Fratres Alumni! from each busy sphere
Once more withdrawing, find we welcome here.
Here, where aforetime—aye-remembered days—
The lists we entered for scholastic bays;
Gathered from this our mother's bounteous store
The facts of science, and the classic lore
Embalmed forever in the glorious tongue
Wherein great Homer and Anacreon sung;
Here, 'mid these lordly hills, these quiet groves,—
Scenes of our earlier rivalries and loves—

Where unschooled notions caught their chastened
tone;
Where, haply too, some last wild oats were sown;
Here, whence departing—boys no longer then—
We hailed our first proud impulses as men;
Here haply gathered, well I know what theme
Lends inspiration to each waking dream.
The realm of Memories, on this day of days,
Outspreads its landscape to our longing gaze;
While she, its queen, of ever changeful face,—
Now lit with smiles—now dark with sorrow's trace;—
She—Hope's twin-sister—emulous to share
Our all of life—all that we have and are—
Extends a welcome hand, while thus we own
Our just allegiance to her mighty throne.

Blessed of mortals is the man whose heart
Preserveth ever from the world apart,
Some choice retreat, within whose sacred walls
The olden memories hold their festivals.
Where fond memorials of the past are hung;
Where thoughts go clasped with fancies ever young;
Echo the lays of home and childhood hours,
And floats the incense of life's vernal flowers.
Before whose guarded, tabernacled shrine,
Maternal prayers attend in shapes divine;

And earlier loves, and joys of long ago
Their sweet notes warble in delicious flow.

Beneath such mortal's form, howe'er uncouth,
Be sure, upsprings the fount of endless youth.
Somewhat that's human, ever in his breast
Asserts its presence as a constant guest;
Something is throbbing, 'neath whate'er disguise,
That may be touched with generous sympathies.
Some such kind motor, brothers,—is it not?
Hath brought ye hither to this cherished spot,—
Of old-time scenes, some transient glimpse to gain;—
Review the by-gones, and be boys again.

MEMORIES my theme: Oh! list kind friends the while;
The gentle muse bespeaks your gracious smile.
Pray don't forget, though this is classic ground,
And these are scholars, learnéd and profound;
Yet he who seeks your transient thoughts to lure,
Is no professor, but an amateur.
Attend, ye doctors! to the dogs give over
Doses of physic, while the men recover;
While Pegasus shall limp before your eyes,
He'll give your patience healthful exercise.
Hear ye, attorneys! don't, for once, demur;
The muse retains you: charge the fees to her!

No doubt she'll serve you as some clients do,
And prove insolvent when the cause is through!
Ye reverend clergy! hearken, I beseech;
Give laymen license now and then to preach;
Your best of sermons, with the listening throng,
Have most effect when sandwiched well with song.
Ye pedagogues! who wear your nerves all out
In teaching those "young idiots how to shout,"
Commit a while the text-books to their shelves,
And frankly own you once were boys yourselves!
And thou, sage critic! drop that dreadful sneer;
'Twill be your turn to poetize next year;
Beware! lest I avenge my jealous muse,
And pluck *your* plumage—in the "Crowville News!"

Sweet memories of childhood hours! how gratefully they steal
Across our minds, as Time revolves his never-halting wheel;
The pleasant thoughts that cluster round the old paternal home,—
Be these our priv'leged visitants thro' all the years to come!

Perhaps it was a humble cot, where frugal meals were spread;
A plain, unostentatious roof above the infant head;

Or, maybe, 'twas a mansion proud, around whose
plenteous board
A generous hospitality its rich libations poured.

But whether cot or stately hall, it needs not to inquire ;
Whether the boy went barefooted, or clad in rich
attire;
Or whether she who gave him birth, was one of
haughty air,
Or patient being, long inured to housewife toil and
care.

Ah, no! it is not circumstance of outward good or
ill,
Can make our past awake within the sympathetic
thrill;
For, whether carved elaborate, or plainly wrought,
the frame,
Our memory's faithful portraiture attracts and
charms, the same.

That was a proud, eventful day, when first the hopeful son
Forsook the age of baby frocks, and put those
trousers on!

'Twas on a pleasant Sabbath morn: e'en now it makes me smile
To think how grand he marched to church, and strutted up the aisle!

That jacket, with the buttons on! their brilliance, I'll be sworn,
Beat every badge or epaulette the fellow since has worn;
And there were pockets big enough for knife, and top, and string—
The boy was hero then, be sure, and happy as a king.

And you'll remember, like enough, about that famous sled,
With hickory runners, natural crook, and painted very red.
'Twas christened the "Excelsior," or some euphonious name,
And had, upon the school-house hill, a quite distinguished fame.

And when you coasted, after school;—I hope you won't deny—
'Twill do no harm to own it now, but boys are precious sly—

'Twas quite your habit, out of which perhaps some others grew,
To offer little Jane a chance to slide down hill with you!

That ancient school-house holds a place in memory still, I trow,
Where tasks seemed so impossible, and time so dreadful slow;
Where "Webster's Elementary" was sadly dogs-eared o'er,
And Peter Parley—good old soul—became an awful bore!

And if, perchance, you overstepped that most preposterous rule,
And stood convicted of the crime of whispering in school;
Ah, me! what childish penitence came trembling from your tongue,
As o'er your head, "you rascal, sir!" that birchen sceptre swung!

Those well-worn desks, if standing yet, I'll venture to declare,
Along their honored surfaces, your famed initials bear.

You thought it was a clever job, done up exceeding brown;
But now, the letters stand askew, and one is upside down!

Of merry Christmas holidays, shall I forget to sing?
When Santa Claus a fresh supply of gifts was sure to bring;
When all the household was aglow with festive mirth and glee,
And each young urchin donn'd his wreath, and decked his Christmas tree.

Those rows of stockings, round the hearth, arranged with partial care;—
What wondrous faith in dear St. Nick's ubiquity was there!
How oft we strove to keep awake, so haply we might hear
The clattering sound on housetop, of the phantom sledge and deer!

And how, as morning dimly dawned, with emulous desire,
Resounded merry welcomings to loving dame and sire;

And o'er each treasure brought to light, its new possessor gloried,
And in its turn each stocking-full was duly inventoried.

The feast, too, was a grand affair ; when all the aunts and cousins
Were congregated round the board in numbers told by dozens.
No Saratoga can restore to us dyspeptic sinners
The appetites that lent the sauce to those prodigious dinners!

The old church, with its moss-grown tower, whose structure you believed
The grandest architectural feat the race had e'er achieved,
Has now a double sacredness, as, after years have sped,
You see what kindly influences about your path it shed.

How grateful on the list'ning ear, on Sabbath morning, fell
The never-failing summons of the sweet church-going bell—

The old church-bell! how, latterly, with pleased surprise, you own
What else-neglected memories wake in freshness at its tone!

There, in the wonted place of prayer, and thankful praise, and song,
You lent a happy, youthful face to that familiar throng.
There oft you stayed with Sabbath-school and village-choir, at noon,
And learned the sacred lesson, and the good old-fashioned tune.

The gathered throng of worshipers is vastly changed to-day;
And many a face is older grown, and most have passed away.
The venerable forms you knew, as rapid years have sped,
Have, one by one, betaken them to regions of the dead.

The parson and the chorister have gone their several ways;
Another voice from pulpit now, its messages conveys;

And Doctor Watts, in some absurd, fantastic garb,
you see,
Whose quaint old costumes charmed you once—
sweet Corinth, and Dundee!

Yet, sometimes, as the ancient bell from out the
steeple rings,
And Signor Fiddle-faddle's choir some old-time anthem sings;
Once more your pulses beat response to welcome
peal and strain,
And home, and youth, and all the dear old past are
back again!

O, all ye scenes of boyhood days; what stories ye
could tell
Of joys ye mutely witnessed once, of griefs that once
befel;
Yet long as time's dominion lasts, it shall not be discovered
Around each spot what cherished thoughts and
memories have hovered.

There's many a patch of earth beneath the over-
spreading sky,
Presents no feature to allure the casual passer-
by;

It is but acre, house and barn, to his unthinking gaze,
Who sees it unillumined with the light of other days;

Yet, somewhere, over earth's expanse, there gleams a human face,
Gleams ever with a brighter glow, at thought of that loved place;
To him, how truly picturesque its scenery appears,
Up through the length'ning vista of irrevocable years!

There was the wanderer's early home; there, oft in blissful dream,
Again he sports upon the knoll, or paddles in the stream;
There each remembered rock and tree its vigil seems to hold
O'er sacred memories of the past—the scenes, the times of old.

This makes the poetry of life; O, doubt not, gracious friends,
On each and all—in some rare moods—the gentle muse descends.
Alas! our words can ne'er repeat those finer strains that roll
Their sweet Eolian harmonies across the captive soul.

Enough for us, if, now and then, some power the
sense o'erwhelms,
And tenderly uplifts us into bright, ethereal realms ;
And almost, in strange melodies, we feel to us is
given
To catch delicious echoes of the symphonies of
Heaven.

To merrier measure and rollicking rhyme,
The versatile muse bids our fancy keep time ;
While, just for the moment, we pass in review
Some prominent scenes which, as students, we knew.

Our college remembrances ;—bless thee, our mother !
Who mad'st us thy children, and each son a
brother—
Not least of thy bounties we reckon the tether
Which binds us as parts of one household together.

Those years spent in college—how brimming the
cup
Which their fond reminiscences serve to fill up ;
No fraction of life-time contributed more
To the treasures our memory holdeth in store.

And gladly to-day, as we joyfully meet,
The old-time acquaintance and class-mate to greet,

I hail the occasion, and bid ye retrace
The fancies that clamor for uppermost place.

Come, then, fellow-students, and banish your fears!
Who cares that your Latin has rusted for years!
Let Pegasus furnish your "pony" and "Smart;"
The lesson's an old one; we'll have it by heart.

No matter to-day how your scholarship stands;
I tell you, the record's in excellent hands;
And as to who "flunked," or with "honors" was flush,
I've some personal reasons for keeping that hush.

That verdant young Freshman:—he's since become "Colonel,"
Or "M. C.," or "Judge," or the "boss" of a journal;
"Professor," or what-not;—but *wasn't* he green,
When he came on to college, a youth of sixteen!

How all the societies bored and beset him.
To see if he'd do, and then—if they could get him.
How kindly the graduates put him in trim,
And sold at one bargain their bedsteads and—him!

How proud when accepted, and bidden to come,
He started in quest of his room, and his chum.

How grandly West College loomed up to his view;—
Of its dense population, how little he knew!

How the Sophomores grinned as he scampered down stairs
At the first chapel bell, the first morning, for prayers.
How he solved from that moment the mystery deep,
How to make most of time, and economize sleep.

How he passed each ordeal of practical joke;
Discovered how blarney ends often in smoke;
And when Sophomores raised their tumultuous din,
And shouted "Heads out!" learned to keep *his* head in!

And, oh, human nature!—the same evermore—
How he relished the fun, as he reckoned it o'er;
And resolved the whole farce should be stoutly revived,
Just as soon as the next batch of Freshmen arrived.

How, little by little, 'mid college routine,
Some marked metamorphoses came to be seen;
And the youth of last year, very verdant and raw,
Came to have, in some sphere, quite distinguished *eclat*.

Perhaps, my dear sir,—you know best as to that—
You became college champion, with ball and with bat;
Perhaps, when you spouted your maiden oration,
They dubbed you next "Moonlight"* with loud acclamation.

Perhaps you were famous for muscle; and so
Whenever the class above yours, or below,
Undertook their superior force to declare,
It was deemed quite essential that you should be there.

Perhaps, from an awkward, unpromising clown,
You became the Beau Brummel of college and town.
No doubt there were chaps who knew more of Greek roots,
But you beat them all hollow on neck-ties and boots!

Perhaps you grew partial to serpents and lizards;
Caught innocent birds, and extracted their gizzards;
Of the College Museum became the curator,
And of natural science, a learned revelator.

Perhaps, of the transits you sought to be certain,
And as each night uprolled its magnificent curtain,

---

* Prize speakers at Williams are called "Moonlights."

You swung that huge opera-glass on its bars,
Tow'rd the orbs overhead for theatrical stars.

Perhaps, of companions right jocund and boon,
You thought more than you did of the man in the
moon;
And while your old chum was intently star-gazing,
Perhaps—maybe not—but perhaps, you were "haz-
ing."

Perhaps you loved ease, and were wont to invoke
Your quiet day-dreams 'mid the incense of smoke;
While, according as fancies grew brighter or duller,
So glowed the pet meerschaum;—pray, how did it
color?

Perhaps with all book-lore your mind was imbued,
Excepting the text-books; and those you eschewed.
So, despite all the treasures you tried to amass,
You reigned without peer at the foot of the class!

But the muse must forbear; though each actor and
scene
Might be colored afresh in her patent machine;
She remembers her mission; 'tis but to suggest,
While your fancies, thus quickened, accomplish the
rest.

Then, once more, ye classic scenes, hail and fare-
well!
Around ye for aye shall our memories dwell;
Nor shall absence nor distance their potency prove,
For these time-honored places to 'minish our love.

And lingering now, with these pictures before me,
Warm, filial emotions steal pleasantly o'er me;
And I seem in glad vision to recognize one,*
Whom to know, was to yield him the heart of a son.

O, smooth be the seas and auspicious the gales,
That shall bear up the ship and enliven the sails;
And again, home-returned from Europa's far shore,
To these scenes and high duties, his presence restore!

And long be the seasons, while yet in his might,
He shall live to do battle for truth and the right;
Till at last, with the great souls departed, at rest,
Thou shalt take him, dear Father, to homes of the
blest!

Of tender memories, fain the muse,
As pensively the past she views,
From out her store of fragrant fancies,
A wreath—a delicate wreath, would choose.

---

* President Hopkins, then absent in Europe.

Romantic memories ; say, proud sir,
Was aught so sweet of joys that were,
As troth to thee by fair one plighted,
And thine, right loyally pledged to her?

How blissful were the moments spent
At eve, to loving converse lent,
Beneath the stars, whose roguish twinkle
Lumined the gorgeous firmament.

Perchance beneath the trysting tree,
Perchance beside the sobbing sea,
Perchance where all the valley echoes
The rivulet's laughter, wild and free ;

Perchance in bower, perchance in grove,
In cloistered court or dim alcove ;
O, ever somewhere, somehow ever
Gushes the tremulous syllable—Love!

I wot she was a maiden fair,
Her bonny face was free from care,
How most angelic seemed each feature,—
How like a halo her wreathéd hair!

And eyes of brown or azure hue
Bespoke a nature fond and true ;
A heart that should, with glad endeavor,
Battle the ills of life with you.

How oft you mused with hands enclasped,
Conversed of present joys, and past,
And hopefully, through all the future,
Happy, adventurous vision cast.

The numerous years, perchance, have flown,
Since first you caught the thrilling tone,
From maiden lips so softly faltered,
Yielding a heart that was all your own.

The lips have lost their ruby now,
That erst pronounced the hallowed vow;
And time has since, with ruthless finger
Written his autograph on that brow.

Perchance—more sad—that form hath found
Its last repose low in the ground;
And Death, remorseless, holds your treasure
Hidden beneath a grassy mound.

And sometimes, as you chance to trace,
In childhood's all-unconscious face,
Some likeness of that fond companion,
Summoned from thine to Christ's embrace;

Fain from itself the soul would flee;
For of God's rare gifts to such as we,
I almost seem to hear you sighing,
"Saddest of all is Memory!"

Of patriot memories in this trying hour,
When bold-faced treason dares assert its power;
When faithless sons, with sacrilegious guilt,
Assail the structure which their fathers built,
The muse might sing, if need were, to instil
In hearts like these a nobler zeal and will.
What glorious memories! how they cluster round
Each towering shaft and olden battle-ground.
What golden letters upon history's page
Immortalize the hero and the sage,
Who saved our country from oppression's load,
And made her Freedom's favorite abode!
What memories hover o'er that ensign proud,
Whose stripes and stars above the battle cloud,
In Freedom's dawn, and high-advancing day,
In glory shone, to glory led the way!
Beneath that banner, how, with lapse of time,
Our land hath gained a prestige more sublime
Than in historic annals can be told
Of all the empires and the states of old.
Happy Columbia! with thy memories crowned,
Though traitors lurk, and envious foes surround,
Yet who that builds thee in his heart a shrine,
But feels—aye, knows—the victory shall be thine!
Those very memories shall thy helmet be,
Thy sword, thy shield, thy scathless panoply.

Hapless the foe, confronts such shining mail!
His arm must wither, and his courage fail.
Said I, "his courage?"—'tis that desperate kind,
Which goes by stealth, and, trembling, looks behind.
It is such courage as would fell to earth
The very form of her who gave him birth.
It is such courage as would pierce the breast,
On which in infancy his face was pressed,
Or level prostrate with insensate clods,
His fireside altars and his household gods.
Oh! sure as truth, and truth's eternal laws,
We hail the issue of so righteous cause,
And see before, as with prophetic eye,
The grand result—the glorious victory.

And that great victory; would that it might come
By war unheralded, or roll of drum.
Nay; better, happier, nobler might it be,
As from her tripod hints the Muse to me.

In thefullness of time I behold in my vision
How a people betrayed shall yet utter their cry;
How the South, their false leaders shall set in derision,
And pronounce their pet dogma an infamous lie.

Then again, I foresee, how from fertile savannah,
And happy plantation, with grateful accord,
All voices shall swell the resounding hosanna—
Hail, blessed re-union ; praise, praise to the Lord !

Then with hearts not more brave than magnanimous ever,
The sons of the North, with a brotherly grasp,
And a welcome embrace that no traitor shall sever,
The sons of the South shall right joyfully clasp.

Then Memory, her mystical chords shall re-waken,
And penitent children shall weep to behold
How precious the boon they had almost forsaken,
How priceless the birthright they almost had sold !

Thou God of our fathers ! O hasten the season,
When once again Memory her incense shall burn
On altars now dim, and when calm-visaged Reason,
To the throne she deserted, shall once more return,

Then as ever, Columbia, advancing in glory,
Of the faith in this trial her children possessed,
To unborn generations shall transmit the story,
Who shall rise up to call us—their forefathers—blest!

Of grand old memories, such as live sublime
In olden history, or in classic rhyme ;
Of legend memories, haply passed along
In dim tradition, or unlettered song ;
Of local memories, we have cherished well
In curious tales we heard our grandams tell—
Of ghost and spectre—dusky squaw and chief,—
Tales wonder-fraught and staggering belief ;
Of social memories, gratefully restored
In rare re-unions round the festive board ;—
Of each and all, the Muse would gladly sing,
But Time speeds onward with resistless wing ;—
So I must cease ; and now to you, dear friends,
The grateful Muse, the parting hand extends.
Your warm assurance, overcame her fear ;
Your partial kindness introduced her here ;
What thoughts and feelings she hath well expressed
Remember kindly, and forgive the rest.

S. B. S.

POEM

DELIVERED BEFORE I. O. O. F., SAN FRANCISCO, CAL., 1863.

Why man through mourning must his joys enhance;
His reason vaunting, yet commit to chance;
Why Hope paints pictures for minds immature
Which manly learnings change not, but obscure,—
In fainter light leaves youth's ideals to men,
To mock what now is, with what might have been;
Why men despise the thing, revere the form;
In sunshine cowards, heroes in the storm,—
Self-torturing, with a vague, fictitious harm,
While life's broad sea is mirrored in a calm,
Rising with strength from morbid fancy's threat,
As serious dangers compass and beset;
Why words by moral costumers are made
Dark dominos in life's grand masquerade,—
Not all concealing, yet a full disguise;
Why single names form constant compromise
'Twixt good and evil, simple truth and lies:
"*Prudent*," the misers' favorite maxim-cry,
By which the world commends them when they die,—
Whilst "Generous," "Noble," "Liberal" and "Just"
Are terms the poor pass to the rich, on trust,—

With "Enterprise," the letter-shield of lust,
And "Charity," incarnate in a crust!
Why sweet content deserts the Monarch's throne,
And claims the peasant's cottage as her own;
Why harmony of thought is frequent found
Amid the discords of contentious sound;
Why calms, proverbial, coming storms presage,
And are but omens of a day of rage,—
At present peace foreshadowing a curse
Which Envies in the deeps of stillness nurse;
Why Sciences pretentiously exact,
Place "new discoveries" on the roll of fact,
Which soon their venerated being give,
That one, firm, honest, steadfast Truth may live,—
Since, brought in contact, they themselves conflict,
And point in focus what they contradict;
Why great inventions follow in the wake,
And often seem the creatures of mistake;
Why relished sin adopts the mode and time
Sought or selected by compunctious crime;
Why sin's last patent notches the degree
At which the average moral stand must be;
Why failure in the marts of trade is less
A synonym for ruin than success;
Why he who seeks peremptory relief
Upon the highway may be held a thief,

Whilst he who plunders from the public vaults
Is merely weak, and amiable in faults;
Why the sage public o'er a fancy frets
While Christian churches dance away their debts;
Why creedless wits, who flatulently sneer
At every dogma which the mass revere,
Attain to fame upon the false pretense
Of doing honor to man's common sense!—

These daily mysteries in the mighty plan
That shapes the growth and discipline of man;
These lighter, modern marvels, which, perchance,
Are sample offspring of strange circumstance;
These contrasts, inconsistencies and frauds
Hypocrisy induces, or applauds,
Contribute in a ratio and concert
To fashion evil we may not avert;
Produce conditions in our social state
Philosophies explain not, nor abate;
Uncertain render temporal needs and gains,
Debauch our comfort and increase our pains;
Confusion cast where purposes are just,
And cripple courage with a hard distrust;
The private and the public prospects shroud
With almost an impenetrable cloud,—
The veil which hides the future from our sight
Prefix with gloom and deepen into night;—

Add to the blindness nature's laws decree
A sad misgiving that the worst will be.

A Faith divine may raise the mind serene
Above the trials of this earthly scene ;
A heavenly Hope may bring the soul repose
Amid the sternest of our mortal woes,
And build a patience that will bravely bear
The ills of time, the promptings of despair.

Yet learn we not from that same gracious Book
Within whose pages saints devoutly look
To find this glorious Faith and Hope revealed ;
The corner-stone of Promise has been sealed
With this inscription,—With the race began
THE UNIVERSAL BROTHERHOOD OF MAN !

At once to aid the spirit in its strife
For noblest elements in human life,
And all the energies of soul incite
To study and exemplify the RIGHT ;
With righteous thought a worthy practice suit,
Confirm and nurture honest faith with fruit ;
Interpret into acts, enlarge the scope
And purify the properties of hope ;
An actual beneficence educe
By schools of principles explained through use ;

In systematic effort teach and prove
The base and product of a catholic love;
Remind the aged, educate the youth
As to the beauty and the power of truth;—
With these grand objects, those who seek will find
ODD-FELLOWSHIP in wisdom was designed.

With no less purpose did our fathers build
This sacred Order;—in whose terms fulfilled,
Themselves and their true children have been blest;—
Their memory, immortal, stands confest,
Well worthy of the reverence we pay
In every ceremonial act to-day.

Our honored Fathers! let no one presume
To think by words he can their names illume.
What of their fitting eulogy we claim
Has not been written in the Order's fame.
'Twould be unseemly to attempt to write,—
'Tis blazoned elsewhere, in the realms of light.
In chapters which no earthly eye can trace,
Their work, unwritten here, has glorious place:
A work obedient to the Order's laws,
Or instigated in its noble cause;
A work of Friendship, so divinely odd,
Its record the prerogative of God!

A work which, in the harvest hour of time
Shall be proclaimed in sweet, celestial rhyme!

We boast of Progress, and we vastly prize
The culture of the arts that civilize.
We pride ourselves that we were haply born
Where science strides and literatures adorn.

Material Greatness is the public theme:
The popular motives are condensed in steam.
Each fresh advancement in mechanic skill
Inflames conceit and magnifies the will.
Once fairly harnessed, genius can prepare
New uses for the elements in air—
Not as of old the marriage rites perform,
But with the tokens and the bolts of storm;
Wing Cupid's arrows with electric fires,—
To Hymen's service consecrate the wires;
The bands the Grecians thought fair Venus wove,
Snatch from her fingers and commit to Jove;
And, for the tariff which the law allows,
Transmit and register connubial vows;
Audacious 'gainst the ancient saying's force:
Whom Lightnings marry, Thunders will divorce!

We boast of Wealth! The privilege to amass
Enjoyed exclusive by no favored class.

Riches increasing at enormous rate,
And swiftly swelling such an aggregate
That, within reason, it must surely seem
To far outstrip the miser's wildest dream.
We know, of late, the precious ores are found
In such profusion as affords no ground
For accurate reckoning of prospective yield ;
But, from the recent opulence revealed,
E'en the imaginative broker lords
Fail singly guessing what their tunnel hoards,—
The sum, so fab'lous, to approximate
With giant digits—must incorporate !

We boast of multiplying paths of trade,
On which with speed large revenues are made ;
Paths so direct, so very smooth and wide,
The poor to fortune regularly ride ;—
Since any knave may pelt his dupe with rocks,
Then thrust his swollen feet in public stocks.

We boast the glory of our common schools ;
With great "improvements" made by modern rules.
Where the stout implements which were in vogue
As fit correctives for a truant rogue,—
To spur the slothful, break the stubborn will,
And measured lessons thoroughly instill,—

Have been converted in their uses here
T' instructive "objects," from dire things of fear!
The lash or rod, which once was thought, forsooth,
A natural stimulant for the sluggish youth,—
When well applied, most potent to obtain
The greatest product from each pupil's brain,—
Is now employed by every teaching Miss,
As in the new Mnemonic synthesis,
Hinting not only what its source must be,
But every purpose of the ox or tree.
Not to the physical emotions bring,
On sight, suggestions of a mortal sting,
But sage suggestions,—which may grow apace
All planetary "objects" to embrace!

We boast a cheap, efficient, speedy mode
Of granting justice through a civil code:
Whose terms provide that suitors, who may feel
Aggrieved at first decisions, can appeal
To grand tribunals, where each concrete case
Is aptly furnished with an abstract face;
Where facts are "features," and the counsel's whims
Concerning cognate issues are the "limbs."
Where lawyers—like experienced miners—fight
For claims which merely have the color, Right,

Where skillful logic is employed to show
The various errors of the court below;
And history, like a criminal arraigned
To show the reason why they are—sustained.
Or the emergencies of present hours
Are plead to prove discretionary powers.
But where by judgments we are not beguiled,—
Unless they are through inadvertence filed.

Cheap is the mode! 'Twas Solomon's advice:
My son, get wisdom at whatever price.
Efficient! Since it thoroughly conveys
Essential knowledge in eccentric ways,—
Aiding the mind by each peculiar turn
To hold the lesson it deserved to learn.
And speedy! When the value and amount
Of wisdom gained is taken in account.

We boast a penal code; which seems to shed
Abundant mercy on the felon's head.
His prison roofed by statutory laws
With open sky-lights of ingenious flaws;
His dungeon door barred gently, on a catch,
Till "justice" nimbly lifts the legal lache!

With conscious pity are our minds imbued
For those who lived when social laws were crude,
When needs were simple, when the arts were rude.

'Twere stupid Folly's part to deprecate
Outspoken pride at our advancing state,
In all that make convenience, comfort, ease,
Save time and labor, or the senses please.
A healthy sentiment of pride is part
Of all appreciative sense of Art;
And great discoveries in themselves denote
To-day's advantage which they must promote,—
Compelling us with flattery to contrast
The present progress with the ignorant past.

Our education, and a force inborn,
Tempt us to see primeval times with scorn;
And with an ever ready reverence bow
Before the genius of Imperial Now!

Thus do we fail to keep in prudent mind,
Favors and burdens are alike assigned;
Thus do we fail to practically own,
With social progress social cares have grown;
Ignore, or—equally at fault—forget,
As our advantage, so our civil debt;
As the complexities of life increase,
So must man's labor for the public peace.

Our Fathers, with a present and a prescient view,
Which history clearly outlined and which reason drew,

Felt and forecast necessities of deepening weight
For some grand system that should serve to mitigate
The individual penalties of common sin,
And link our neighbors in the ties and bonds of kin.
—For in their skillful, moral plan, they recognize
Anarchial dangers from mere, sordid enterprise.
—The holy impulse which their hearts and conscience fired,
Seems to have almost made their beauteous work inspired;
And following history, thro' a lengthened lapse of time,
Has crowned their efforts as successful and sublime!

Then, brothers! let us votive offerings bring,
While manual outlines we attempt to sing;—
Now, while we celebrate a natal morn,
And larger Opportunities are born;
Now, when our banner proudly is unfurled,
And we avow our precepts to the world.

Come, Stranger! ere ye seek a closer name,
Lend audience to the doctrines we proclaim:

How do we learn our life? how read the page,
As Time's hard finger quickly throws it o'er?

With what reflections do we grow in age,
  And near the sands of th' inevitable shore?

Full soon we find that Heaven has well decreed
  To every man his own peculiar fate :
With following hours contrasting thought and deed ;
  With years all barren, and with moments great.

Full soon we learn a law of equal birth,
  To which, without incongruous act, we give
A holier homage in the scenes of earth :
  Unto himself no man can truly live.

A thousand times the precious truth we hear ;
  Still from our practice it remains concealed ;
Till blessed sorrow makes our wants appear,
  And all adapted uses are revealed.

The general lessons gathered 'mid the din
  Of worldly conflict, triumph or defeat,
Provoke the "Delphic Oracle within,"
  To call the mind to Fellowship's Retreat.

Not to the hut of hermit or recluse,
  Where misanthropic sentiments are nursed ;
Not to retirements where the mean excuse
  For selfish ease is Avarice's sated thirst :

But to the cloistered company of those
  Whose purpose is to thoroughly equip
Good soldiers for the battles 'gainst life's woes,—
  That test the champions of Odd-Fellowship.

Here, man is separated from the world;
  No longer burdened with fictitious cares;
No more within Dissension's eddies whirled;
  No longer threatened by Ambition's snares.

Here, Vice no more is potent to allure;
  Here, Hates and Envies can no more alarm;
Here, every object, motive, work is pure,
  And Virtue's signet is the regal charm!

Here, Love and Friendship hold the sovereign sway,—
  Their mild dominion gloriously assert:
Thy promise all their precepts to obey
  Insures the benediction they concert.

Here, Faith and Charity combine to bless
  The weary mind with heavenly balm of Peace;
Assuage with sympathy the heart's distress,—
  For sorest trouble give or point release.

Should any round this sacred altar bow
  Who will not cherish what they here declare;

Who will not follow the initiate's vow
  With earnest hopes in resolution's prayer ;

Presumptuous Mortal ! Wouldst thou dare approach
  Where on the recreant falls a fearful ban ?
Canst thou a talismanic secret keep ?—
  Then show the fortitude becomes a man !

Alas for man ! In darkness and in chains,
  In moral blindness and by passions bound :
A mournful spectacle where folly reigns,
  And wisdom's voice is an unheeded sound.

There is a time most fitting to confess—
  When stern ordeal of trial is at hand—
The grievous errors which the mind oppress,
  And give to conscience sceptres of command.

O ! sad remembrances of wrong, awake !
  Now is the hour, repenting, to reveal
The sins which by their recollection break
  From retrospect the dark, funereal seal.

If ever thou hast mean advantage gained ;
  O'er-reached thy fellow with a plann'd deceit,—
His honor blasted while in friendship feigned,
  His fortune ruined by a studied cheat ;

If thou hast robbed the widow's house, and made
  Long prayers in public an availing cloak
Against that knowledge thou wer't well afraid
  Would just and quick retributive provoke ;

If thou hast caused the orphan's tears to flow,
  Hast sought his golden portion to purloin ;
And then, a savoring charity to show,
  Heaped shallow saucers with the smallest coin ;

O ! answer truly,—at thy soul's expense !
  Confess, if guilty, and at once retire :
For else than innocent of grave offence
  Thou mayst not bide the dreadful track of fire !

Life's painful end life's duties best can teach.
  Emblems of mortal struggling and of death
The heart not lost to human hope must reach,
  And touch the conscience with compunctious breath.

He who is fit and able to endure
  The early discipline of bonds and night,
Deserves for recompensing to procure
  The fullest liberty and clearest light.

In this true Light may Brothers ever walk ;
  This Liberty without abuse enjoy.

May no false signals tempt them but to mock,
  No sensual charms solicit and destroy.

Hail! master workmen, who to-day unite
  In services of dedicating power.
In ample form conduct the solemn rite,
  And consecrate the building and the hour.

May the grand invocations which ye raise
  The gracious favor of our God obtain;
And may your choral symphonies of praise
  Ascend to Heaven in an accepted strain.

From out the bustle of the crowded street,
  From out the tumult of the business mart,
May yonder house be our beloved retreat,—
  The home we cherish with the mind and heart.

Within its walls may harmony abound;
  May Honor's court be firm established there;
May royal truth be there enthroned and crowned,
  And glorious visions for her sons prepare!

O! may our brethren be exceeding glad
  Before the shrine erected there to wait;—
In regal vestitures of scarlet clad,
  Rejoice to stand within our temple's gate!

Brother, Grand Herald of the North! Proclaim
A consecration in pure FRIENDSHIP'S name;
And, sprinkling water, dedicate this place
To constant practice in that heavenly grace.

Brother, Grand Herald of the South! Approve
This work,—a Temple of enduring LOVE;—
And typify our kindled hearts' desires
With brilliant lightings of the altar fires.

Brother, Grand Herald of the East! Declare:
Here TRUTH'S good seed shall fall, and spring and bear
An hundredfold,—to widely save and bless,
And wreathe with honor in a right success.

Brother, Grand Herald of the West! Foretell:
Faith, Hope, and Charity alike shall dwell
Within these consecrated scenes of ours;
And fill the common air
With fragrant incense, as the scattered flowers
Breathe perfumes everywhere.

And Brothers all! Unite in earnest prayer
That this grand work may have a heavenly care:

That with the Father's blessing, this good Order
may increase,—
"Whose ways are ways of pleasantness, and all
whose paths are Peace."

C. A. S.

LINES,

READ AT A SUPPER GIVEN BY PARLEY A. R——, TO HIS MASONIC BRETHREN, IN CELEBRATION OF HIS MARRIAGE.

Our worthy Senior Deacon, boys, has had a fit come o'er him,—
As many a worthy fellow has, who's gone this way before him:
In short, he's joined another lodge, with obligations new,
Whose secrets can be given in the presence of but two.

I know you'll think it mighty strange that such a tender passion
Should overcome so stout a heart in such a wondrous fashion;
You'll think the deuce is in it, when you find that aught can weaken
The stoical proclivities of this our Senior Deacon.

Just lend your ears, then, for a "jiff," and listen while your "Master"
Relates the actual history of this singular disaster:

How Parley came to parley with the lass that's now
his bride:
How Molly plied her arts until the youth was mollified.

'Twas on a pleasant Sabbath eve—it seems to linger
yet,
With balmy odors, soft as when that loving couple
met;—
The world was mostly gone to rest; the "witching
hour" drew nigh;
And still this pair were strolling forth beneath the
starry sky.

Our brother, for a deacon, seemed in quite hilarious
mood.
No doubt the learned discourse that day had done
him "heaps" of good.
"Love one another," was the text the parson had
selected;
Its queer effects the reverend man could hardly have
expected!

"You are a Mason, I presume?"—began the curious
Molly;—
"I hardly thought you'd ever stoop to such a piece
of folly;

But, since you've gone and done this thing, I'll tell
you what I'll do :
I'll e'en propose to have you make of me a Mason
too !"

"Well, really !" said our startled friend ; "if now,
upon your word,
You make this proposition of your free will and accord ;
And if you'll keep the secret from the ears of all creation,
I'll e'en proceed this very hour to your initiation."

He clasped her hand within his own ; he drew her
fondly to him ;
His heart began to palpitate ; a rapturous thrill went
through him ;
And from their lips, as stood the pair upon the
grassy lawn,
There came a sound—as if a cork were being slowly
drawn.

This most delightful ceremony thrice repeated
there,
Gave out its tell-tale whisper on the circumambient
air ;

Then spake the Senior Deacon, beneath the trysting tree,
In accents low and tender: "Molly, that's the first degree!"

I rather think she liked it; at any rate she said
She didn't see so very much in Masonry to dread;
And if he'd only promise her to be a faithful brother,
She'd pass on from the first degree, and undertake another.

I saw it not, but I suspect that if the truth were known,
'Twas on the second step that most the fellow's craft was shown;
'Tis said he gave her lectures on the liberal arts and sciences,
Relieving the monotony by Cupid's soft appliances.

And, finally, it came to pass, in proper course of time,
That he conferred, and she received, the third degree sublime.
It was a famous wedding, and we all beheld with pride,
How Molly was transfigured from a maiden to a bride.

There, brothers, that's the story; the Deacon's still
our own;
Still stands within our circle, but no longer stands
alone;
For the pledge that we have taken, and shall cherish during life,
Now protects beneath its aegis yet another Mason's
wife.

Then here's a cordial health we drink to Parley and
to Molly:
May all their days be free from grief and sombre
melancholy;
Till that Celestial Lodge above shall ope its golden
portals,
To welcome them, both bride and groom, among the
blest immortals.

S. B. S.

LINES,

READ AT A DINNER GIVEN BY DR. C. T. COLLINS TO THE BERKSHIRE MEDICAL SOCIETY, AT INDIOLA PLACE, GREAT BARRINGTON, MASS., JULY 30, 1862.

THAT Collins is the nurse for me; he gets one's diagnosis,
And then prescribes his medicines in allopathic doses.
In fact, so great his faculty for treating lung and limb,
The very Faculty itself is "treated" now by him.

I met the Doctor on the street; he grasped me by the hand;
He looked me over, felt my pulse, then spoke in accents bland:—
"How are you, friend?" but, strange to tell, he absolutely laughed
To learn that I'd been ailing since—they talked about a draft!

"Well," said the Doctor, "your complaint is dreadfully contagious:
I find the neighborhood is full of men who talk courageous;

Their tongues are loud enough to make you prick your ears in wonder,
But there's some kink about their legs to make them run like thunder!

But this is neither here nor there; the war is quite exciting;
But my affair, as you shall see, is vastly more inviting.
The Berkshire Doctors, one and all, from valley, hill and heather—
I'm going to have them, Wednesday week, around my board together.

Of flesh and fowl I mean to have a bountiful selection,
And let these chaps just try their hands at *post mortem* dissection.
I'll show our folks a clever trick, and let the people see
How, under certain circumstances, doctors can agree.

And then, to give the dinner some celebrity, you know,
I want the village parsons, and the lawyers, in a row.

The three professions all combined afford a thorough
teaching—
You see, ours do the practicing; the clergy do the
preaching.

Our neighboring men of letters, and a few "F. F.
G. B's"—
I shall surely lay some covers, and reserve some
seats for these;
And chaps whose wives, like yours and mine, have
rather wholesome faces,
Must give their spouses, as of right, the most con-
spicuous places.

I shall prescribe a dose all round, adapted to revealing
'The warm, champagny, old-particular, brandy-pun-
chy feeling;'
And when the heavy masticating processes are done,
We'll have a little flow of soul, and sentiment, and
fun.

There's Duncan, way from Williamstown—you knew
him when in college,—
His head's a perfect reservoir of sparkling wit and
knowledge;

And there's the veteran Doctor Childs—God bless
him! he enjoys,
At four-score years, to hold his youth, and be one
of the boys!

* * * * * *

I'll have these fellows trotted out, and make them
show their paces,
And put them through an exercise of intellectual
races;
And those who hold allegiance to some other learned vocation,
May add their tribute to the flow of mutual admiration.

And as for you, pray bring along your little play-
ful muse,
And let her dance a lively jig in lightly-stepping
shoes.
Don't let her fear the wise old heads with whom she
comes to mingle;—
I'll warrant she can fool them all with her delusive
jingle."

I tried to have myself excused, and all that sort of
thing—
The same as nice young ladies do when importuned
to sing;—

But "No, you simply must," was all the Doctor had
to say;
Then left me in a mute surprise, and went his homeward way.

And so I come; and just to take some vengeance on
my friend,
I tell you the whole story, from beginning unto
end.
You now perceive precisely, what the Doctor was
about—
His notion was—to call us in, and then, to call us
out.

But, notwithstanding, since we're here, and feeling
somewhat mellow,
We may as well own up at once that he's a first rate
fellow.
He plies his arduous calling with a wondrous skill
and vigor,
And keeps a big establishment, but keeps a heart
that's bigger.

And once or twice in every year, as sure as the returning
Of planets through their giddy paths, the festal
lamps are burning

Around the Doctor's board; and not to be of those
who go there,
To use a vulgar idiom, is simply "to be nowhere."

A health, then, to the Doctor! may genial skies be
o'er him,
And troops of friends around him, and pleasing hopes
before him;
"May his heart preserve its freshness, and the light
of life's young day,
With softened, radiant glory shine upon his evening
way."

In freedom, peace and plenty, may it be his to dwell;
May he have hosts of patients, and may they all get
well;
And of that favor'd number, may all here present
be;
And when he does this thing again, may we be here
to see.

S. B. S.

WORDS.

LINES READ BEFORE THE SACRAMENTO LIBRARY ASSOCIATION, FEBRUARY 3, 1860.

NECESSITY, that stems all law
  And brooks of no delay,
Engulphed the gentle friend I saw
  One week ago to-day.

His modest way, his honest smile,
  His 'customed accents bland,
Had given place to stoutest style
  Of summons and command.

It was the old, old tale of woe,
  Since Lyceum Leagues began;
That will not tolerate a "No",
  'Gainst that committee-man.

When bureau stars beguile, betray,
  And leave in wretched plight,
Who else must save from blank dismay
  But some domestic wight?

His prose may lack Athenian grace;
  His rhymes may be "the worst;"

Nor mother wit nor wisdom's trace,
  In either product nursed;

A youth, perchance, who early met
  His all-sufficient test;
And only asks they may forget
  Who heard him at his best!

Well known for all he is and ain't,—
  For all he can't and can;
He is a lecturer, poet, saint,
  To that committee-man.

Such was the basis of salute
  And orders to attend,
Which brought me here without dispute,—
  Obedient to my friend.

In choosing a topic, why need I be driven?
The goddess of rhyming was specially shriven.
First principles always supply the best plan,—
My groundwork, all-spanning, is primitive man.

So, out from your Eden, old Adam of kin!
Before you e'er fell in the pitfalls of sin;

While faith in your heart—then the fountain of
truth,
Endowed thee unselfish, immortal in youth.
Before having learned o'er foul flesh-pots to gloat,
The core of your system was fixed in your throat.
Your palate delighting in nuts and herbs raw,
And your bones benedictive of pallets of straw.
Thy paradise dwelling and service should teach
Beginning, and object, and evils of speech.

For every living animal was set a certain voice,
In different tones and emphasis of which they could
rejoice.
Distinctive as their outward forms was each one's
range of sound;
The treble and the screech on wings, the roar upon
the ground.
And these beyond the mere physique declared the
race and kind;
Fixed key-notes for each temper, from the panther
to the hind;—
For each, by laws of harmony phrenology employs,
Expressed in fullest narrative their natures in their
noise.

But what was his peculiar voice who ruled above the
beast;
Who walked amid perennial fruits, sole monarch of
the feast?
What single tone could indicate his majesty and
might;
Assert at once his scope of will, his purpose for the
right?
Not all the various instinct sounds which from the
herd ascend,
Not all the sweetest songsters' notes that did enchanting blend,
Could form a language for the man:—a mirror to
disclose
A record for the earnest thoughts that in his roam-
ings rose.

The first commission given to man, in which his
speech was made,—
The last self-gift of Him who spake, and all things
else obeyed,
Was when the creeping things of earth in trains before him came,
And what man chose to check them off, to each one
was the name;
Which natural history catalogue proved Adam not
a mute:

As tickled to articulate, his voice invoiced the
brute.
But tho' the earth bore fruits and flowers, regardless
of expense,
Yet was no help-meet found for man within the
garden fence.
One night he slept a deeper sleep than he had ever
known,
And when he woke, and conscious breathed, he miss-
ed a bosom bone.
While pondering on this sudden loss, resolved a
cause to draw
For this exsection of a rib, his Arab wife he
saw!
Then as man slept and woke betimes, we must, per-
force, believe,
'Twas early on a cloudless morn when Adam first
knew Eve!

Speechless he stood! and when for words, new-syl-
labled, he strove,
He learned himself spell-bound, enrapt, o'erwhelmed
in mastering love!
Through his suspense at last he broke,—exclaimed
in lordly tone:—
"O, woman! we are flesh of flesh and bone of very
bone!"

Thus did the man the woman call; their union thus
decide;
And with these words unbridled he the sweet tongue
of his bride!

Which, from the day it was unloosed, has never
ceased to go—
With words of kindness and content; but very rarely
slow.
Indeed, it seems as tho' it was implanted in her
heart,
Not to forget—if e'er forgive—that Adam had the
start!

Such was Eve's fancy to converse for conversation's
sake,
That when her spouse was tired of talk she gossiped
with a snake;—
Whose sinuous counsel caused her fall, and brought
a common woe
On all her offspring, who persist in sinning here below.

* * * * * *

It came to pass the sons of Noah were traveling to
the west;—
They cried: "Go to! come let us build a tower and
city, lest

We should be scattered all abroad, upon the planet's face,
Instead of bound in unity of residence and race;
And let the tower's top ascend, a monument of fame,
Which, to all coming sons of men, our craft'ness shall proclaim.
Aye, let the apex of the tower to Heaven in glory reach:
For can we not make well-burnt brick, and have we not one speech?"

But lo! go to! the sons of men are suddenly dispersed;
For their rash plan, with languages a thousand times accurst.
What awful force was manifest in words of close intent,
When persons parted as they called adobe for cement!
Amazed, confused, enraged, they sloped,—each family alone;
And on their toil in Shinar's land the sun no longer shone.

* * * * * *

Now, with a leap across the years—with your kind approbation—
We leave the scattered ancient tribes for our folks' Yankee nation.

No matter what has passed between, we have this
sure conclusion :—
And those who litigate the point remain in weak
delusion :—
Words are our staple, and produced in wonderful
profusion.

In pulpit and upon the stump, in market and in forum,—
Wherever two or three may chance to make a business quorum,—
There you will find some smart pretense, for wealth
or honor seeking ;
And, nine in ten, his capital exhausts itself in speaking.

The wordy man ! I know him well, and I have known
him long—
Proportioned to his lack of brain, his lungs are large
and strong.
The wordy man ! I know him well ; his temper and
his fashion ;
His drawling trick for wisdom's calm, his simulated
passion.
For, shine or storm, 'tis all the same ; his plethoric
condition
Responds with hopper evenness to every feed petition.

His logic rests on simple stress of cop'lative conjunction;
O'er sense of tense he rides rough-shod, with rhapsodizing unction.

Some simple man, reputed well about his native village,
Where he has gained a competence in store-trade or in tillage,
Has nursed the thought for many a year, in honest meditation,
That he was born for eminence in councils of the nation.
In farmers' clubs and miners' leagues he leaks his "proud ambition;"
Suggests what Congressmen should do, on such and such condition.—
Premises or concludes with hints about a vain oblation
Of solid truth, when feeble minds control our delegation!
His hour at last! The neighbors say: "John Smith's an honest nature—
Let's send him down to 'represent' in this year's legislature."

"Agreed," say all; agreement is in caucus forms
perfected;
And in due course John Smith is hailed "Assem-
blyman elected."
Now squarely on the road to fame, he must assume
a standing,
In manners and in dress, alike respectful and com-
manding.
For weeks before the session time, that nothing may
be lacking,
His new boiled shirts and broadcloth coat are placed
in careful packing.
Once at the capital, he feels his genius hugely swell-
ing,—
And what may be his final post there's no prophetic
telling!
Now, all his energies are taxed, his brain is overladen
With matter from the choice of which to pick phil-
lipics, maiden.
Lo! now this legislator shouts, 'mid wild expectoration;
His eye dilates, his breast upheaves with dreadful
respiration.
The hall is close with crowding sounds, with words
is atmospheric;—
He gains his climax with a shriek that borders on
hysteric.

He ends! and ends his public life—for, with the term expiring,
He finds his "painful duty" is to beat a sad retiring.
His age consoles: his efforts were abortive from their lateness!
And so he bids a "long farewell" to politics and greatness.

The man of words! I know him well; his every form and feature
Present to me, in simple guise, a most familiar creature.
While prominent upon the list—by general concession—
The actual act of public talk is not in his profession.
In short—for short is his address—his business is the writing
Of speeches in the proper shape from very poor inditing.
He takes a threadbare piece of cloth; re-weaves it, clean and shining—
Ah! mysteries and miseries of his acute refining!
Who knows of his alchemic toil? who thanks him for his study
O'er crucibles of ugly signs;—expressions rank and muddy?

Evolving from a jumbled mass some thoughts of useful meaning;
From loads of innutritious chaff, some wheaten kernels gleaning.
Is gratitude for such a work, from wordy men expected?
Where toughest skill is exercised, least debt is recollected.
I've seen unnumbered Solons gloat, in halls of legislation,
Because the text constituents quote enhanced their reputation;—
Until their fame collapsed in shame, from one good, square translation!

Words for the million! Who will get a patent right for pumping
The greatest number in the space allowed for party stumping?
Where Norman French derivaties, promiscuous and excessive,
Are used to stilt a tedious talk, and render it "impressive."
Where truth is not so much ignored as set in cool defiance;
Where often on the naked howl is placed a cheered reliance.

Where men of cultivated taste descend to black-
guard diction;
Where convict scoundrels patronize their patriots' conviction!

Words for the thousands! Simpering dames who resolutely tarried,
Despite all calls, beyond the time in which they should have married;
And men and women out of sorts in marital condition,
Who think their private griefs confer a special foreign mission,
Pry out their neighbors' evil days, and picture trifles glaring;
Knock down the stool of penitence, and set reform despairing;
Destroy the hopes of some fond girl, whose keenest heart affection
Was justly placed,—tho' not assumed to be on earth's perfection.

And who shall now for cotton bales or gold the pæans sing?
We hail the royal council board:—The man of speech is king!

I speak not now of babbling fools,—of those who
throw away
Their own and other people's time in lingual display.
I speak of such as Henry was,—of Webster and of
Clay.
I look to him, the eloquent, inspired New England
son,
Whose words have saved the home and tomb of
Father Washington!

Words for the hundreds! Blessed few; in Honor's
house devoted:—
Each one determining his choice,—admitted or promoted!
Words that the seeds of fire contain for nations now
complaining;
Words that when victory is won, disclose the skill
maintaining.
Words breathing peace, and hope, and faith, through
earthly time enduring,—
For every listening soul a hate of morbid thoughts
procuring:
THEIR speech we yearn to hear; for truth gleams
radiant in the hearing,
And in the trance we grasp the love that casts out
pride and fearing.

But here a thought compunctious stays; and in its candid telling,
I make avowal consonant with most congenial spelling.
Should I permit my rhyming muse to longer test your favor,
I might reduce a note of praise to feeble semi-quaver.
So while there's merit in the act, I'll make a timely ending;—
That when 'tis said, "it was not much," the phrase may be commending.
Declaring that a favor found in some such exclamation,
Will more than double all the capes of her best expectation.

C. A. S.

EXPERIENCES AFLOAT.

VERSES WRITTEN ON BOARD U. S. TRANSPORT, ILLINOIS, OFF FLORIDA COAST, JANUARY, 1863.

O GENTLE Muse! O gracious Muse!
Bestow thy smile on me;
While I describe the wondrous sights
I see upon the sea.

Old Ocean is a heavy swell;
A deep old salt, for that;
You'll find your error, if at first
You take him for a flat.

No rower can withstand his roar;
For blows he's ever ready;
And whoso keeps his company,
Is apt to get unsteady.

He brags what flags wave o'er his waves;
He boasts his ships are whalers;
With gales regales us, just to show
How he assails the sailors.

Ah me! I'm six days out from shore;
A cleaned-out, luckless rover;

Another six-days cruise ahead;
  And so, I'm half-seas-over.

I feel so "cabin'd, cribbed, confined,"
  I scarce can draw my breath;
There's no more comfort in my berth,
  Than if it were my death.

I go upon the upper deck
  They call "the hurricane;"
I spy a seat hard by, I strive
  With all my might to gain.

The passage thither seems up hill;
  I'm just a'going to soar;
When lo! there comes a sudden lurch,—
  I'm sprawling on the floor!

With stern resolve I seek the stern,
  The ship's in mad carouse;
The masts as to their master nod,
  The bow is making bows.

The smoke-stack is exceeding sick,
  It vomits forth a cloud;
A deathly pallor seems to sit
  On every sail and shroud.

I look down in the engine room ;
  The struggle there is fine ;
The old ship's stomach seems disturbed
  Almost as bad as mine.

An afterthought conducts me aft,
  How very queer I feel !
The things go dancing round me so,
  My brain begins to reel.

Then comes the strange sensation on,
  The like you never knew ;
There's nothing for it, but to run,—
  Eugh ! Eugh ! ! E-e-u-g-h ! ! !

O grim old Neptune ! once release
  Your precious hold on me ;
And you may play your pranks at will,
  I'll never go to see !

S. B. S.

CHARGE OF THE FORTY-NINTH.

[The Forty-ninth Mass. Vols. participated in the attempt to carry by storm the rebel works at Port Hudson, La., May 27, 1863, losing in killed and wounded more than one-third of the number who went into the action.]

"Forward now the Forty-ninth!" the General's
mandate came;
"Attention, Third Battalion!" was the Colonel's
prompt exclaim:
"Now, ye sons of Berkshire, your crowning hour
has come;
Prove your fond fidelity to ancestry and home!"

Straightway from the undergrowth, our gallant boys
upsprang;
Rapid and sonorous the familiar accents rang;
"Right face! Lively! Forward march!" meanwhile, in each eye
Mark the firm resolve that dareth both to do, and
die.

Through the tangled bushes stealthily we tread,
While the shells are shrieking madly overhead;
Now we reach the open; and, across the plain,
See the rebel cannon, spouting leaden rain.

"On the right, by file in line!"—rapidly we form:
"Forward march! Guide centre!"—now the fiery
storm
With redoubled fury vexes earth and sky,
As our glorious banner greets the foeman's eye.

Gallantly before us, in the thrilling scene,
March the storming party, with musket and fascine;
See! their steps they hasten! "Double quick!"—
now then
Comes the tug of battle; 'quit yourselves like men!

Ah, what rebel cunning had prepared the way!
Felled trees, logs and branches in our pathway lay;
Still our flag moves forward; aye,—and not alone;
For our line of battle bravely holds its own!

God of mercy help us! Twice the murderous balls
Strike our hero Colonel; ah, he reels; he falls!
Our Lieutenant-Colonel, "Onward! Onward!" crying,
In an instant stricken, on the field is lying!

Yet our boys, undaunted, with their might and main
Strive to gain the ramparts, but, alas! in vain.
From those fatal ramparts, looming still afar,
How the foe, exultant, hurl the bolts of war!

Through our ranks, where glittered bayonet and blade,
See what deadly havoc shot and shell have made!
Of that proud battalion,—fresh-lipped men and brave—
Scores now groan in anguish; some have found a grave!

Strive no longer vainly, now that hope is past;
Let the logs and pit-falls be your shield at last:—
Down, then; down for safety; ye who still survive;
Thank the God of battles ye are yet alive!

Softly soon the Day-King sinks unto his rest,
And the grateful twilight deepens in the west.
Hushed the din of battle—now, with footsteps fleet,
Weary, saddened soldiers make their swift retreat.

Lo! what scenes confront them, as they rearward tread;
Here a comrade wounded; there a comrade dead!
Friends at home, and kindred; ah! what would ye say,
Could you see your petted FORTY-NINTH to-day!

This, at least, in future, say with honest pride,—
"Berkshire boys right nobly fought, and bled, and died."
Ever let their actions be preserved in story,
And their names encircled with a wreath of glory.

S. B. S.

LINES,

WRITTEN FOR IMPROMPTU CELEBRATION, JULY 4, 1863, ON BOARD STEAMSHIP CAHAWBA, AT SEA, OFF COAST OF FLORIDA, EN ROUTE HOME FROM NEW ORLEANS.

THE glorious Fourth has come again; 'tis ours to hail the day
Afar at sea, as o'er the waves our good ship speeds its way;
And while our staunch "Cahawba" floats in majesty along,
From grateful lips let us uplift our patriotic song.

Well cherished day; how bright the fires on memory's altar burn,
As, each revolving year, we greet its annual return!
Our country! with what pride we trace her onward, upward way,
Since first our grandsires hailed the dawn of Independence day!

In conflict born, in faith sustained, baptized in blood and fire,
Exposed in tender infancy to Britain's haughty ire;

Still our Columbia lived and thrived, and came at last to be
An empire whose dominion stretched from sea across to sea.

Beneath her banner, science, art, and each fair enterprise
Thrived, like exhuberant fruits, beneath the most auspicious skies;
Here Justice held her scales aloft, and with benignant mien,
Religion, with her mitred front, o'erlooked the gladsome scene.

Upon that banner, earth's oppressed from lands afar have gazed,
As on some sign of healing by some modern Moses raised;
And unto it with joyful hope, and with a faith sublime,
Have flocked a countless multitude, from every shore and clime.

Blest, O, how blest! beneath that flag, we lived, nor thought nor dreamed
How much of discord lay concealed, where all so cheerful seemed;

Dreamed not there breathed a soul so base,—to human sense so closed,
As dare profane the citadel where all our hopes reposed.

But times have changed; this very scene reminds us that the foe
Hath risen in his might to deal the fratricidal blow.
The uniforms we wear to-day, and many a well-earned scar,
Tell that the nation writhes beneath the crimson foot of war!

But, God be praised, the hour hath shown, that when, in years gone by,
Heaven oped its gates to greet our sires, true valor did not die.
O, let our faith and hope grow strong, as in our ranks to-day,
We recognize the sons of sires, as brave, as true, as they!

And now, as comes the season round, when every bosom glows
Afresh with love of country, and with wrath against her foes;

O, let us at a common shrine our sacred vows re-
cord,
The contest never to give o'er, nor sheathe the right-
eous sword,
Till once again, from Kennebec to distant Rio
Grande,
Our Flag shall spread its ample folds, unchallenged,
o'er the land;
And everywhere, the wide world round, that glori-
ous Flag shall be
In very deed, and very truth, the Ensign of the
free!

S. B. S.

TO JULIA, IN HEAVEN.

Sister! we mourn with ceaseless grief thy going,
Since thou hast left us;
With each recurring day our tears are flowing,
More deep the yearnings in our hearts are growing,
For that loved presence, whereof—God's bestowing—
He hath bereft us.

Thou wast, but art not here forever more;—
Such thy brief story;—
Thy life was bright and joyous, but 'tis o'er;
Thou hast gone seeking dear ones gone before,
And from the slopes of that celestial shore,
Hast risen to glory.

Say, in those upper mansions, didst thou meet
Sister and brothers?
And in the first bright throng that came to greet,
And brought thee glad embrace,—swift-winged and fleet,—
Was there not that dear face,—serene and sweet—
Our sainted mother's?

Oh! I do seem to see new joy in Heaven,
As she who bore thee

Saw thy pure soul from earth's frail vesture riven,
Safe at the goal towards which it well had striven,
And, joyous in this child-companion given,
          Bent smiling o'er thee ;

And to the Father, on His white throne seated,
          And to the Son,
And to the Spirit—God Triune—repeated
Glad hymns of praises, nor in vain entreated
Welcome to thee, O rapturously greeted,
          Thy Life-work done !

There, as eternal cycles roll away,
          Thou art at rest.
Around, the everlasting sunbeams play ;
Through golden streets, through sweet fields, thou shalt stray,
And in yon Heaven shalt spend an endless day
          Among the blest.

Yet e'en from Heaven's ecstatic joys, I know
          Thou wouldst look down,
And gaze in fondness upon friends below,
And fain wouldst woo them from this world of woe,
And higher joys portray, and fain wouldst show
          The victor's crown.

But, oh, how swift the years will wing their flight
In thy esteem!
Our life is but a day—soon past—then night
Comes, whispering of the morn, or else with blight;
And all—the old, the beautiful, the bright—
Pass like a dream!

And, shortly, all the friends and kindred known
On earth to thee,
Must cross the stream which thou hast crossed, alone,
Must stand in judgment at God's awful throne,
And, in its bliss, or terrors, must be shown
Eternity!

Spirit departed unto realms above,
I pray, look hither;
Watch o'er and guard me with that sister's love,
Which erst I know thy tender heart did move;
From God and Heaven permit me not to rove;
But lead me thither!

And, haply, He who lives to intercede
At God's right hand,
To my poor prayers may graciously give heed;
O'er sins like mine, His wounds afresh may bleed,
And I may gain, obedient to His lead,
The promised land.

Yet not to gain it, when I know what guest
Inhabits there ;—
What greater torment for the human breast,
What greater woe wherewith to be oppressed,
What greater grief, or sorrow, or unrest,
Than such despair!

Dear sister! Earth is less since thou hast died,
And Heaven is more.
From Heaven look down and be my constant guide.
So may I 'scape the snares of sin and pride,
And reach at last, beyond Death's gloomy tide,
The shining shore.

There, as the tireless centuries come and go,
No fate shall sever ;—
Supernal joys shall have perpetual flow,
Loved ones of old shall throng with hearts aglow,
And bid us taste of pleasures, we shall know
Are ours forever.

S. B. S.

MUSINGS IN A CEMETERY.

I.

I STOOD within the consecrated ground,
Where hundreds sleep th' inevitable sleep;
In thoughtful mood I strolled at leisure, round
The sacred place where mourners come to weep;
Where sculptur'd stones their constant vigils keep;
Where solemn trees their drooping branches wave
O'er prostrate forms, consigned to slumber deep;—
The old, the young, the good, the base, the brave,
All to one common level come at last—the grave!

II.

How populous grown, thou city of the dead!
Within the period of a few brief years.
How short the time since first a lifeless head
Was here laid low with many sighs and tears!
Yet, day by day, upon our careless ears
Fall sad the tones of the funereal bell,
As, here and there, some fated mortal hears,
Sounding for him, th' inexorable knell—
"Hence to the regions where departed spirits dwell!"

III.

So, one by one, the marble columns rise,
And for its tenant yawns another tomb,

And some new shaft points upward to the skies,
And new-wreathed flowers exhale their sweet perfume—
As fain to rob some grave of half its gloom.
Here speaks a stone of aged worth passed away;
There, of a youth cut down in early bloom;
There, of a child called from its infant play—
Blest one! so soon let in to realms of endless day!

IV.

'Tis a fine impulse—worthy of a race,—
The foremost, doubtless, of the sons of earth,—
The habitations of the dead to grace
With fitting tributes to departed worth.
How meet that one who had a common birth
With me; whose youth ran parallel with mine—
Who sat beside the same paternal hearth—
When called at last his being to resign,
Should find a grave o'er which these hands should place a shrine!

V.

Yes, honored be the instinct which incites
To decoration of the sacred spot
Where the dead rest, with something which invites,—

Which seems to say, "Thou art not clean forgot;
Though gone from earth, thy name hath perished
not;
But o'er thy ashes, the memorial stone
Some place to thee in memory shall allot—
Record a life in which some virtues shone
Too bright to pass away unchronicled—unknown."

VI.

It makes the living look with lessened dread
On death, and scenes which its approach attend,
To see attractions multiplied and spread
Around each tomb by some surviving friend.
'Tis sweet to feel that, when one's life shall end,
He shall not sleep within a nameless grave,
But o'er him some inscription shall defend
Awhile his record 'gainst the Lethean wave,—
Prolong his influence, and his good example save.

VII.

And there's incentive in the pleasing thought,
That whatsoever hath been grandly done,
In panegyric letters may be wrought
Upon the shaft, or monumental stone,
To tell the pensive passer-by of one
Who, in some noble sphere, held high command;

Who, in mankind's affection, held a throne ;—
Endowed with gifts of head, and heart, and hand ;—
Whose life was one long benediction o'er the land.

VIII.

But monuments are feeble bulwarks all
Against the havoc and the waste of time ;
They serve a purpose, but decay and fall,
Ere they who built scarce reach th' eternal clime.
Some living truth disclosed—some deed sublime—
These be the monuments that shall endure.
Great Cæsar's valor,—greater Homer's rhyme
Give each a place in history secure,—
Beneath Fame's temple-dome, a habitation sure.

IX.

The prophet, Moses, towards the mountain height,
At God's commandment, lifted up his face ;
So passed forever out from human sight,
And no man knoweth of his burial-place.
Yet not till men have lost the power to trace
In holy writ, the record blazoned there,
Shall he,—the leader of a chosen race,—
The homage of the ages fail to share,
Or crowns of everlasting splendor cease to wear.

X.

Of good and bad taste, it may well be said,
Our cemeteries make a vast display.
Like living cities, cities of the dead
What sort of folk inhabit there, betray.
The architecture of the present day,—
The ancient models setting all at nought—
In various style—grave, cumbrous, graceful, gay—
Some fair, some execrable shapes hath wrought—
The chance embodiment of each contriver's thought.

XI.

Yet 'twere a simple thing to keep within
The bounds of proper taste and cultured sense;
Build some substantial structure o'er thy kin,—
Against time's ravages, the best defence,—
And shun, of all things, vulgar, base pretense.
Did he die rich? be modest, ne'ertheless,
Nor strain to typify his opulence
By something that shall only make men guess
What share it cost of all that Dives did possess.

XII.

I can perceive a fitness when men build
Their costly tributes to great Washington;
Or, lavish of expense, adorn and gild

Their proud memorials to each gifted one,—
Soldier or sage, or patriot, whose life done,
Seems to become the property of all
Within whose midst his grand career was run ;
Who, o'er his dust, or in the classic hall,
Or in the market-place, his sculptur'd form install.

XIII.

But when old Jones, whose riches were amassed
In manufactures, or in merchandise ;
In prosperous venture, or some signal cast
Of fortune, pays stern Nature's debt, and dies,
And wills that o'er his ashes there shall rise
The most imposing of memorial stones,—
His name, forsooth, to thus immortalize ;
I really can but think that Mr. Jones
Is paying overdue respect unto his bones.

XIV.

And mark the folly of the vast outlay !
This man would fain perpetuate his name ;
But, ah ! how soon his fabric will decay,
And time will mock his weak, pretentious claim.
Wealth can find better shifts to purchase fame.
Jones spent a fortune ; he might have endowed
A charity or college with the same,

And bought applause from no ignoble crowd,—
Conceived a generous act, and won distinction proud.

XV.

Rich Amos Lawrence;—honored be his name!—
A poor boy once,—became a millionaire;
Then, thoughtful founder of a fragrant fame,
On charities bestowed a zealous care.
The tomb that shrines him is a plain affair,
And yet his name on many a structure shines,
Goes linked with benefactions here and there,
And, until Time his sovereignty resigns,
On Fame's bright scroll shall be inscribed in living lines.

XVI.

When I must answer to the final call,
I'd have no costly pile above my head;
But I would be remembered, if at all,
For something nobly done, or fitly said.
But, should I join the multitudinous dead,
Who leave no footprints on Time's treacherous sands,
Enough for me, to have my children shed
Sometimes a tear beside the spot where stands
The simple stone placed o'er my dust by friendly hands.

XVII.

While thus I mused, lo! the descending sun
Began to cast his shadows, dark and long;
And so, with one accord, were quickly done
The day, my stroll, my reverie, and my song.
To the near city I made haste along,
Through avenues proud, and bustling thorough-
fares,
And once more mingling with the busy throng,
Ah, me! how soon life's round of paltry cares,
Re-ent'ring all my thoughts, possessed me una-
wares.

S. B. S.

POEM,

DELIVERED AT GREAT BARRINGTON, JULY 4TH, 1865,
AND ON SAME DAY IN PITTSFIELD.

No MORE to chronicle fraternal wars;
No longer hand-maid of the furious Mars;
No more to beckon to a soldier's grave
The youthful warrior,—the heroic brave;
No more with classic tread and ireful mien,
To lend thy presence to some battle scene;—
Goddess of song! with gladder notes attend;
Here in our midst, with radiant brow descend;
On happier themes, O let thy zeal increase—
The HOUR OF TRIUMPH, and the DAWN OF PEACE!

Dark was the cloud, which, gathering thick and fast,
For many years the Nation's sky o'ercast;
And fierce the storm, whose pent-up wrath broke forth
O'er desperate South and o'er determined North,
When the defiant flag was first unfurled,
And civil war's hot thunderbolts were hurled,
Waking the echoes of the startled world.

Sad was the day, and evil was the hour,
When Reason left her throne and lost her power;

When first the impious madman dared begin
The strife in which he could not hope to win;
To fire the nation's temple dared presume,—
Whose flames, once lighted, must himself consume;
Too glad this common heritage to mar
With all the havoc of tremendous war,
And drown the sacred ties of brotherhood
In swollen rivers of fraternal blood!

It was to be; the God who rules above,—
Alike the God of justice, as of love,—
Doubt not, was witness with omniscient eye,
Of all the scene; and from His throne on high,
Beheld what man saw not, nor yet foresees,—
Results, far-reaching through the centuries!
Nay, e'en to us, of finite, feeble sense,
Comes now and then a glimpse of recompense,
And all the sacrifice of toil and blood
Seems cheap in prospect of the coming good.
Men die, but nations live, whose men are great,
And fit to found and regulate a state;
And nations are the mighty instruments,
Beneath the wondrous rule of Providence,
Wherewith to hasten that consummate end,
To which all time's events and changes tend;
And whoso with a pious trust essays
To give his nation power and length of days;

To make her nobler, and of higher worth,
Among the thrones and kingdoms of the earth,
Fulfills a mission ; and may lay him down
Where death o'ertakes him ; he hath won a crown.
And thou, whose eye to-day can only see
That far-off grave 'neath the magnolia tree,—
O cease thy grief ; for though no more the boy
Comes back to mingle in these scenes of joy,
Nor joins his comrades,—proudly welcomed now,
The laural wreath encircling every brow,—
Yet, one day, when God's Bugle in mid-air
Shall sound " Attention ! " he too shall be there ;
At that last roll-call, " ADSUM ! " shall reply,
And join the Grand Encampment in the sky !
His work was done ; he had not reached life's noon ;
He died too soon, you think, yet not too soon.
A hero, died, who might have lived instead,
To die, a riddance, in an old man's bed.
Peace to your ashes, brave, departed ones !
Sleep well ; though now the sun may bleach your bones
By Mississippi's stream, or down beside
Where the James rolls his deep, historic tide,
Our hearts go out and up to you to-day,
And bid you God-speed on your heavenward way ;
And fresh and green your memories we shall keep,
Till ours to sleep the same mysterious sleep !

Thank God for our glorious, gallant dead!
On history's page we have often read
Of the wondrous deeds of those,
Who at famed Thermopylæ fought and fell,
And at Marathon struggled long and well,—
Whose story the grand old writers tell,
In immortal verse and prose.

And we thought that the age was forever past,
When spirits so noble could still be cast
In a like heroic mould;
And we did not dream that here and there,
Each in his little round of care,
Breathing with us the common air,
Were youths, whose courage to do and dare,
Occasion might unfold.

We have read in old books, of classic ground,
And have longed to visit and linger round—
As pilgrims round a shrine—
Each famous spot, where, in days gone by,
Proud Greek met Greek with a dauntless eye,
In haughty contempt of death, to die,
With an impulse that seemed divine.

But no longer we need to gaze afar,
To where the grim-visaged god of war
Hath stalked with ponderous tread.

On the hither side of the ocean foam,
Where the young Columbia hath her home,
Sacred indeed hath the soil become,
With the graves of the deathless dead!

Let the Old World now be the New World's guest,
As the long line moves from East to West,
In procession vast and grand
Of pilgrims from far beyond the sea,
In this favored home of the brave and free,
By the graves of martyrs for Liberty,
In reverent awe to stand!

Inscribed on a new-built Arch of Fame,
Shall stand forever each honored name
Of that unselfish throng;
And the unborn millions shall be taught,
What deeds sublime these heroes wrought,
And how with patriot zeal they fought,
And conquered a giant wrong.

And of that proud Arch, the white keystone
Shall bear the shining name of one,
Whose death was the august crown
Of the sacrifices a nation gave,
In a perilous hour, its life to save;—
Sleep well, great Chief, in thy hallowed grave,
On the heights of the world's renown!

Sleep well, O, martyred President!
  The dastard blow that struck thee dead,
  New lustre on thy record shed,
And wrought thee good, where ill was meant.

Thou hadst the plenitude of fame,
  And heart of friend and whilom foe;
  There seemed no higher boon below,
Or short of Heaven, for thee to claim.

So all-symmetric thy career,
  To live, was but to jeopardize;
  For oft would busy envy rise,
And seek excuse to carp and sneer.

So, like a fully ripened sheaf,
  The reaper, Death, at God's command,
  Did cut thee down with furtive hand,
And all the world was plunged in grief.

O, how the nation wept for thee!
  While fast in sympathetic flow
  Fell stranger tears, and tones of woe
Came wafted o'er the sobbing sea.

With calmer eyes we now discern,
  In this event, the hand of God.
  We place thy ashes 'neath the sod,
And shrine thy deeds in history's urn.

Full at the zenith stood thy sun,
 Betokening grateful afternoon;
 Yet none shall deem inopportune
That swift eclipse; thy work was done!

Now let us turn the picture round, and view the brighter side,
And gather as we gaze, some food for patriotic pride.
The crisis o'er, our country lives;—in vigor yet survives,
A thousand-fold more dear for all those consecrated lives.

Four years—four pregnant years have passed, since war was first begun;—
The mightiest war that ever yet was waged beneath the sun;—
And every Independence Day, as year succeeded year,
Still found within our anxious hearts alternate hope and fear.

But, God be praised, the scene is changed; the clouds have rolled away;
'Tis ours to hail the dawning of a more auspicious day;

The atmosphere is purer far,—the nation smiles again,
And Peace o'er all the fair expanse resumes her glad domain.

Our "erring sisters" have come back,—at least they say they're coming;
The busy wheels of enterprise on every side are humming;
The boys come home to breathe the northern air so fresh and balmy,
And each one struts, and brags about—"When I was in the army!"

The contrabands are freemen all; it seems so strange and new,
The situation puzzles them; they don't know what to do:
But let them all lay down to-day the shovel and the hoe,
And shout and sing, "De kingdom's come, an' de year ob Jubilo!"

The rebel States come back so fast, for re-admission asking,
The powers of the President they're greatly over-tasking;

But let each wandering star once more upon our banner shine:
To err is human, it is said;—but to forgive, divine.

But as for "Jeff," the head and front of all the wicked plan,
I'll e'en express my sentiments as mildly as I can.
I know you'll think me too severe; I know I shall be blamed;
And yet I vow and do declare—*She ought to be ashamed!*

And there's our old friend, Johnny Bull; my recollection's dim,
Or else the Yankee nation owes a trifling debt to him.
The poor old fellow has the blues, and bitterly desponds,
And gets no interest, now-a-days, on those Confederate bonds!

And there's the Third Napoleon, and the Sovereign Castilian;
And there's the new-fledged Emperor, the Archduke Maximilian;
Some doctrine we'll expound to them—they call it "the Monroe,"—
Unless they very shortly take French leave of Mexico!

We have some little tubs afloat, and now and then
a gun,
And boys enough, both north and south, who'd like
to see the fun ;
And Montezuma's halls, methinks, will witness quite
a scare,
When cook-stoves from Connecticut come hissing
through the air!

I tell you what: I do believe this mighty Yankee
nation,
When once it gets its "dander" up, can whip the
whole creation;
And since our family quarrel's done, and things are
quiet now,
If people don't behave themselves, there'll be a precious row!

But I must stop my Pegasus, before he does his
worst ;—
He gets so full of patriotism, I fear the nag will
burst;—
He wants to give a toast or two, and then his story's
told:
It's time to close ; for I suspect the dinner's getting
cold.

Then here's to Grant, and Sheridan, and Farragut, and Sherman;
The Yankee boys, the Irish boys, the steady, fearless German;
And all the gallant officers, and all the noble men,
Who fought the fight; what land shall look upon their like again!

Long life, and health, and every good, be theirs in bounteous store,
Till they shall join their comrades upon Jordan's farther shore;
And when the soil of centuries upon their graves is pressed,
Still may the grateful generations rise to call them blest!

And now, to glorious UNCLE SAM, let's give a rousing cheer!
The dear old Patriarch has reached almost his ninetieth year.
Let every heart and tongue unite to give the toast *eclat*,
And join each voice with mine: Hip! hip! Hurra! Hurra!! Hurra!!!

S. B. S.

LINES,

READ ON THE OCCASION OF HON. AND MRS. WM. D. BISHOP'S CRYSTAL WEDDING, BRIDGEPORT, CT., OCT. 20, 1865.

["Our tokens of compliment and love are for the most part barbarous. The only gift is a portion of thyself. Thou must bleed for me. Therefore the poet brings his poem; the shepherd, his lamb; the miner, a gem; the sailor, coral and pearls; the painter, his picture; the girl, a handkerchief of her own sewing."—*Ralph Waldo Emerson.*]

O GENTLE muse! who deignest oft thy presence to bestow,
Where Hymen celebrates his rites, and Cupid bends his bow;
Descend and linger here awhile, thy grateful influence shedding,
To give this glad occasion voice, and grace our Crystal Wedding.

No crystal offering I might bring, could hold the least compare
With those we witness here displayed, so tasteful and so rare;
Be mine, instead, to shape the thought which animates the throng,
And bring it hither, wrought in verse, and crystalized in song.

The Crystal Wedding! fitting theme for poet's gladsome rhyme;
Bright spot upon the borders of the rapid stream of time.
What memories and what hopes surround this point upon life's way,
Betwixt the veiled To-morrow, and the beauteous Yesterday!

'Twas Hope that crowned the nuptial hour, when first the wedded pair
Set forth together, hand in hand, the vast Untried to share;
Now Memory too attends the feast, with gladness in her mien,
And lends new interest to the time, new beauty to the scene.

'Twas fifteen years ago to-night, the mystic knot was tied,
Which bound in holy wedlock, the bridegroom and his bride;
And some were there, who now are here, and some in death lie low,
Who bade the happy pair Godspeed, but fifteen years ago!

And some are here who were not there,—for so the
world wags on;
New friendships, and new ties are forming ever and
anon;
And some new comers I perceive, of tender ages
rather,—
The eldest is'nt yet fifteen;—they all look like their
father!

The bride and groom betray no serious ravages of
time;
Of manhood, and of womanhood, they scarcely reach
the prime;
And yet for them so prosperously life's fickle stream
hath run,
The prizes most can never win, already they have won.

For he, in legislative halls, hath mingled with the
great,
And aided to administer the grand affairs of State,
And much goods hath laid up in store since wedded
life began,
And is a Railroad President, and was—an Alderman!

And she hath lent the magic charm of beauty and of
grace
To many a proud assemblage, and many an honored
place,

And been a ready helpmeet unto him in life's endeavor,
And greets us now, a courtly dame, and handsomer than ever!

Fifteen years wedded; no divorce; no "spats;" no shattered nerves;
No jars—except that harmless kind, for pickles and preserves;—
Bright children; very pleasant home, and well-to-do in life;—
'Tis well; I yield assent, and do pronounce them man and wife.

(I tell you in parenthesis, this ceremony's binding.
I know full well that latterly, there has been much fault-finding,
Because ambitious laymen played the deuce in one or two setts,
But I was made a Justice, when I lived in Massachusetts.)

Now here's a health, twice-wedded pair, to you and yours we proffer;
Life's bounties may you richly share, in basket, store and coffer;

No crystal gift that sparkles here, but silently rehearses
The hearty benediction I would fain repeat in verses.

And when the years—a decade more—have swiftly passed away,
And time perchance hath silvered o'er your brows with lines of gray ;
Though weeping friends o'er many a tomb, tears meantime shall be shedding,
May it be yours, as bride and groom, to keep your silver wedding !

Nay—rarer chance to mortal lot—still let the wish be spoken,
May the silver cord be looséd not, nor the golden bowl be broken,
Ere at life's even you shall stand, inspired by memories olden,
To join each faithful hand with hand, in nuptials that are golden !

And finally, we wish you all the joys vouchsafed to mortals ;
May the shades of life unfrequent fall on these domestic portals ;

May every tongue your deeds extol; may friends prove true and stable,
And Heaven grant you numerous olive-branches round your table!

And when the promised Bridegroom comes, O may we all behold
The crystal stream, the silver thrones, the city of pure gold;
And join that august, shining throng, before the Great I AM,
To celebrate eternally the Marriage of the Lamb!

S. B. S.

POEM,

DELIVERED AT THE RE-UNION OF THE FORTY-NINTH REGIMENT, MASSACHUSETTS VOLUNTEERS, AT PITTSFIELD, MASS., MAY 21, 1867.

How strange a thing is memory: as I gaze
This night on comrades of those fruitful days,
When arméd cohorts thronged on every hand,
And war's alarms and thunders shook the land;
I am not here,—but backward, far away,
My inmost thoughts and recollections stray,
And bygone scenes are passing in review,
Which, haply, I may reproduce to you.

And first, Camp Briggs* attracts my gaze; the spot whereto we rallied,
When forth from peaceful hearths and homes, as raw recruits we sallied;
When, having stumped the county o'er, for men to aid the nation,
We undertook the rudiments of martial education.

---

* Camp Briggs, Pittsfield, so named in honor of Brigadier-General H. S. Briggs.

And first, there came the "Allen Guard,"* with Captain Israel Weller,—
A whilom three-months sergeant, and a funny, whole-souled *feller* ;
With Clark and Francis for his aids, he fired the opening gun,
And straightway boldly issued "General Order Number One!"

Then Garlick, Plunkett, Sumner, Train and Morey followed fast;
Then Parker, Shannon, Rennie; and then Weston came the last;
And so, ten goodly companies encamped upon the green,
While tents and shanties multiplied, enlivening all the scene.

O then 'twas drum-beat, morn and night, and tramp tramp, all the day,
And not a little arduous toil, and very little play;

---

* The "Allen Guard," a militia company in Pittsfield, named after Hon. Thomas Allen, who had contributed largely to its organization and support, was the first company of the Forty-ninth to go into camp. It established itself at Camp Briggs on Sunday, September 7, 1862, which was the day when the Thirty-seventh Regiment left it for the seat of war.

The boys complained of homesickness;—the discipline seemed hard;
And ever and anon, at night, the rascals ran the guard.

What stunning dress-parades we had, at every close of day,
When all the Pittsfield gentry came to witness the display;
When Captain Weller put us through the exercises fine,
And "R. R. Noble, Adjutant," went strutting down the line!

And then, what everlasting drills, and marches up and down,
Eliciting the compliments of all the belles in town;
And as we marched in column on, about a score abreast,
Good Lord! how Plunkett's towering form loomed up above the rest! *

Pete Springsteen† served the rations round, according to our means.

---

* The Forty-ninth was known wherever it went as "the regiment with the tall major." Major Plunkett was six feet six in his uniform.

† Peter Springsteen, whilom landlord of the United States Hotel, Pittsfield, furnished rations for officers and men, when the camp was first established, and accompanied the regiment South as its sutler.

The beefsteak was exceeding good, and eke the pork
and beans.
Our appetites were glorious, and we minded not the
odds,
And quaffed our coffee piping hot; 'twould kill at
forty rods!

Of Pittsfield hospitality, I hardly need remind;—
This grand old town, whose people were so generous
and kind;
Where many a mansion, with the warmth of welcome, was aglow,
As, through the "witching hours," we tripped "the
light fantastic toe."

And here, the pensive muse would pause, in sadness
to deplore
The death of Sarah Morewood, who shall greet us
here no more.
Deep on the white entablature of memory, we record
Her virtues, yielding now, we trust, exceeding rich
reward.*

---

* Mrs. Sarah A. Morewood, late of Pittsfield, now deceased, was a lady of ample means, and proportionate generosity. The Thirty-first and Thirty-seventh Regiments while encamped at Pittsfield had received many favors at her hands, but the Forty-ninth were especially indebted to her for many acts of kindness

At first, the clear October days were mild and warm enough;
But, by-and-bye, the nights grew cold, and winds blew chill and rough;
The guard-house was a populous and thriving institution,
And all the while our rank and file betrayed a diminution.

We shall not soon forget the day, when orders came to leave,—
To 'pack all up for Worcester, and go that very eve.
Our tents were struck, our knapsacks slung,—and then,—lo, and behold,—
Our train came not, and there we stood, a' shivering in the cold!

On th' horrors of that dreadful night, I need not here to dwell,—
The men were all disgusted, and the officers as well;

---

and attention. Before leaving Pittsfield every officer was presented by her with a portfolio with writing materials, in convenient form for camp use, and also a copy of the Scriptures, and a number of miscellaneous books. The whole regiment was the recipient of her hospitality on many occasions, at Pittsfield, and while in barracks in New York, and in camp on Long Island.

But, what with show of coffee and refreshments, brought from town,
And sharing with the men the "gloom," we kept their temper down.

The welcome morning dawned at last; the tardy train arrived;
We gave Camp Briggs a parting cheer; our spirits quite revived;
With many a benediction from many an anxious friend,
Away we sped:—and so I bring this chapter to an end.

And now, at Camp Wool, Worcester, we tarried for awhile.
We came at night, and travel-worn for many a weary mile.
That snow-storm you'll remember, and the wintry winds that blew,
And the hospitable snow-drifts that we had to stumble through.

But the commodious barracks, and the host of generous friends
We found down there in Worcester, soon made complete amends;

The drilling-grounds were spacious, and the winds
 began to lull;
Oh! after traveling farther, we sighed for old Camp
 Wool!

And Colonel Ward,* who held command, and afterwards who died
A hero's death, we here recall with sorrow, yet with
 pride.
A courteous gentleman was he; a soldier true and
 brave;
Long let memorial flowers bloom above his honored
 grave!

And here it was we organized; and for our leader
 chose
A private at the war's outbreak—a General at its close.
He needs no cheap insignia now—of eagles, or of
 stars,—
His badges of nobility are honorable scars.†

---

* Colonel George Ward commanded the camp at Worcester when the Forty-ninth arrived. The Fifty-first Massachusetts Regiment was also there. Colonel Ward had been in active service, and the artificial leg which he wore testified that he had been to the front. He afterwards returned to active duty, and eventually fell in battle.

† Major-General Bartlett was in the Junior Class at Harvard when the war broke out. He enlisted as a private for the three months' campaign; then he became Captain in the Twentieth

The "Bay State"* was a famous place for sociable resort,
Where Captain Shannon took by storm the grand Piano Forte;
Where Weller improvised the dance, and Doctor Rice grew mellow,
And spun his yarns, which made him out—a devil of a fellow!

Massachusetts, and was acting much of the time while in that regiment as Field Officer. At the battle of Ball's Bluff he showed great bravery and skill, and succeeded in bringing off from the field a small remnant of his men, crossing the river himself in the last boat, after seeing his command safely out of the clutches of the enemy. While before Yorktown he received a wound in his leg, requiring amputation above the knee. Subsequently he was appointed Commandant of the post at Camp Briggs, and although an entire stranger to the officers of the Forty-ninth, so favorably impressed them, that they chose him as their Colonel. He served with the regiment, and was severely wounded in the attack on Port Hudson, May 27, 1863. After the Forty-ninth was mustered out, he became Colonel of the Fifty-seventh, and served under Grant in the long campaign of 1864–5 against Richmond. He was wounded at the battle of the Wilderness, and for his bravery promoted to be Brigadier-General. At the attack on Petersburgh, at the time of the explosion of the mine, General Bartlett was captured, and was a prisoner in the hands of the enemy for some time. At the close of the war, he was brevetted a Major-General, at the age of twenty-five, a most merited compliment, most fitly bestowed at the termination of so remarkable and brilliant a career. He has since died of diseases contracted in the service.

* The Bay State Hotel, Worcester, was the place where we went occasionally to get a "square meal," and have a social time.

The ladies came in troops, to do our necessary stitching,
To glad us with their charming smiles, and manners so bewitching;
In truth I deem it very sure, had we much longer tarried,
Each bachelor would then and there have been decoyed and married!

But orders came to move again;—again we watched in vain
From day to day, the coming of the transportation train;
We lingered through Thanksgiving, and were happily surprised
By dinners which those same dear creatures quickly improvised.

Next day we took the Norwich cars, and then the "Commodore,"
A steamboat staunch, which bore us straight to old Manhattan's shore;
And so, one drizzly morning, fatigued and hungered all—
We stretched our line across the Park, before the City Hall.

The barracks up in Franklin street, became our next
resort,—
A place to study insect-life of every phase and sort;
We tarried but a week or so—but plenty long enough;
The best accommodations there—to draw it mild—
were "rough."

Behold us on Long Island next, at Union Course en-
camped;
The ground was wet, and so our feet and ardor both
were damped;
However, we contrived to live and flourish passing
well,
For Hiram Woodruff's was hard by, and Snedeker's
Hotel.

And here it was we lingered on for quite a length of
time,
And many a day experienced the roughness of the
clime;
At East New York we had a row, the Sutler grew so
mean,
The boys confiscated his goods, and smashed up his
machine.*

---

* The allusion here is by no means to our old friend Springsteen, but to the rascal who contracted to feed the troops on Long Island *by the job*, and served the boys with rations of rancid pork and beef, that were "an infringement of Goodyear's patent for Vulcanized Rubber."

But, by-and-by, they placed our boys,—their comfort to increase,—
Where trotting nags had quartered in the piping times of peace ;*
And here we stayed, and here we drilled, and kept our snug abode,
And marched our soldiers back and forth, along the smooth plank road.

And now, a large detachment was assigned for provost work,
In picking up deserters in the City of New York.
Our boys resolved themselves into a Vigilance Committee,
To watch that mythic "Elephant," that stalks about the city.

At length there came an order, to our most unfeignéd joy,
To embark our troops for Dixie, on the steamer "Illinois ;"

---

* The barracks in the rear of Snedeker's Hotel, consisted of the stalls which had been used for trotting horses, in connection with the races at Union Course. The names of many celebrated nags were posted up in the stalls which they had respectively occupied ; and the use to which these accommodations had come to be appropriated, was matter of considerable remark and merriment.

We set sail in high feather,—but, arrived off Sandy
Hook,
A feeling slightly singular our senses overtook.

A disposition seized us, to keep the vessel's side,
And cease our conversation, and only watch the
tide.
We found some strange attraction the briny surge
beneath,
And many a mouth was wide agape,—and Charlie
lost his teeth!

And when we reached Cape Hatteras, our symptoms
were redoubled,
And many a fellow's diaphragm with dreadful qualms
was troubled;
O ever since, when I desire my veriest foe to be
With heaviest penance visited, I wish him out at
sea!

We gained at length the South-west Pass, of Mississippi's stream,
And once more, of smooth waters and green fields,
began to dream;
But our voyage seemed prosecuted beneath a luckless star,
And our ship was over-freighted, and we couldn't
cross the bar.

We telegraphed to New Orleans, and soon with joy espied
The Yankee boat, "New Brunswick," at anchor alongside.
She bore us up the river, and beneath the clear moon's light,
Louisiana's sacred soil regaled our gladdened sight.

Next morning, as we trod the deck, with interested eye,
We gazed on fine plantations, as we swiftly floated by.
The sweet abodes of peace they seemed, nor could we, from afar,
Discern as yet the havoc wrought by fratricidal war.

And now, upborne in heaven, the Day-king held his throne,
And in the glorious sunlight, a hundred steeples shone.
There sat the Crescent City on the river's eastern shore,
O how unlike the City it had been in days before!

Its levees all unoccupied for miles along, save where
A federal transport lay in wait for orders, here and there;

While in mid-stream the gunboats lay, with ever threat'ning frown,
And iron fingers pointing towards the proud but conquered town.

And here we ate fresh oranges, and, after noon sailed on,
A few miles up the river, to encamp at Carrolton,—
A place, by no means such as that for which our hopes were looking,
The most attractive thing to us, was Madame Schraeder's cooking.

But here we met the Thirty-first; and glad enough were they
To welcome us, so lately come from Berkshire homes away;
And many a spot we talked about, where we would like to peep in,
Of dinners that we used to eat, and beds we used to sleep in.

We took some trips to New Orleans along about those days,
And studied its geography, and learned its devious ways;

And dined at the St. Charles Hotel, and looked at
octoroons,
But, others having been and gone, we brought away
no spoons.

For Baton Rouge we started next,—the night was
chill and dark,
It took us until past midnight, our baggage to embark;
The Major's horse fell overboard; we bivouacked
on the shore,
And the Colonel vowed those cook-stoves should
encumber us no more!

We floated up the river all the following day and
night,
Till we saw afar the State House, with its massive
walls of white;
And the Hospital we wot of, and the Arsenal, all
standing
Along the river's eastern shore, the noble stream
commanding.

And here we joined the First Brigade, in Augur's
famed Division,
And carried on our strict routine with order and
precision;

And here, I recollect, we all financially were *busted*,
But Train and Morey came across some sutlers there, who trusted!

And here, until the fourteenth day of March, we lay at ease,
When General Banks conceived a plan, with force and arms to seize
The stronghold of Port Hudson;—but here let the Muses rest,
I'll sing that olden ballad; it will aid our memories best.

THE PASSAGE OF THE MONTESINO.*

Banks, of Shenandoah fame,
By the Crescent City swore
That Port Hudson, on the river,
Should defy his might no more.

---

* This ballad, "The Passage of the Montesino," was written at the time, and on the spot, and contains scintillations of more than one genius. Several officers had a hand in its production. In fact, nearly half of it was written before we were invited to take a share in the intellectual effort necessary for its completion. The several authors would prefer not to publish their names, but we are bound to state that the regiment could boast a good deal of undeveloped poetical talent. The ballad was read by a great many within and without the regiment at the time it was written, and we are glad to put it in shape for preservation, after eliminating some local allusions and hits, the printing of which would be matter of doubtful propriety.

By the Crescent City swore it,
And sent without delay,
An order to his Chief of Staff,
To summon his array.

He summoned to him Farragut,
And gave him orders sealed;
Then, girding on his armor,
With his staff he took the field.

Attend ye to the story,
Which I will now relate;
It happened in the Lowlands
Of Louisiana State.

'Twas on a cool March morning,
When we our steeds bestrode;
And, just as day was dawning,
Struck the Bayou Sara road.*

We crossed the Montesino
By plank bridge, and pontoon;
And halted for the bivouac,
Some three hours after noon.†

---

* The road leading out of Baton Rouge, northerly towards Port Hudson, some twenty-five miles distant.

† The Bayou Montesino is a small stream or creek, about six miles north of Baton Rouge. The place where we "halted for the bivouac" is some miles further north.

We plucked the rails from off the fence—
Of boards there were but few,—
And spread our scanty shelter tents,
To shield us from the dew.

The air was filled with squeal of pigs,
And cackle of the geese;
While stalwart oxen lost their hides,
And simple lambs, their fleece.*

And now the night was falling,
Soon rose the evening star;
And through the deepening twilight,
Gleamed camp-fires from afar.

But hark! what noise arises!
This night we sleep no more;
For the tide of battle surges
On Mississippi's shore! †

---

* The "gobbling" done by our men on that expedition, was something tremendous. It was strictly forbidden in orders from Headquarters; but hunger knows no law, and officers were obliged to wink at some depredations upon private property in the enemy's country, especially as an occasional rare bit thereby found its way into their own mess.

† There was heavy cannonading during the night, as Farragut was attempting to pass the batteries on the river, and did succeed in passing Port Hudson with the Flagship Hartford, and the Albatross. The head of our column was also near enough to Port Hudson to make some demonstration on land, and divert as much as possible the attention of the enemy from Farragut's operations.

And now, an aide from Chapin,—
  The Driller of Brigades—*
An order brings to form the line
  In haste, without parades.

Upon his own black stallion
  Sat the gallant Brigadier;
And he called to him the Colonel,
  And he whispered in his ear;

"Our army has attacked the Fort,
  And been repulsed;"—they say—
"In haste o'ertake the Forty-eighth,†
  And homeward lead the way!"

The bivouac of our brigade was probably three miles east from the river, and some miles south from the outer line of fortifications of Port Hudson. The explosion of our gunboat, Mississippi, on the river, lighted up our camp with the glare of day: and the report, which was not heard until the lapse of a minute, as it seemed, was terrific. This was about three o'clock in the morning, and an order coming nearly simultaneously, to fall in, and march back the way we came, created a temporary panic which is cursorily described in the verses which follow.

* Colonel Chapin, of the One Hundred and Sixteenth New York, Commander of our brigade; and, as is hinted, an inveterate driller thereof. He was a brave and faithful officer, and was killed at the storming of Port Hudson, on the 27th of May. President Lincoln appointed him Brigadier-General, of date the day of his death.

† The Forty-eighth Massachusetts; which, together with the One Hundred and Sixteenth New York, Twenty-first Maine, and our own regiment, constituted our brigade.

The road is blocked with wagons,
  The darkness settles down ;
But swiftly marched the FORTY-NINTH,
  In silence back to town.

The FORTY-NINTH marched swiftly ;
  But swifter far than they,
Beneath their feet, the Forty-eighth
  Let no grass grow, that day.

Their Colonel had been ordered
  By General Banks, they say—
To hold the Montesino,
  And keep the foe at bay.

*   *   *   *   *

The Bayou Montesino reached,
  No foe was there discovered;
And silence was the deity,
  That o'er the valley hovered.

Ah, then, the gallant Forty-eighth
  Did mighty deeds of valor ;
And courage on each countenance,
  Assumed the place of pallor.

And now their Colonel, homeward bent—
  Their manly zeal arouses;

"Press on, brave boys, and seize and hold
  Our lumber and cook-houses!"*

And so, for many a weary mile,
  In toilsome march, we find them;
Before them were their household gods;
  The FORTY-NINTH behind them!

And now, a short half mile ahead,
  The old camp greets their vision;
And each indulges sweet foretaste
  Of sleep and dreams elysian.

But look! behind, a cloud of dust
  Our eyes are now discerning;
It cannot be;—it is, it is
  An order for returning!†

The Reverend Chaplain—worthy soul—
  Had trotted on before;
And so he did not hear his flock,
  How dreadfully they swore!

---

* The old camp of the Forty-eighth at Baton Rouge, had been very comfortably arranged, with elaborate cook-houses, etc., and the regiment seemed to feel great apprehension, lest some other regiment should arrive there first, and establish "squatter sovereignty."

† Just as we came in sight of our old camp that day (the 15th) we received orders to march back, and encamp at Bayou Montesino.

The sun was near his setting—
  The clouds betokened rain,
When, having reached the Bayou,
  We pitched our tents again.

And now, in all their fury,
  The elements are roaring ;
And down in copious torrents,
  The watery flood is pouring.

O, orange groves and palm-trees!
  O, land of milk and honey!
Where "zephyrs were so very soft,
  And skies so bright and sunny ;"

We thought to spend a winter here,
  Should fortune so decree it,
Would be the thing :—but, on that night,
  We really couldn't see it!

All o'er the deeply-furrowed field, *
  The waters rose so high,
Our boys could neither make their beds,
  Nor keep their powder dry.

---

* We encamped on "Pike's Plantation," in a field where cane had been grown the year before. The furrows were very deep, and the rain soon filled them with water. Here we were nevertheless tired enough to sleep ; but many a poor fellow contracted the fever that day and night, which, within a fortnight, consigned him to a furrow in which he still lies.

The guns with rust were covered o'er,
  And many a luckless wight
Began to think his chance was slim,
  If forced into a fight

But if he dared to try his piece,
  And if it chanced to go;
He had to stand at "shoulder arms,"
  For half a day or so.*

At Bayou Montesino,
  For six long days we stayed,
To tempt the rebel foemen
  Our precinct to invade.

We gobbled up their sugar,
  We licked their syrup fine;
And longed to lick the rebel
  Who dared approach the line.

---

* It was contrary to orders for any one to fire off a piece in camp, as false alarms were to be deprecated. One of our officers was under arrest for a week for firing off a pistol. The boys were sometimes *very sure* that their guns were so rusty that they wouldn't go off, and the cartridges couldn't be drawn with a wormer; and, furthermore, an attack from the rebels was hourly expected. Yet if an unlucky private *tried* his piece, and it *did* go, he was summoned up in the front of the Colonel's quarters, and ordered to do penance by standing there under arms till duly released. The muse records this as an instance of dilemmas in which soldiers were sometimes placed.

But only to O'Brien's* gaze,
  And the gallant cavaliers,
Who hailed from "Little Rhody,"
  The enemy appears.

In vain did General Dudley
  His whole brigade deploy,
And execute manœuvres,
  The rebels to decoy.

For, as that famous army
  Aforetime, marched in vain;
So, Dudley did go forward,
  And bravely back again.†

Of all that week's adventures,
  We lack the words to tell;

* Lieutenant-Colonel O'Brien, of the Forty-eighth Massachusetts; an impulsive, but brave Irishman, who commanded the storming party at Port Hudson, May 27, was killed. On one occasion, while at Bayou Montesino, he was officer of the day; and a company of Rhode Island cavalry, who were out on picket, thought they discovered the enemy approaching, and reported accordingly to Colonel O'Brien, who rushed to Headquarters and made such representations that Dudley's brigade of our division was ordered out to meet the intruders. It proved to be a false alarm.

† "The French marched up the hill with an army of ten thousand men, and then—marched down again!"

"I never see that!" says she with "Jock"
  And sighs "Ah! well! well! well!"*

At length there came an order—
  On dress-parade 't was read;—
'T was General Banks who sent it,—
  Now what do you think it said? †

"My valiant boys; take courage!
  Our object is attained;
Your cue is to be jubilant,
  For victory has been gained.

"Perhaps you deemed it 'running,'
  The morn you were so fleet;
But the truth is you were making
  A 'masterly retreat!'

"You see, I only wanted—
  While Farragut passed through
The gauntlet on the river—
  That you should halloo 'Boo!!!'

"I came a week beforehand,
  To Baton Rouge, you know;

---

* Favorite expressions of astonishment with Frenchman "Jock," the Colonel's servant.

† General Banks issued a congratulatory order, saying the object of our march was accomplished, etc., but as we had failed to capture Port Hudson, we could hardly "see the point."

And had a very grand review ;—
  But that was all for show.

"And now, my boys, I thank ye,
  For gallant deeds ye've done ;
Go back to camp and rest ye
  On the laurels ye have won.

"And in the long hereafter,
  Be this your glorious boast ;—
'We went with Banks's army
  To Port Hudson . . . . . . almost!'"

Then there came a thrilling order in the following month of May,
To take by storm Port Hudson, with ardor to essay.
It was a fearful struggle, and the muse forbears to dwell
On that momentous conflict, and the fate which there befel.*

---

* On the 27th of May, the Forty-ninth had one company (G) on provost duty at Baton Rouge ; Company F was guarding the baggage train ; about one hundred men were on picket duty, and a large number in convalescent camp and hospital, so that but two hundred and thirty-three men took part in the assault. Of this number, sixteen were killed and sixty-four wounded, making eighty in all—more than one third of the whole number. The

For memory will remind us of the gallant boys who
died,
While with us there contending, fighting bravely,
side by side;
Who sleep in nameless graves afar beneath that
Southern sod,
And whose souls were thence uplifted to the presence of their God.

O, if no other impulse moved our hearts to gather
here,
To hold one brief communion, with each recurring
year;
Our duty still were plain enough, since, haply, we
survive,
Their sacrifice to count, and keep their memories
alive.

O, such a brotherhood as ours, we shall not find elsewhere,
And ours are obligations that we never may forswear;

Colonel and Lieutenant-Colonel were both wounded, and every company had one or more officers killed or wounded. Officers and soldiers who served throughout the war, and who participated in the assault of May 27, have pronounced it one of the severest and bloodiest engagements in the history of the war.

The warm, fraternal flame within our breasts can ne'er expire,
For our initiation was THE BAPTISM OF FIRE.

From the threshold of Eternity, amid the battle's din,
We did hardly meet dismissal, as our brothers entered in;
They have crossed the stream to where the fields with lasting verdure smile,
And we, upon its hither shore, are lingering yet awhile.

Yet not unscathed did we escape the battle's angry storm,—
I stand surrounded here by many a scarred and shattered form.
The grim Death-Angel, hurling forth his missiles thick and fast,
Gave some of us the tokens of his presence as he passed.

Then let us praise the God of Hosts, whose overruling power
Did shield us, and deliver us in that portentous hour;
Nor let those heroes moulder there, unhonored and unwept,
In that mysterious sleep which peradventure we had slept!

Thus, brothers, in numbers less brief than intended,
  I have sung, as my impulses moved me ; and now,
Ere the harp be unstrung, and its minstrelsy ended,
  Let us banish the sadness that sits on each brow.

The conflict is over ; and Victory, descending,
  Is perched on the Banner, so proudly we bore ;
And the white Dove of Peace its glad presence is
    lending,
  And we list to the clamor of battle no more.

I have sung of our perils by land and by water,
  And glimpses of by-gones have sought to unfold ;
Of scenes of enjoyment, of hardship, of slaughter ;
  Yet how much, after all, there remaineth untold !

But while memory lasts, though our heads become
    hoary,
  The events we were part of, we shall not forget ;
But to our childrens' children shall narrate the story,
  While with tears sympathetic, their eyes shall be
    wet.

And as time shall roll on, let us happily gather,
  Now and then one more glance retrospective to
    cast ;
With a fondness and longing, unlessened, but rather
  More deep, as our years recede into the past.

And now, let the generous cup be o'erflowing
  With grateful libations, potential to cheer;
The rapture of social enjoyment bestowing,
  As we strengthen the ties of our fellowship here.

S. B. S.

LINES,

READ AT GREAT BARRINGTON, MASS., JULY 4, 1867, ON THE OCCASION OF THE VISIT OF AMERICUS HOSE COMPANY, OF BRIDGEPORT, TO GREAT BARRINGTON, AS THE GUESTS OF HOPE COMPANY, NO. 1.

THOSE sempiternal editors, on both sides of the border,
Who, sometimes, for the lack of news, concoct a batch to order,—
Have been proclaiming all along, that, previous to the races,*
My Pegasus would volunteer to show the crowd his paces.

I wish those editors could know how serious a thing
It is, on all occasions to be advertised to sing;
And, furthermore, that Pegasus, when once you try the rule
That—will he, nil he—he shall GO:—is staky as a mule!

And yet, upon this festal day, when, on my native heather,
So many new and old-time friends are haply met together;

* The exercises of the celebration that day, concluded with races on the Housatonic Fair Grounds.

I fain would clothe the sentiments which to the hour belong
In drapery of fitting rhyme, and comely garb of song.

I stand upon my native hills; and once again behold
Familiar scenes—all redolent of memories of old;
The grand old elms in majesty the smiling landscape crown,
And on the sweet vale, as of yore, the lordly hills look down.

I clasp the hands of early friends; while, answering to my gaze,
Gleam genial stranger faces here,—the friends of latter days;
The present and the past unite;—the mountains greet the sea,—
The rare occasion is replete with poetry to me.

Here did my young eyes look their first on things beneath the sun,—
Here were my earliest lessons learned; my earliest prizes won;
Here the delightful school-boy days flew onward all too fast,
And here my early manhood years in sweet content were passed.

And many a merry, glorious Fourth, as year succeeded year,
Have I, in unforgotten days, enjoyed and welcomed here.
There's many an "old inhabitant" can testify, I trow,
What annual racket I helped make—say twenty years ago!

We boys were wont to congregate in force the eve before,
And make the whole night hideous with glare, and din, and roar.
I met some of them,—older grown—last evening at the train,
And, for the nonce, I could but feel that we were boys again!

But those old times have passed away;—their very memories seem
Far down the distant retrospect, like some mysterious dream.
No more those primitive affairs in once secluded vale:
For, now-a-days, we celebrate upon a larger scale.

No sanguine orator unto my boyish ears foretold
In highest flights of prophecy, the scene we here behold.

The "woolen works" in Barrington were then but sheep and lambs,
And Bridgeport, an obscure resort for men in quest of clams.

The steam-car was unknown up through the Housatonic vale;
'Twas deemed a quite indecorous thing to ride upon a rail;
The man who lived in Berkshire, and had seen Long Island Sound,
Was no small "pumpkins," you may bet, in all the country round!

But, by-and-by, the thought occurred to some sagacious mind,
Old Berkshire to Long Island Sound, by railroad ties to bind;
So, Barrington's the depot now for many a thriving town,
And Bridgeport has become, indeed, a city of renown.

And so it was a pleasant thought for Berkshire boys, to-day,
To bid us hasten hither from a hundred miles away.

I know a heartier patriotism each stranger bosom
thrills,
Inhaled with this sweet atmosphere among the
Berkshire hills!

* * * * * *

And now, may this acquaintanceship, so pleasantly
begun,
Retain a lasting friendship in the breast of every
one;
And when the day is over, and we seek our homes
again,
May each have added one bright link to memory's
golden chain!

S. B. S.

POEM,

DELIVERED BEFORE THE GRAND CHAPTER OF THE ZETA PSI FRATERNITY, AT DELMONICO'S, NEW YORK CITY, DECEMBER 27, 1867.

I GO back twenty years to-night, and bring to mind
the days,
When with my college peers I strove to win scholas-
tic bays;
And varied the routine of tasks laborious and dry,
By joining in the mystic rites of glorious ZETA PSI.

I see, in that far retrospect, that little band of ours,
Which held its conclaves just beyond where lordly
Greylock towers:—
For I'm a Berkshire boy, and gained my academic
knowledge
In what you might be pleased to term, a mere "fresh-
water college."

O, very pleasant were the hours we spent within the
place
Where our enthroned Hierophant alone unveiled his
face;
Vouchsafing intellectual food to each and every one,
And eke the generous dessert of good-fellowship and
fun.

What rousing times we used to have, electioneering, then,
When each commencement-day brought on a bevy of fresh men;
When every society disparaged all the others,
And reaped the annual harvest of its new-inducted brothers!

I've been a politician since, and mingled in the brawls
Of primaries, and caucuses, and legislative halls;
And watched political machines, and been within the ring,
And button-holed the Governor, and all that sort of thing;

But ne'er within my memory did affairs of such concern
Depend on human strategy, or fate's capricious turn,
As those contentions, who should hold the favorite positions,
And bear away the honors at the college exhibitions.

And when it chanced,—to gladden my enthusiastic eye,—
That on the victor's person flashed the badge of ZETA PSI;

I tell you, 'twas a prize unmatched by many later toys,—
For men still clutch their playthings, and are simply older boys.

The college is a microcosm; and if we don't inherit,
We're sure as students to imbibe enough of party spirit;
The tree inclines precisely as at first you bend the twig—
A. Oakey was a "Kap," I'm told, and Hoffman was a "Sig."

The youth who leads a college clique, will, doubtless, lead a clan
Somewhere, upon a larger scale, when he becomes a man;
And he whom all his cronies hailed, a jovial, genial fellow,
Will hold his own, e'en when the leaf of life is sere and yellow.

The boys of twenty years ago! as I recall them now,
Alternate shade and sunshine seem to flit across my brow;

I follow down the catalogue the old names, one by
one,
And note with varied sentiments what time for each
hath done.

There's one, is U. S. Senator; and two or three de-
termine
The weighty matters of the law, and wear judicial
ermine;
And some have found the source of wealth remarkably prolific,
Upon the far Nevada heights, and shores of the Pa-
cific.

Some argue causes at the bar, and legal quibbles
moot,
And some—Lord help them!—strive to "teach the
young idea to shoot;"
Some deal in goods and merchandise, with manners
bland and pleasing,
And some the tortured purse of poor old "Uncle
Sam" are squeezing.

Some grace the pulpit, and proclaim the everlasting
Word;
Some, in the latter pregnant times, have wielded well
the sword;

And one—a mighty handsome chap—a veritable Paris—
Has simply raised a fine moustache, and—carried off an heiress!

Some boast a goodly heritage, and live aloof from cares;
Some operate in fancy stocks, among the "Bulls and Bears;"
Some scribble for the papers, and employ the art phonetic;
Some wake the oratoric strain, and some the strain poetic.

And some, in life's bright morning, have responded to the call,
Which, soon or late, shall send forth its alarum to us all.
I count upon that little list, the death stars;—they are seven;
So many old-time friends have sped from earth—we trust, to Heaven.

But turn we now to witness, after lapse of twenty years,
How fair a thing, and vigorous, our ZETA PSI appears;

From tiny seed, on welcome soil, the forest monarchs grow,
And they who plant, do oftentimes plant wiser than they know.

The tender shoot, whose destiny no mortal might foresee,
Hath grown, and flourished, and become a very Banyan tree;
And hundreds of ingenuous youth, beneath its bowers have strayed,
To hear the whispering of its leaves, and linger 'neath its shade.

We build our own best monuments; our own deeds, after all,
Outlast the brass, or marble, or the niche in storied hall.
Well saith the Poet—"We ourselves can make our lives sublime,
And, dying, leave behind us footprints on the sands of Time."

I know not whether simple slab, or more pretentious pile,
Repeats the tale that Sommers* lived, and wrought on earth awhile;

* John B. Yates Sommers,—Founder of the Fraternity.

What recks he, since in hearts like these shall be enshrined his name,
And Time itself shall only add fresh laurels to hi· fame!

And now, dear brothers, standing here, within your midst, I seem
Like mythic Rip Van Winkle, softly wakened from a dream.
Emotions passing sweetest song my inmost heart o'erflow,
As I renew the vows to-day of twenty years ago.

I feel it was a kindly act, rejuvenating me,
Who watched the infant stem erewhile, to now behold the tree.
The choruses of bygone years repeat their glad refrain,
And I am Heaven's favorite—a college boy again!

And now, long live our ZETA PSI! and as the years roll round,
May roots and branches new on our fraternal tree be found;
And ever and anon, beneath its overhanging boughs,
May it be ours to congregate, and ratify our vows.

And you, my younger brethren, pray remember, that
to me,
And my compeers, you owe it now, to cultivate the
tree;
So shall it thrive, and may kind Heaven vouchsafe
that you and I,
May live to see our grand-sons wear the badge of
ZETA PSI!

S. B. S.

A LEGEND OF BLACK ROCK.

AN OWER TRUE TALE.

'TWAS on the first of April, and the sun had just gone down,
And the shades of night were falling on a certain sea-coast town;
When a few congenial spirits somehow happened to combine,
At the Doctor's to assemble, and discourse of turpentine.*

Now, these chaps who thus assembled, we may just as well premise,
Were a parcel of stockholders in a famous enterprise,
To extract from out a cord of wood, when duly baked and fried,
Turpentine, tar, coal, and acid, and no end of gas beside.

But like all contrivance human, this had had its ups and downs,
And dame fortune had cajoled it with alternate smiles and frowns,

* Dr. J——, an enthusiastic stockholder.

And the sessions at the sanctum where the Doctor
sat in state,
Had been frequent as the changes and vicissitudes
of fate.

When the "Holmes"* came in all laden with a car-
go worth the while,
It was better than his doses to behold the Doctor's
smile.
When 't was thought the "Holmes" was cast away,
and every one felt blue,
'T was the Doctor who could, best of all, their flag-
ging hopes renew.

Now, on this same first of April, there had been a
lucky fry,
And the hopes of all the party were proportionately
high,
And the Doctor was foretelling, with the wisdom of
a prophet,
How this would beat all frying pans elsewhere this
side of Tophet.

Just then there came a knocking at the Doctor's office door,
And a rather stout man opened it, and stalked the
threshold o'er;

---

* The "Madison Holmes," a schooner bought by the Company for transporting pine from North Carolina.

Said he, "Get up your horse, Doctor, as quick as
e'er you can,
Our deucéd works are all a-fire, as I'm a living
man!"

Up rose the frightened company, in consternation
all,
And on each countenance at once there came a solemn pall,
But the Doctor cried, "Sit still, my boys; no April
fool am I,—
There's no such thing; and as for you, I tell you
sir, you lie!"

But the stout man called the negro man, and bade
him go ahead,
And get the best nag harnessed, and the buggy from
the shed;
And the Doctor compromised so far, he'd go at least
to see
What, under heaven, all that flame and ominous
smoke could be.

They westward drove—the Doctor and the stout
aforesaid man;
A lurid light the while had come, the western sky to
span;

They reached, they crossed Division street; in mad
career they flew,
When all at once the dreadful scene burst forth upon
their view!

"My God! my God!" the Doctor cried; "and do
I wake or dream?
And can that be our kindling wood which makes that
awful gleam?
And must they burst, those tender chords, that bind
this heart of mine,
To all those cords of wood, and eke that tar and
" turpentine!"

Meanwhile the stout man cocked his eye, and with
poetic gaze,
Regarded Nature's grander moods, and watched the
gorgeous blaze.
"Behold!" said he, "my friend, behold, how awfully sublime,
Up toward the stars, to contemplate those blazing
cinders climb!"

"Oh, dear! oh, dear!" the Doctor said, "why overflow my cup
Of sorrow, as I only see my fondest hopes go
up.

Untold per cent., softest of things, and almost here
in pocket,—
Spirit of Shadrach! there it goes, brief, brilliant as
a rocket!"

In rage the Doctor lashed his steed; they quickly
cleared the mile,
Which brought them to the fated spot where they
had staked thei. pile.
'Twas nothing but a funeral pile; they could do
nought but mourn,
For that which was, but now had gone to that proverbial "bourne."

* * * * * *

The pensive pilgrim, as he wends his way along the
coast,
May note to-day an inlet, whose good harborage is
its boast;
A splendid shaft there towers, inscribed, "A.–D.,–
1–8–6–9."
Which means to say—"This classic field is soaked
with—TURPENTINE!"

S. B. S.

ROSE COTTAGE REMINISCENCES.

TO MRS. JOSEPHINE ——.

You threw me down "the glove" one day—
(The "mitten" long before!)
And bade me in some simple lay
Recall the times of yore;
When you and I were lass and lad,
And life-tints all were rosy,
Whose pleasures were in common had,
By "Samivel" and "Josie."

So, Josie, dear;—for e'en so now
I'll venture to address thee,—
Tho' other lips returned thy vow,
And other hands caress thee,—
A ballad of the olden time
I'll sing;—but since our houses
Are side by side, pray keep the rhyme
A secret from our spouses!

And to begin: two decades back
Along the vale of years,
A distant speck on memory's track,
"Rose Cottage" school appears.

The place is strangely altered now,
  And where the roses flourished,
There stands a shrine where sinners bow,
  And hungry souls are nourished.

I mind me of the "corridor"—
  A sort of masked embrasure,
Behind which maidens waited for
  And spied the beaux at leisure.
I mind me of the houses twain,
  Between, the cosy arbor,—
When "Tommy" chased some venturous swain,
  'T was no ungrateful harbor.

O, peaceful scenes! O, classic shades!
  Where precept and example
Were both combined in *three staid maids*—
  'T would seem the means were ample
To keep those cloistered nuns intent
  Upon the tasks before them;
And yet how many a smile was lent
  To lads who dared adore them!

And oh! what various, nameless arts,
  And how much necromancy,
Did occupy those loving hearts,
  To circumvent "Miss Nancy!"

How, in a trice, on many a night,
  That lawn became Sahara,
As dawned on some fond couple's sight,
  The spectre of "Miss Sarah!"

I recollect the serenade
  Was quite a favorite cover,
'Neath which the old, old game was played
  'Twixt lady-love and lover:
For, while the song allured each ear,
  And melodies were blending,
The *billets doux* to windows near
  Were covertly ascending!

But as for me, I quite despised
  The rash, adventurous measures,
By ardent lovers improvised
  For amatory pleasures.
To me opposed no envious space
  Those fairy realms to gain;
For, 'twixt them and my dwelling-place
  Was nothing but a lane.

Lord! how my heart went pit-a-pat,
  And all that sort of thing,
As 'neath that portico I sat,
  To hear my charmer sing.

I studied law,—or so professed,—
  But now, at this remove,
The truth were just as well confessed,—
  I learned no law but love.

O yes! I fell in love, of course;
  But did not dare to tell it,
For fear 'twould make the matter worse,
  Should my beloved repel it.
'Twere bad enough to lose my heart,
  But vastly better so,
Than have my darling say "depart!"
  And tell me—"not for Joe!"

And so, no doubt, it came about
  That when school-days were over,
"*That other fellow*" found you out,
  And proved a bolder lover.
But, sometimes, as my thoughts recur
  To that "Rose Cottage" garden,
I heave one sigh for "hours that were,"
  And feel like——"ENOCH ARDEN."

S. B. S.

LINES.

READ AT THE CLAM-BAKE WHICH WAS GIVEN AT THE RE-UNION OF THE FORTY-NINTH REGIMENT, MASSACHUSETTS VOLUNTEERS, AT PITTSFIELD, SEPT. 11, 1873.

STRANGE! how a clam, a closed-mouthed thing, and undeclamatory,
Should make you all so clamorous for speech, or song, or story;
But observation goes to show, at divers times and places,
The stillest fellows, oftentimes, turn out the hardest cases.

A missive from the adjutant, a week or so ago,
Announced that you would shell to-day your old bivalvous foe;
And then, apparently to make the invitation louder,
He added, with significance, "there'll also be clam-chowder!"

He bade me join the festive crowd, and gulph a clam or two,
Since, when the war was raging, I was on the Gulf with you.

Said he, "there'll be a chowder mixt of mirth and
speech and song,
And clams with toast, and toasts with clams; so,
prithee, come along!"

"Oh, no you don't!" at first methought; "I know
what you're about—
You only want to ope my shell, and then, to draw
me out.
I see what you are raking for; I do, by the Eternal!
And after you have shelled the clams, you mean to
shell the Colonel!—

And yet, upon reflection, it will never do,"—
thinks I—
"To let so glorious a chance for feed and fun go by,
I'll chew upon 't; for maugre all apologetic shams,
Clam-av-i de profundis—I am always death on
clams!"

And so I come; and knowing well how very apt I
am
To overeat, and thus become as stupid as a clam,
I bring my post-cœnatic toast, all ready-wrought in
song,
Done up like clams, compact and round—I never
liked them "long!"

So here's to you, my gallant boys—old Berkshire's noble sons,
Who erst amid the battle's din, stood firmly by the guns,
And oft on many a well-fought field, made every "Johnny" stare,
When something worse than clam-shells went careering thro' the air!

Right bravely did ye clamber up the heights, where lurked afar
The foe, amid the horrid din and clamor of the war;
And over-stayed your term, until Port Hudson's pluck had died out,
Resolved to break their boasted shell, and sworn to "clam the tide out!"

Oh, how as yesterday they seem—the old familiar scenes,
Of which we each and all were part, way down at New Orleans!
No slight fraternal kinship binds us henceforth to each other,
In every one I recognize a comrade and a brother.

A health to each and every one, and as the years
roll round,
May each one at the annual feast continue to be
found,
And live to see a grand career attend our Uncle
Sam,
And spend his days in sweet content, and—happy
as a clam!

S. B. S.

EXTRACT FROM A POEM ENTITLED

MILK.

WRITTEN FOR THE SOCIAL AND LITERARY ENTERTAINMENT, BRIDGEPORT, CONN., JANUARY 6, 1870.

WE'RE something like those funny fish we see beneath the tide,
Which often, as we watch them close, display a whiter side.
This whiter side, which seems a part of every human being,
When once we get a glimpse of it, is always worth the seeing.

You think yourself familiar with some cross and crabbed neighbor,
Because you see him come and go about his wonted labor,
Till some day you shall meet him with his harness off, and mellow,
And find him, to your great surprise, a downright genial fellow.

I knew a man, I thought so mean, 'twas simply his to grovel,
Until I caught him laughing o'er the contents of a novel;

And such a knack that fellow had, at anecdote re-
peating,
He'd turn into high carnival, the stiffest quaker
meeting!

Men's very foibles often make their most attractive
features,
To tell the truth—'twixt you and me—I hate these
perfect creatures!
I honor each embodiment of goodness, truth and
meekness,
But hang the chap who won't confess one amiable
weakness!

The life of every mortal man is more or less a rid-
dle,—
Why, Nero must have had some soul; because he
played the fiddle!
The hardest, driest human plant which Nature e'er
produces,
Would not be human, did it not exude some fragrant juices.

All men are poets—it is said—and 'tis a saying
trite,—
There must be poets who can feel what other poets
write;

Ah! those unwritten hymns the soul unto itself hath sung,
In tabernacles not of clay, may one day find a tongue!

The whiter side of every man—no matter how renowned,
However brave, however great, or gifted, or profound—
It is the side which gives the zest to biographic story,
And rounds at least the hero's fame, and supplements his glory.

The hero soon becomes a myth, who shows no whiter side;
Of whom grave history simply states, he lived and wrought and died;
Some altogether human traits their added light must shed,
Or else, although his works survive, the man is very dead.

His whiter side, when all the scenes of mortal life are past,
I reckon will best satisfy the man himself at last.

We may find sermons everywhere;—behold the fishes even,
How, when they die, they always turn the whiter side to heaven!

And now I come to tell you why we are, or should be here—
To sink our selfish selves, and let our better selves appear;
To linger for a little while on one of life's oases,
And help each other cultivate our most redeeming graces.

Come, let us then be human, and deal gently with each other,
And find in every one a friend, and every friend a brother;
What sweets the cup of life affords, O let us freely share—
A few more kind or selfish deeds, and we shall be—elsewhere!

Here let us interchange the gifts vouchsafed us from above,
Of wisdom, wit, or melody,—at any rate, of Love,
And have our hearts impregnated with Charity's sweet leaven,
A little purged of earthly dross—a little nearer Heaven.

So, I've discoursed of milk; like mercy's quality,
not strained—
From far beyond the milky-way, like gentle dew-
drops rained;
Perhaps the song has been obscure; perhaps it was
your blindness—
You recognize the theme at last—"The Milk of Human Kindness."

S. B. S.

GAGROW.

WRITTEN IN A GREEN HOUSE, UPON HEARING OF THE ILLNESS OF A TENDER PLANT, WHICH HAD BEEN NURTURED IN A WARM CLIMATE.

If the Dutch Flora thinks he floors,
Or, if the Florid thinks he's floored,
They know not well the subtle powers
By which the brightest color's lowered.

Far and Forgot are sweet with mist;
Shadow and sunlight, still I'm game;
My vanished head-piece struck Grow's fist;
He 'scaped; I fell, but take the blame.

They reckon ill who count me out;
When quick I fly, I triumph bring;
I am the router and the rout—
Alone the bully of the ring!

Galusha trespassed on our aisle,
I knew not of his sacred art;
Now a meek Christian do I smile—
I heard no sound, I feel no smart.

ARGUMENT.

For ; If a Dutchman thinks he hits,
  Or, if the fallen feels a blow,
They know not well the subtle pits
  That keep, and stub a brave man's toe!

C. A. S.

POEM,

READ ON DECORATION DAY, AT BRIDGEPORT, CONN., MAY 30, 1869.

ONCE again, O faithful comrades, we are welcoming the hour
When the spring-time lingers only to resign her floral dower;
And with tenderest emotion, and with reverent steps, we tread
Where the proud earth shrines the ashes of our brave, heroic dead.

In the hallowed burial-places, other loved and lost ones lie,
But we do not heed their presence, as to-day we pass them by.
And the harvest of the roses with a jealous hand bestow,
Where the partners of our own best deeds are mouldering cold and low.

Let republics prove unmindful of the love they once professed,
And withhold the meed of honor from their noblest and their best;

And to newer idols turn them with unseemly haste
aside,
And forget those who but yesterday so gloriously
died;

We have sworn that long as unto us remembrances
shall come
Of the sad adieus to cherished ones, and dear delights of home;
Of the hardships of the prison, of the pestilence's
ire,—
Of the weary march, and battle's awful baptism of
fire;

That the comrades who endured with us the labor
and the pain;
Who in youth's high flush went bravely forth, but
came not back again,
Shall be heroes of a treasured past, we shall not
cease recall,
Till ourselves shall clasp in close embrace the mother
of us all!

And to all else we give pause to-day, that vernal
flowers may bloom
In a superadded beauty on the patriot's early
tomb;

And we gather 'neath these fresh-clad boughs, that,
vocal as of yore,
Now repeat Æolian dirges for the brave that are no
more!

Nor with us alone to-day do scarred and shattered
forms attend,
Where the voices, sweet at once, and sad, of grateful
memory blend;
For in all the land, from Kennebec to Mississippi's
shore,
Do the roses shed their fragrance for the brave that
are no more.

And by many a widowed hand to-day, in mansion
and in cot,
Hath been twined the fair anemone with sweet
forget-me-not;
And in many a nameless orphan-girl hath 'wakened
proud desire,
To assert, in this mute eloquence, the valor of her
sire!

O! the wealth of buried heroes that our nation boasts
to-day,—
In the soil where we were nurtured, on the prairies
far away,—

In the town and in the hamlet, and by every mountain side,
They are sleeping 'neath the altars for whose sanctity they died.

But, my comrades, we would ne'er forget, nor could we if we would,
What a multitude unnumbered of our glorious brotherhood
Are asleep in rude, unnoticed, undiscoverable graves,
In the regions that the Cumberland or Mississippi laves;

In the lone graves, hollowed darkly, where the camp-fires dared not burn,
And by hands that on the morrow should be lifeless in their turn;
Or in trenches, where in hot haste, when the battle's rage was spent,
Horse and rider, friend and foeman, in red burial were blent!

Little dreamed he, youth ingenuous of twenty years ago,
Gazing out upon a future with auroral hopes aglow,

Thinking only of a life-work, o'er which Peace her
rays should shed,
And of Death, beside the hearth-stone—children's
faces round his bed;—

Little dreamed he, little dreamed ye, who had known
him as ye thought,
How much God-like and heroic in his nature was
inwrought,
Which occasion should enkindle, till from mean and
trivial things,
He should rise to deeds that challenge envy in the
breasts of kings!

Thus we sometimes may discover, how, while prison-
ers of time,
From resources deep within us, we can make our
lives sublime;
And we see, although but darkly, and with dim and
finite eye,
When this chrysalism endeth, what we may be by-
and-by!

Let them sleep, those nameless heroes, where so gallantly they fell,
Where I seem to see the wild-flower bloom, their
resting place to tell;

Where the earth, enriched with noble blood, seems dressed in brighter green,
And our thoughts in ghostly forms to-day, are hovering o'er the scene!

And the wild-birds sing their requiem above their lowly graves,
And the sad magnolia, weeping there, its solemn branches waves;
And the voices, inarticulate, of Nature's choir, declare
That the soil around is hallowed ground, for the warrior dead are there!

Let them sleep, while roll the centuries in ceaseless tide away,
Till at last the grand Reveille sounds to usher in the day,
When the whole of Earth's Grand Army shall betake them to their rest,
With the armies that encamp around the cities of the blest!

Let this hour repeat the lesson—ever old, yet ever new,—
That at best we are but shadows, and what shadows we pursue.

What are we among the millions of the universal spheres,
That are going and are coming, through the wilderness of years?

Here to-day, the waves of Lethe we would gladly hold in thrall,
But its dark, oblivious waters, must ere long engulf us all;
And our story in the distant future ages shall be told,
As we tell of Babylonians, and Babylon, of old!

Yet we know there are implanted deep in every human breast,
Germs of noble aspiration, and mysterious unrest.
The economy that shapes the orbs, yet notes the sparrow's fall,
In the everlasting Drama, hath a part for each and all.

After all, then, life is earnest, and in life's severe review,
Many years do not so signify, as what we are, and do;
For the years are oft-times squandered, gathering shells along the shore,
While the ocean, undiscovered, lies in vastness just before.

These our heroes, who thus early sleep beneath the
silent sod,
Have lived longer, as I reckon the arithmetic of God,
Than the selfish one, whose days have eked out life's
extremest span,
Yet who never was accounted, and who never was,
a man.

Do not mourn, O stricken widow; do not mourn, bereavéd sire,
For the loved one, swift-ascended, pure from the
funereal pyre;
As these flowers to-day betoken, scattered o'er his
lowly tomb,
In the Paradisean gardens, evermore his soul shall
bloom!

In the lapse of generations, we shall surely be forgot—
But I tell you that our actions, good or ill, shall perish not.
As the stone sunk in mid-ocean, sends a ripple to
each shore,
So each deed, once done, is making larger circles
evermore!

In the Registry of Heaven, every act is noted down,
And for every cross we carry, there is treasured up
a crown;

And for every noble sacrifice is waiting a reward,
And for each courageous soul, the benediction of
its Lord.

O ye shades of the departed! if perchance ye hover
near,
Looking forth from yonder Heaven, our apostrophe
to hear;—
Tarry not; we bid ye rather to celestial bowers return,
While we only guard your ashes, safe in history's
golden urn.

Now from these sweet ceremonies, friends and comrades, let us go,
Somewhat wiser, somewhat better, and with hearts
that overflow
With a love, benign and catholic, whose promptings
shall not cease
Till we reach at last the Outposts, where the coun-
tersign is "Peace!"

S. B. S.

HYMN,

SUNG ON DECORATION DAY, AT BRIDGEPORT, CONN.,
MAY 30, 1869.

Air—PLEYEL'S HYMN.

Sound the dirge, the requiem sing;
Floral wreaths and garlands bring;
Scatter roses o'er each grave,
Where in glory sleep the brave.

Passed away before life's noon,—
Who shall say they died too soon?
Ye who mourn, O, cease from tears.
Deeds like theirs outlast the years.

Crown the sod with beauteous wreath,
While our heroes sleep beneath.
Softly, sweetly, let them rest,
With our benedictions blest.

Let our voices hymn their praise,—
Martyrs of illustrious days;
While their spirits hover near,
Pleased our grateful song to hear.

Lord of Hosts! whose guardian care
Both the dead and living share;
When life's conflicts all are past,
Bring us unto peace at last.

S. B. S.

POEM.

MEMORIAL DAY, BRIDGEPORT, CONN., MAY 30, 1870, AND AT STAMFORD, CONN., MAY 30, 1876.

AND now, my comrades, faithful still, again we welcome here
The saddest and the gladdest day of all the rolling year;
And come once more to decorate with sweet memorial flowers,
The early graves, the honored graves, that haply had been ours.

The grasses thicken o'er those graves: more thickly intertwined,
The roots have grown above each form, the sacred sod to bind;
And so our common love hath grown a thing more hardly riven,
And sturdier faith points upward to the heroes' rest in Heaven.

On every hand, throughout the land, with measured tread, and slow,
I seem to see our serried bands in sad procession go;

And yet, not sad; they do but go to bid the roses
bloom,
And plant the flag for which he died, above the
soldier's tomb.

But grander army, statelier pomp, and spectacle
more rare,
With sweeter strains than here awake the circumambient air—
Procession of the memories—the muse would lead
this hour,
But words are base interpreters, and song hath lost
its power.

And yet, as one some tiny seed on eager soil might
throw,
Whence some rare plant should quick upspring, and
into beauty grow;
E'en so, perchance, some words of mine, almost at
random strown,
In every soul may help beget a poem of its own.

We say this is "Memorial Day;" 't were but a lost
day then,
Did we discern or heed no more than greets the
outward ken.

The scene may gratify the sense; grand may the
pageant be,
But O, 'tis neither all nor what we long to feel and
see!

Our unobtrusive place in life we each resign to-day,
The while our thoughts take rapid wing, and beckon
us away;
Swift vehicles of memory are translating us afar,
As once again we share the pomp and circumstance
of war.

Once more we wear the blue, and wield the musket
or the blade;
Once more at morn, the mounting guard—at eve the
dress-parade;
Once more the drill, the camp-routine, inspection
and review,
Once more, at break and close of day, reveille and
tattoo.

And yet once more we hail the call to gallant feats
of arms,
And gather the experience of battle's fierce alarms,
And watch the war-cloud's awful frown, and hear
the shrieking shell,
And view once more the blood-stained fields, where
cherished comrades fell.

Once more, sad little funerals are seen to wend their
way,
As one by one our martyr boys embrace their kindred clay;
Once more, by night, the bivouac beneath the starry
dome,
The silent prayer, the brief repose, the wistful
dreams of home.

O, tell me, in an hour like this, in what o'erwhelming flood
Do they not all return—those scenes of toil, and fire,
and blood!
O, as we enter Memory's fane, and tread its echoing
floors,
What pictures line its walls; what spectres haunt its
corridors!

This day is theirs, and no less ours, who, from the
hither shore
Of that dark Stygian stream, beheld their spirits
wafted o'er.
The dead are with us; we do feel their presence as
a spell;
The memories we invoke are theirs, but yours and
mine as well.

Nor theirs, nor ours alone, who did the brunt of
battle bear,
For in the rites we celebrate, yet other hearts must
share.
Ah! not alone by those in martial panoply arrayed,
Upon our country's altar were the sacrifices laid.

The sire, who with his blessing bade his boy that
last "good bye;"
The mother, who yearned after him, as he went forth,
to die;
The maid, who gave the honeyed kiss, as bravely
from her side
He hastened, who should ne'er return to claim her
as his bride;

Or she, the mother of his babes, and partner of his life,
Whose boon it was to bear for him the sacred name
of wife;
Who sadly—oh, how patiently!—the weary months
beguiled,
And wears to-day the widow's weeds, and clasps the
orphan child;

Have these no part in all the scene which greets the
vision here?
Shall we not hush while they bedew these garlands
with a tear?

Have they no dear-bought right, these sweet observances to keep,—
O'er which, if there be tears in Heaven, the pious angels weep?

Alas! dear friends, sad thoughts must come this hour to each and all;
Somehow on every heart and home, the shadows seem to fall:
Each breast some missing idol shrines, we would nowise disown,
Nor with iconoclastic hand dissever from its throne.

And yet, somewhat of pride, I ween, awakes in every heart,
Which feels that in this mighty grief it justly claims a part.
Some Spartan spirit yet inspires: some patriotic glow
Still warms the stricken breast, and bids it bravely bear the blow.

In years to come, as older grown, the orphan boy shall read,
How in some grand, terrific hour, was wrought some matchless deed;

O, what a flush of filial pride his radiant brow shall
wear,
If he can say to all the world; "My father perished
there!"

And you, my comrades, tell me now—how e'er your
lines be cast,—
As life is short, and you survey the record of your
past;—
Say, is it not the darling thought in grateful memory's store,
In that our country's trying hour, the faithful part
you bore!

'Tis seven brief years, almost this hour, with some of
you I stood
Before Port Hudson, midst a sea of carnage and of
blood.
A chief rode down the shattered lines, and kindled
every brow
With these proud words: "Press on, my boys;
you're making history now!"

Thank God! that history hath been made; and
brighter yet shall shine,
As consummating ages roll, on blazoned page and
line;

And mark in all the storied past, a most illustrious
day,
Whose crescent influence shall be felt, when we have
passed away.

And now, dear friends, I know what fond emotions
in each breast,
At such a season still remain, voiceless and unexpressed.
Each heart in all this gathered throng goes somewhere out alone,
And seeks, beside some single grave, a treasure of
its own.

And here and there some noble deed, some few remember well,
Whose glory passed unheralded, and history shall
not tell;
Which, done by some pet general, had handed down
his name
To wondering posterities: so dear, so cheap is
fame!

I mind me of a noble boy, whose mother's sad consent
Enrolled him with the heroes of a gallant regiment;

Dark day for her, bright day to him, when that career began,—
Sixteen years old, but every inch a soldier and a man!

There came the battle summons as in hospital he lay,
Where yet the fever threatened to consume his life away;
The army moved; the tidings reached the sick boy's ears anon;—
Straightway he rose: the dangerous way, alone, he followed on!

There came a call for volunteers, with musket and fascine,
To first assault the hostile works, and fill the ditch between;
Whose courage in that solemn hour should stand the dreadful test?
The roll was quickly filled with names,—that boy's among the rest!

Next morn, awaiting hasty rites of sepulture, was laid
A row of heroes—stark, cold forms—beneath the forest shade.

Each rigid face looked heavenward with fixed and
stony stare,
And—saddest sight of all to me—the noble boy lay
there!

The blanket in his knapsack found, his winding-sheet
was made,
And, all uncoffined, in the trench his mangled corpse
was laid;
With reverent hands the clods above his lifeless
form were pressed,
And so, his work well done, the youthful warrior
was at rest!

Above his dust the stranger treads to-day, and heed-
eth not;
I know in all that lonely waste I could not find the
spot;
Yet, unforgetful of the life that boy his country
gave,
I tell you, here and now I place a wreath upon his
grave!

So, each and all, bring flowers, bring flowers, whose
perfume shall arise
From graves of heroes near and far, to scent the very
skies.

Where these our dead do live again, and keep their
 blest abodes,
And smiling Hebe serves for them the banquet of
 the gods.

S. B. S.

MY AMANUENSIS.

INSCRIBED TO MISS LIZZIE HAND.

A HANDSOME maiden here at my right hand,
A sonnet for her album doth command.
She's trebly handsome;—for, you understand—
She writes, and has, and is, a handsome Hand.
To phrase it handsome;—handsome little "Liz"
Not only handsome does, but handsome is.

S. B. S.

SUNRISE FROM THE SIERRAS.

THE gentle lustre of the morning star,—
  The sweet submission in its fading rays
The rising radiance of the golden bar,
  The eastern sky in grayish fields displays :
The leaping up from some great sea of fire,
  Of mighty lances of resistless light,—
Betokening the Day-King's fierce desire,
  With martial pomp to slay the hosts of night!

C. A. S.

FAREWELL HYMN TO REV. J. B. F——.

SUNG BY SUNDAY SCHOLARS, CHRIST CHURCH, BRIDGEPORT, CONN., APRIL 17, 1870.

Tune—SWEET HOUR OF PRAYER.

FAREWELL! sad word repeated oft,
As through life's pilgrimage we wend;
Farewell! kind guardian of our souls,
Belovéd Pastor, guide and friend.
Our infant voices gladly join
In grateful blessings, ere we part;
And bid thee bear to other scenes,
The thankful tribute of each heart.

Thy faithful toil through all the years
Here in thy Master's vineyard spent,
This hour we linger to recall,
With sad and glad emotions blent.
And thou, where'er thy lot be cast,
In sweet remembrances, we know
This consecrated place shalt keep,
And us, the friends of days ago.

Farewell! still in thy Lord's employ,
Elsewhere his message mayst thou bring,

And other young disciples teach
  His grace to seek, His praise to sing.
O blessed work, and workman blest!
  We bid thee Godspeed on thy way;
Glad be thy harvest, late thy rest
  In realms of everlasting day!

And in that day, and in those realms,
  May we at last together meet;
And, at the shining throne of God,
  Pastor and flock, each other greet.
There, as the endless ages roll,
  May we in radiant splendor shine
Among the jewels—ransomed souls—
  That deck the crown that shall be thine.

S. B. S.

HYMN.

SUNG AT DEDICATION OF JULIA SUMNER HALL, GREAT BARRINGTON, MASS., JUNE 28, 1871.

Air—GREENVILLE.

Now let gentle memory lead us,
  While this hour our thoughts recall
Forms of loved ones who precede us
  Whither we are hastening all.
Weak we know our best endeavor,
  'Gainst the Lethean wave to strive,
Still with human fondness ever,
  Would we keep our dead alive.

His behest this hour obeying,
  Who, for sake of memory dear,
Crowned an earnest life, essaying
  These memorial walls to rear.
Thus we gather, while we listen
  To familiar tones of yore,
And while eyes in sadness glisten,
  Here to glisten nevermore!

Side by side they now are sleeping,—
  Sire and daughter, in the tomb;
Kindred from afar stand weeping,
  And all hearts are filled with gloom;

She, in womanhood's first dawning,
  He, of ripe three score and ten,
Both lie waiting that bright morning,
  When God's own shall wake again.

'Neath the flow'rets o'er them blooming—
  Summer's verdure, winter's snows—
Only faith our souls illuming,
  We must leave them in repose.
So, wherever God shall call us,
  Wide world o'er, our lines to cast,
And whatever fate befall us,
  Death shall claim us all at last!

Father, sister, our sad pleasure,
  With fraternal, filial care,
This fair cenotaph to treasure,
  So its walls your names shall bear;
And when loved ones gone before us,
  Wave for us their welcome wands,
Each and all, may God restore us,
  To the "House not made with hands!"

S. B. S.

PROLOGUE

TO TABLEAU OF CAGLIOSTRO'S MIRROR, BRIDGEPORT, CONN., OPERA HOUSE, DECEMBER, 1873.

KIND friends, we bring you, in a waif of rhyme,
A curious story of the olden time.

Know then, there lived a hundred years ago,
Where yet the Arno, and the Tiber flow,
One Cagliostro, by whose magic skill,
Loved ones, and lost, were re-produced at will
Upon his mirror; which he did contrive,
By sorcerer's art, to make the dead alive.
Tradition adds: it pleased him to discover
This power occult unto a sighing lover,—
Whose mistress, early snatched from his embrace,
Among angelic beings had a place.

So, one by one, within the magic glass,
The youth beheld, in bright procession, pass
Beings divine, recalled from their abodes
In far-off regions, habited by gods.
And, one by one, he saw, but to ignore,
Until at last, the field of vision o'er
A beauteous image moved; and on him shone
A rapturous glance, responsive to his own.

No more, can Heaven itself the maid retain,
Whom Love, transcendent woos to earth again!
Mortal, but radiant with celestial charms,
Once more she calls her idol to her arms!

Enough: the story hath been briefly told,—
What you have heard your eyes shall now behold!

S. B. S.

POEM,

READ AT THE OPENING OF THE BRIDGEPORT OPERA HOUSE, DECEMBER 26, 1870.

ONE moment let the play abide; for 'tis not meet to hear
A stranger voice first break the spell, and greet th' expectant ear.
Would some more graceful song than mine, its message might indite,
To bid ye WELCOME, each and all, this glad, auspicious night!

This night 'tis mine to speak to you first words of joyous cheer,
Within these walls, we trust shall stand thro' many a prosperous year.
Almost we know, when he who built, and we and ours are not,
This temple still shall crown its site, and beautify the spot.

All men are builders; in their day all men must builders be
Of some creation, good or ill, their fellow-men may see,—

Of wood, or stone, or thought. or deed;—some fabric
they must give,
To speak for them when passed away, and their own
lives outlive.

But, not to court didactic strain—I deem his fortune
kind,
Who, hence departing, haply leaves some monument
behind,
Built, not to crumble o'er his dust, apart from
haunts of men,
But to present him where he wrought, and living
still as then.

So I regard the rare old man,—our neighbor and
our friend,
Whose lot has been, amid these scenes, these fifty
years to spend,
And now on soil acquired by toil, in earlier, lustier
days,—
Postponer of a fruitful life, this cenotaph to raise.

Events oft happen as we wend our way along time's
shore,
Which bid us pause, and look behind, and round us,
and before;

And so, this night, we can but list to voices of the past,
And scan the present, while we strive the future to forecast.

So, with our aged friend, we take the wings of memory,
And almost from its birth o'erlook this nineteenth century;
Behold the quiet bay, where here and there the sail boats glide,
While peacefully the hamlet sleeps, the watery waste beside.

But less remote, the scene is changed, and now the bustling town,
With marts of trade and numerous spires appears, the slope to crown.
On the horizon, far away, the eye discerns a speck;—
It nears; the NIMROD! and we see JOHN BROOKS upon the deck!

Again the panorama shifts; a city greets our ken,
With freighted vessels at her wharves, and streets alive with men.

And now we hear the engine's shriek, along Pequonnock's shore:—
George Griswold blows the stage-horn at the Franklin House no more!

One step—a lapse of twenty years—and now, upon the green,
The massive halls of justice rise benignant o'er the scene;
Excited suitors help to swell the bustle and the din,
And—sure sign of prosperity—how lawyers do flock in!

Nearer we come, apace with time, until, on every hand,
The palaces of industry—the mammoth workshops stand;
A busier aspect everywhere distinguishes the scenery,
'Mid rush and ring and roll and roar and rumble of machinery!

And meanwhile,—we begin to note,—arise on every side,
Abodes of wealth and luxury, magnificence and pride;

And, better still, abodes we see, whose plain exterior tells
Where modest means keep "home, sweet home," and frugal comfort dwells.

The school-house rears a loftier front; the church more grandly towers;
(I say my prayers at old St. Johns;—of course I don't mean ours.)
The Library out-grows its shell; the city hall looks gayer,
It's "some" to be a councilman; it's famous to be mayor!

Æsthetic taste is manifest; the city's pride and boast
Are centred in the loveliest park on all New England's coast.
Kind charity opes wide her doors; the orphan need not roam,
Nor widow weep: here each may find a haven and a home.

The alms-house wears a winsome look; and oftentimes, when floored
By impecuniosity, I'm wondering how they board—

Nay more, 'tis pleasant to reflect, when all resources
fail,
And worse grows worst; one refuge still—a most delightful jail!

The city borders widen out, and every truant son
Who sought a Fairfield for his home—we captured every one!
Our Black Rock neighbors deemed it first a chastening from the Lord;
They've now some sixteen candidates for Alderman, First Ward!*

Across the harbor, hope deferred long saw an uncouth ridge;
But now it bears symmetric shape, and Bridgeport boasts a bridge.
Right glad the muse records its birth, and gives it place in rhyme;
Long may it stand, and long defy old Ocean and old Time!

Now, shall we lift the envious veil wherethro' we dimly see,
And in our fancy, picture forth the city that shall be,

---

*Allusion to annexation of a part of Fairfield to Bridgeport.

When fifty superadded years shall shed their leaves
and snows,
Still making the waste place rejoice, and blossom as
the rose?

Well may we hope, that long as Peace shall hold
her gladsome reign,
And Industry her hosts deploy throughout her vast
domain,
This busy port, so close beside the gateway of the
world,
May write "Excelsior" on its flag, and keep its folds
unfurled.

Meanwhile, as other structures rear their walls on
every hand,
This edifice, unspoiled of time, and beauteous still,
shall stand.
Tradition says, its site was once the dowry of a
bride.
We prize it as the builder's gift to us, this festal-
tide.

Here, many and many a year, as generations come
and go,
Science and art shall prophecy, and wit and wisdom flow;

Here eloquence shall charm the ear, and melody outpour,
While roll the seasons, and when we shall tread life's stage no more.

For so we go; our life is all a drama and a dream—
The muse would gladly linger still to dwell upon the theme.
I crave your pardon; you shall see blithe Ida Vernon soon;
Years gone, 'twas my delight to hear her play "The Honeymoon!"

And now—interpreter between recipients and giver—
For him,—long life and walk serene, this side of Jordan's river;
For you;—with patriarchal love, he greets your presence here,
And bids you "Merry Christmas," and a "Happy, Glad New Year!"*

S. B. S.

* The Opera House was erected by the venerable Lewis C. Segee, present on the occasion, but since deceased.

"I HOPE TO HEAR SPEEDILY FROM YOU, AFTER WHAT I TRUST WILL BE A PROSPEROUS VOYAGE TO AND SAFE ARRIVAL IN AMERICA."

Affly [illegible]

IN MEMORIAM.*

O PRICELESS hours were thine and mine.
Dear Brother! in that far off land,
Where last, together, hand in hand,
We stood beside the banks of Rhine.

Together, through the storied halls
Where Art its lavish treasures brings;
Amidst the homes and tombs of kings;
Within renowned Cathedral walls,

We strayed; until where, grim and hoar,
Old Heidelberg its tale repeats,
And Neckar aye his Brother meets,
We parted, who should meet no more.

I know it now, how I did yearn
From those loved scenes to bid thee come;
And o'er wide ocean bring thee home,
Nor speak "Farewell," but plead "Return!"

'Twas all unselfish; for methought
How unto gentle studies wed,
And how by fine ambition led,
Thou would'st not leave thy work unwrought.

---

*Perished at the wreck of steamship Atlantic, off Halifax, April 1st, 1873, Albert Increase Sumner.

So, tarrying in that glorious land,—
Where heavenly music seems foretold,
And pours its floods o'er shrines of gold,—
I gave to thee the parting hand.

Since then, with fond fraternal care,—
Expectant of bright days to come,
A throne within my own dear home,—
I've kept for thee the waiting chair.

Within Westminster's gorgeous Urn,
Last litany thou didst repeat;
Then swift foreran the message sweet,—
The harbinger of glad return.

Now in familiar Minster walls
The Organ waits thy wizard hands,
And tuneful choir, thy skilled commands
To hail the Easter festivals.*

My God! as thunderbolt the shock!
Too well I knew that gentle form
Could ne'er withstand the furious storm,
The frenzied wave, the heartless rock.

---

* Albert was returning from Europe, to fill an engagement as organist in St. John's Church, Bridgeport, Conn.

I madly cried: " Can God be good,
And grudge that little meed of care
From His Omnipotence; nor spare
My darling from the dastard flood?

And He who walked the billowy sea
Aforetime; and, with shining hand
Did wave majestical command,
And whisper 'Peace' on Galilee;—

Could He not, with benignant arm,
Uplift from out that yawning grave
One more—just one—and pitying save
That tender, harmless boy from harm?"

'Tis past, and I am calmer now,
As here, upon this moaning shore,
He lies so still; and bending o'er,
I note such calmness on his brow.

And, in that better " Fatherland,"
Faith pictures ALBERT, disenthralled;—
Among the heavenly choirs installed;—
An angel's harp is in his hand!

S. B. S.

HALIFAX, N. S., April 7, 1873.

THE DIAL.

We separate ; the girls and boys divide—
  Each to a place distinct, or quite alone ;
Our ruthless passions 'neath the altar hide
  The sacrifices, till the hours are flown.

We hear by chance, in a far distant land,
  That John and Mary have long since been wed ;
The babes we left, at manhood's portals stand,
  And ah, God help us ! some sweet friends are dead.

Then comes a flood of unrestrainéd grief ;
  Upon our past, our common hours, we dwell,
Our retrospect is cheated of relief,
  Remorse encircles like the flames of hell.

But Heaven will help us ; as we meditate,
One star sheds comfort, and our pangs abate.

C. A. S.

LINES,

READ AT A DINNER OF FAIRFIELD COUNTY BAR, CONNECTICUT, GIVEN TO CHIEF JUDGE ORIGEN S. SEYMOUR, FEBRUARY, 1874.*

[Judge Brewster, of the Court of Common Pleas, was called on to respond to the toast "*Courts of Limited Jurisdiction;*" but he said Judge Sumner presided over a court of still more limited jurisdiction than his own, though it is one which Sumner claims is the court of last resort; whereupon Judge Sumner responded as follows:—*Bridgeport Standard.*]

I KNEW, I knew these lively chaps would stop at nothing short
Of seeking, in this dreadful strife, the court of last resort;—
In other words, the court that waits the drainage of life's cup,
And then inquires, for all his pranks, how much the man "cuts up."

---

* This dinner was tendered to Chief Justice Seymour on his retirement from the Bench,—he having reached the age of seventy years, which—very absurdly—disqualifies one from holding judicial office in Connecticut. The Court being in session, all the judges were present, and speeches were made by the succeeding Chief Justice, Hon. John D. Park; Ex-U. S. Vice-President, Lafayette S. Foster; Judge Woodruff, of the U. S. Circuit Court; Governor Charles R. Ingersoll; Hon. G. H. Hollister; Col. Nelson L. White, State Attorney, and many others. Hon. J. C.

I tell you, when you probe the Court of Probate, you shall find,
In consequence of consequence, it isn't far behind.
It wants a man of parts, be sure, to understand the rules,
To care for all the widows, and the infants, and the fools.

I magnify my office, then, as everybody should,—
And say that, in a quiet way, I'm doing heaps of good.
It's all the speech I'll make for my constituents' dissection;
You see it's only two months hence, there'll be a new election.

But this is neither here nor there; I chiefly rose to say
How pleased I am to meet our proud Fraternity to-day,
And help entwine a graceful wreath around his honored brow,
Who, having fought a noble fight, puts off his armor now.

Loomis presided, and made the introductory speech. At a subsequent meeting of the Fairfield County Bar, a committee was appointed to publish all the proceedings in a permanent form; but as the committee (of which the author of these lines was a member) has never done its duty, these remarks will not be deemed out of place.

Thrice blest the man who, counting up his three
score years and ten,
Presents a model in himself, unto his fellow men ;
And in the plenitude of all his varied, ripened powers,
Beholds a gladsome retrospect of unneglected hours;

And, gazing forward, can discern a pleasant pilgrimage
Adown the smooth declivities of a serene old age ;
Assured that, when his day is done, he shall but
sink to rest,
As summer sun, with all his radiant banners, in the
west.

E'en such the man, whose patriarchal presence here
we greet,
As round the festive board to-night, his fond disciples meet,
To here pronounce o'er him our benedictive word
" well done ! "
And for ourselves uplift the prayer, " God bless us,
every one ! "

Let wiseacres and shallow fools deny the truth who
can,
The thorough lawyer can but be, and is, the thorough man.

What cultured gifts must all combine, and in his
being blend,
Not all mankind, I ween, are fit to gauge or comprehend.

What arduous toil, what anxious care; how rigorous
the school
Wherein our jealous mistress holds us subject to her
rule,
Is ours, who strive our best within this sphere of life
to go,
Let those, and those alone, recount, who best can
feel and know.

I've made a brief upon this point; and from statistics, say—
The lawyers, of professionals, do most for smallest
pay.
The average lawyer—overhaul the record, and be
sure—
Works always hard,—lives pretty well,—and goes to
Heaven, poor.

And yet we lead a pleasant life; the company is
good,
And gentle fellowship obtains within our brotherhood.

Exceptions but confirm the rule; and, take us all together,
A nobler band, I dare declare, were never bound by tether.

And all the world, whate'er it says, respects the legal calling,
And must confess, that but for us, its state would be appalling;
The very man who finds in our pursuit the biggest flaw,
If he can boast a boy with brains, will have him study law!

My time is up,—a health to all; and unto him erewhile
Our honored chief; who now returns to join the rank and file,—
Long life;—and when in heavenly courts he stands at last, be then
His children's children's proudest boast—illustrious ORIGEN!

S. B. S.

POEM,

READ AT A DINNER GIVEN TO P. T. BARNUM, AT ATLANTIC HOTEL, BRIDGEPORT, CONN., 1874.

I'M no pianist; ne'ertheless a pæan I must sing
This night in honor of our guest, the famous Money King;
The man who keeps informing us that poverty's a blunder,
And rolls up wealth before our eyes, while we look on and wonder.

If Alfred Mantalini could have chanced this man to see,
His first ejaculation must have been, as you'll agree,
"Of all demnition wonderments that swell his fame and pelf,
There never was a demnder one than Barnum is, himself!"

There's no such thing as ciphering the gauge of such a man;
To-day its business in New York—to-morrow in Japan:
One day beneath the sea, to find some learnéd, lovely shark,—
The next, way off, on Ararat, for pieces of the Ark!

Sometimes he calls for quarter, with the giant Fe-
Fo-Fum;
And then again he captures us with General Tom
Thumb;
One day in Bridgeport, staking out new streets across
his farm,
The next, in Windsor Castle, with Victoria on his arm.

One day upon the prairies, looking out for freaks of
nature;
The next, in Hartford, speech-making before the
legislature;
One day, the Bearded Woman; next, the Mermaid
with her comb;
And now, the Hippopotamus, and now, the Hippo-
drome.

To-day, recalling from the deep, oblivious shades of
death,
And so, rejuvenating and rejoicing old Joyce Heth;
To-morrow, showing all at once, the wondrous twins
of Siam,
And Julius Cæsar's boxing-gloves, and fish-pole used
by Priam.

One day, the fiery element his big Museum slashes,
But next day, lo! it rises as a Phœnix from its ashes;

And while the croakers shake their heads, and dubiously figure,
The Crocodile gives broader smile,—the show keeps growing bigger!

I never, NEVER, saw his like; and so I might as well
Give o'er at once the vain attempt all his exploits to tell;
It's all recorded—read of all—on everybody's shelf;
"Biography of P. T. Barnum, written by himself."

There's not a journal round the world, whose columns haven't known him;
Nor board-fence, on whose superfice, bill-posters haven't shown him.
No savage or philosopher; no Gentile, Greek or Roman,
But knows of this ubiquitous, inevitable showman.

But "showman" though he style himself, we know the word but tells
A vulgar fraction of what force within his manhood dwells.
An orator of wide repute, a poet and a preacher,
An author and an editor; a student and a teacher;

A wit, of never failing fund within his storehouse
ample;
Of Temperance, alike renowned Apostle and example;
Philanthropist, with human kind, not merely sympathetic,
But generous and bountiful, and grandly energetic;

And last—by no means least—of all;—and that is
why we come
Thus heartily to welcome him—a lover of his
home;
A home that proudly crowns to-day a whilom barren
waste,—
The triumph and the marvel now of fine æsthetic
taste.

But prouder monument for him; within the city's
bound,
Full many a score of happy habitations may be
found,
Whose owners will not soon forget the prudent head
that planned
The homes they ne'er had builded, but for Barnum's
helping hand!

Oh! when the leaf of human life is turning sere and yellow.
One's best reflection can but be, that he has served his fellow.
How many a man had been a wreck, whose fate had quite undone him,
If Barnum hadn't raised, and put wheels under him, and "run" him!

Now if our fellow-citizen had been a sordid hunks,
Who hoarded all his treasures in old stockings, and in trunks,
We simply should have set him down a flinty-hearted sinner,
Instead of voting him a "brick" and complimental dinner.

And so we wish it understood, and thoroughly inferred;—
These testimonials of esteem—we mean them, every word.
We toast not wealth, nor simply brains; but, as we proudly can,—
The qualities that always make the hero and the man.

Long life and health to him and his, to do and gather good;
And when at last he shall be called to cross the Stygian flood,
Surviving friends with tearful eyes, beholding him embark,
Shall place his statue, I predict, within the Seaside Park;

And every boy who looks thereon, the record shall review,
And learn what steady Yankee pluck and industry can do;
And as our city grows apace, an ever crescent fame,
As halo, shall surround her pristine Benefactor's name.

And meanwhile, he'll be ransacking the Universe for "stars,"
And lay a cable through the air from Jupiter to Mars,
And institute a comet-race, on some tremendous wager,
And cage up Taurus, Scorpio, the Whale, and Ursa Major;

And hire the Twins—oh Gemini!—to manage a
balloon,
And make an exhibition of the old man in the
moon;
And in the vast arena, pit the Sickle of the Lion
Against the vaunted sword and belt of arrogant
Orion;

And, finally, discovering the brink of Hades' crater,
Put out the conflagration with his Fire Annihilator;
Exorcise from the neighborhood, the "cussed" imps
of evil,
Nor rest, till he has raised, reformed, and then—ENGAGED—the Devil!

S. B. S.

MARTYRDOM IN THE TEMPLE.

A BERKSHIRE BALLAD.

IT was the town of Otis,—
  It was a Sabbath day,
To which I call your notice
  In sympathetic way.

An August sun was shining,
  In temper most intense;
The clock was near defining
  When service should commence.

At chapel we were greeted,—
  My Brother Sam and I,—
With courtesies, and seated
  Conspicuously high.

A stall-pew on the bow aisle,
  Assigned to us alone,
Presented us in profile,
  As victims on a throne!

For every waiting creature,
  Who knew the native sire,*
On each resembling feature
  Must searchingly inquire.

* Our father, Increase Sumner, was a native of Otis.

With painfullest reflection,
 Concerning how and why
We were on this inspection,
 Sat Brother Sam and I.

With Corsican refinement
 Of mutual sense of woe,
We kept up our alignment,—
 Well, how I do not know.

But there, our fate bemoaning,
 We silently implored
The help the Rector's coming
 Would naturally afford.

And when the aggregation
 Of thoughts we must defy
Suggested suffocation,
 Or some explosive cry ;—

Right then, when for the Rector
 We could have jumped and cheered,
At fartherest door a spectre
 Obtrusively appeared!

Forthwith our whole attention
 Was conquered and converged :
The act of apprehension
 Foregoing fears submerged.

A tall and slender woman;
  Not less than seventy-five;
Who looked just less than human,
  And scarcely more 'n alive.

She was so slim and bony;
  The blood so spare in her!
A true synchronous crony
  For the ancient mariner.

Her bodice had descended
  From portraits of Queen Bess;
But many fashions blended
  Throughout her satin dress.

A reticule of netting
  Was dangling from her waist;
A brooch of oroide setting
  Resplendent gleamed with paste.

A climbing ivory jocko
  Adorned the shade she lugged;
And, bound in red morocco,
  A prayer-book huge she hugged.

In color of the carrot,
  Her ringlets were aflame;
In pattern of the parrot,
  Her nose was much the same.

Her eyes were fierce reminders
  Of sprite and goblin dreams;
Her glasses, flanked by blinders,
  Were cased in tortoise beams.

But speech seems disappearing,
  And memory shrinks with dread,
When I approach the gearing
  She wore upon her head.

It was a close-thatched lean-to;
  It was a prompter's lair;
It was a sounding screen to
  An olden bishop's chair.

It was a miller's crater;
  It was a tavern shed;
It was a radiator
  For gas-lights overhead.

It was a Leghorn tunnel,
  Resembling in degree,
The ventilating funnel
  Of steamships of the sea.

The trimmings on a fraction
  Of that stupendous plan,
Were fit to cause distraction
  In simple-minded man.

Across the skull-close bonnet,
  And slightly up the grade,
With spangled gauze upon it,
  Were knots of crimson braid.

Between these cones upspringing,
  Were grasses, leaves and stalks;
Two blue-jays, couched for singing,
  Surmounted hollyhocks.

It was a dreadful vision;—
  Flashed on us all in all,
With that acute precision
  Most likely to appall.

She paused a moment,—blocking
  That narrow doorway; then
Recovered from the shocking,
  Our woe began again.

She turned her awful awning,
  As she advanced apace,
And caught us without warning,
  And held us,—face to face.

And drawing near the pulpit,
  Her calcium lights were seen
To blaze on either culprit
  In incandescence keen!

And when in act of kneeling,
  She still maintained her glare,
We trembled ; and the feeling
  Was not akin to prayer.

And when the verse for quiet
  Was solemnly intoned,
"Please read the act for riot ! "
  My brother faintly groaned.

The fire of our affliction
  Abated not a jot ;
From psalm to benediction
  'T was more intensely hot.

Full oft a spell mesmeric
  Was fastened on us twain,
Till on the brink hysteric
  I caught my reeling brain.

By reverent recitation,
  By vaulting tricks of thought,
By back enumeration,
  Delivery was sought.

Perhaps the earnest struggle
  Had braved the general stare ;—
But sacred plea, nor juggle,
  Obscured *her* anywhere.

Call this a profanation,—
  A mockery and a sin?
Retributive temptation
  In God's house will begin!

Why ended not that session
  In ignominious race,
Requires a deep confession
  Of mystery and grace.

Who e'er in judgment sitteth;
  How far excused or blamed:—
"Survival of the fittest,"
  May reasonably be claimed.

C. A. S.

MY BROTHER'S RING.

It glistens not with ruby,
Nor flaunts the diamond's glare,
Nor emerald nor sapphire
Bedecks the ring I wear.
Of simple gold 'tis fashioned,
And on its sable seal,
The family initial
Is all it doth reveal.

Yet not a gem that sparkles
Afar on India's strand,
Or blazes on imperial brow,
Or proudly sceptered hand,
So precious a memento,
So priceless boon could be,
As you shall know, but listen,
This bauble is to me.

Within the Palais Royal,—
For seeming miles ablaze,
As fabulous Aladdin's
To court the 'wildered gaze,—
He told us he had bought it,
With reverent desire,

To wear it as a token
In memory of his sire.

And so he kept and wore it;
I saw it on him last,
As o'er the keys of melody
His fingers deftly passed.
As rolled the swelling volume
Of sound, my eyes grew dim;
I wept to see the signet,
But not—not then—for him!

Alas! within a twelve-month,
On that disastrous shore,
Whose very rocks are shedding
Their tears forevermore,
Brave ship and base commander
Rushed fearfully awreck,
And fearfully and wildly
Rushed hundreds to the deck!

And shivering and shuddering,
In darkness, cold and storm,
Amid that doomed assemblage
There stood our poor boy's form;
And as he leaped in horror
And vain hope to withstand

The mocking waves that clasped him,
This ring was on his hand!

Far down within the caverns,—
Drear tenements of death,—
To note the last pulsation,
The last expiring breath;—
Forever mute, mute witness!
Thou knowest, but dost spare
Those tales—hads't thou but language—
Of heart-break and despair!

Rude hands from out those caverns,
The precious corse upbore,
And tenderly disposed it
Upon the pitying shore.
Kind strangers and survivors
Saved all for us with care;—
All, all they could—his body,
This ring; a lock of hair!

The months have flown and vanished,
And in the haunts of men
I move, and ofttimes gaily
Discourse with tongue or pen;
But sadness, like a shadow,
In night-watch and alone,

Unceasingly steals o'er me,
And claims me for its own,—

And sometimes, as, abstracted,
I gaze upon this ring,
The home of childhood re-appears,
The scenes of life's bright spring:—
Sire, mother, sisters, brothers,
Gone hence beyond the sky;—
I feel we all must meet again,
I almost long to die.

It glistens not with ruby,
Nor flaunts the diamond's glare,
Nor emerald nor sapphire
Bedecks the ring I wear;
Yet naught so dear memento,
So priceless boon could be,
As this sad tale hath told you
This bauble is to me.

S. B. S.

POEM,

DELIVERED AT THE ANNUAL BANQUET OF ST. GEORGE'S SOCIETY, BRIDGEPORT, CONN., APRIL 22d, 1875.

Now I'm a Yankee, born and bred, as any one may guess,
Who gives a moment's heed to what my lips and looks express;
But every Johnny Bull I hail as cousin—nay, as brother,
And while Columbia calls me "son," Britannia's my mother!

Indeed it makes one smile to think how races sub-divide,
And seek their ancient individualities to hide;
As if a hundred years or two could so outspread the tree,
The branches couldn't find the root, or trace their pedigree!

Each son of these born Englishmen, like son of mine, must be
A genuine American; it can't be helped you see;
But each and all,—we still may trace the same historic line;
Recall the days of "auld"—and not so *very* "auld—lang syne."

And "English," "Teuton," "Scot," or "Celt," or
"Yankee"—what's a name!
A bridge across the paltry years, and we are all the
same.
And here, according naught but love to Kaiser or
to Queen,
We work new problems, whose results are with the
Great Unseen.

So, starting with our brotherhood, I think we can
agree
To quaff the cup of fondness for the Isle across the sea;
The Isle, whereto, where'er the fifth of all Earth's
peoples roam,
With faithful love their hearts revert, as their an-
cestral home.

The very "hub" of all the earth; commanding, as
of course,
Centripetal, centrifugal, and every other force;
"Whose morning drum-beat,—comrade of the troop-
ing hours and sun,—
Sounds one reveille round the world, until the day
is done!"

A mound upon the globe's expanse, which other-
wheres upsprung,
Might simply have supported wives and saints for
Brigham Young;

But as the wondering Frenchman cried, its potency to see,—
"Zat leetle patch of earth is one vast meeracle to me!"

As empires of the Orient, her history fades away,
Far back among traditions of a half-forgotten day;
And when the Sphynx itself its hidden story shall unfold,
Then, only then, the origin of Stonehenge shall be told!

What armies, from great Cæsar's time, with awful tread have trod
Athwart her soil, and fought above, and slept beneath her sod;
What navies, charged with thunderbolts from out her flaming forge,
Have borne, transcendent, round the world, the banner of St. George!

What Art and Science in her halls have found auspicious birth,
To educate, to civilize, and gladden all the earth;
What speech hath made her forums thrill; what bards sublime have sung
Immortal measures to embalm for aye her classic tongue!

What monuments on every hand record historic
things ;—
Cathedrals, builded to enshrine sarcophagi of
Kings ;
Tombs, so renowned, that in their midst, in royal
state to lie,
What Albion's son, but craves the boon deservingly
to die!

And statues, that commemorate their ever deathless
dead,
And castles hoar, with amaranthine memories o'erspread,
And palaces, within whose courts earth's noblest
ones have stood,
And towers, whose moated battlements have soaked
heroic blood!

But no effete, decaying realm evokes our laudful
song;
Within her bounds to-day, what homes of wealth,
of comfort, throng;
What industry, what enterprise, throughout her
pent confine,
Hold sovereign reign, from Isle of Wight to New-
castle-on-Tyne!

What commerce, at her teeming ports, awaits each fav'ring gale,
What network o'er her fair expanse, of highway and of rail;
What bustling cities everywhere; and then,—the whole to crown,—
Immense, imcomprehensible, bewildering London town!

O, whoso in a single glance, and in a breath of time,
Would gaze on stores consolidate of every land and clime,
And note a thousand things, his every school-boy book recalls,—
Ascend the dome, and reach with me the summit of Saint Paul's!

There, rolls beneath, the teeming Thames, by mighty bridges spanned,
And Ludgate slopes to Temple Bar, and Fleet street and the Strand—
And just beyond is Charing Cross, from out whose station run
Incessant locomotive trains, like missiles from a gun.

Beyond, the halls of Parliament and Westminster
you see.
There's St. James Palace, Buckingham, and Marlborough, all three.
This way, Trafalgar Square, and Nelson's Monument
you know;
There's Picadilly; there's Hyde Park; Pall-mall
and Rotten Row.

Come back by way of Oxford street, past Lincoln's,
and Gray's Inn;
Again you near the "City," and you catch the roar
and din;
While now and then, above it all, mellifluously
swells
The tocsin of the Cockney's soul—sweet, musical
Bow-Bells!

Past Cheapside, stands the Bank, whose notes do
not belie their worth,
But speak for English gold in every corner of the
earth.
Hard by, Lord Mayor's Mansion House; and in
the Mart between,
The Iron Duke on Iron Horse, o'erlooks the
whirling scene.

And here, Cornhill, Threadneedle and King William
streets converge;
Innumerable multitudes, like waves and billows
surge;
And rampant men and rampant steeds contend with
mad uproar,
And thunder over London Bridge, and all along the
shore.

And farther east—O let us pause with vision rapt
awhile!—
In seeming isolation there, looms up that sombre
pile,—
Long time the seat of kingly pride, and kingly lust
and power—
It stands,—with walls whose very stones do seem to
speak,—the Tower!

And now, one glance on Surry side, vast workshops
to behold—
Whose myriad chimneys belch their flames, and
smoky clouds unfold;
While Crystal Sydenham illumes the far horizon's
crest,—
Resplendent Diamond, blazing there, on Albion's
buxom breast!

There! that will do; and now, my boys, I'll take my
seat and hat.
To sing all night, I couldn't turn a neater verse than
that;—
Shake hands all round! bring cakes and ale; this
once, ourselves we'll gorge,
And give the tankard one long pull, for England, and
St. George!

S. B. S.

LINES,

READ AT RE-UNION OF CONNECTICUT VETERANS, AT HARTFORD, CONN., 1875.

I KNOW precisely what you want: you thought 't would do for me,—
As being what we lawyers call, a sort of an "*ex re*,"
To hold position, by brevet, in this association,
And so contribute to the flow of mutual admiration.

I'll do it! from my childhood's hour—I mean since I was fledged,
And hung my hopeful shingle out, seductively gilt-edged—
I've always said "give me, beneath the ægis of our laws,
A first-class client, one strong fact, and I'll insure the cause!"

So, hailing from the old Bay State—God bless her, there she stands!
I clasp with unfeigned pride to-day, adopted brothers' hands;
And fain, from out these flowers of hope and memory that throng,
Would weave, so you might bear it hence, a fragrant wreath of song.

But where, in all the blooming fields of your illustrious story,
Shall I cull out, most redolent, the roses of your glory?
I read the faithful record o'er with wonder and amaze,
Of this one little plucky State in those eventful days.

I read the roll of martyred dead; and in the foremost van,
Behold one, who so early gave "assurance of a man,"
Chivalric ELLSWORTH! o'er whose corse, with new resolve uprose
The warrior legions of the North, to smite the nation's foes.

And I behold, in retrospect, another manly form,
Which, all too soon, fell prone beneath the battle's angry storm;
The gentle scholar, born to tread serener paths to fame;—
But brighter halo than he dreamed encircles WINTHROP'S name.

One foremost martyr still, our verse may not this hour forget;
Whose life-sun, like a meteor fall'n, in sudden splendor set;—

Of simon-pure Colonial stock, the bright, consummatic scion,—
O, favored Commonwealth, that shrines his dust—heroic LYON!

To SEDGWICK, FOOTE, and all the rest, whose names to us belong,—
Whose lengthened roll transcends by far the limits of our song,—
Not unremembered, do our hearts go proudly forth to-day,
And yield their throbbing benisons above their hallowed clay.

Go now with me, where'er the shock of battle rends the air;
Aloft, defiant, you shall see the tri-vined banner there;
The first unfurled at New Orleans, and waving in the blast
Its saucy folds at Bull Run, o'er the first gun and the last!

The first on Mississippi's soil; the first to kiss the breeze
Beneath the "sacred shadows" of the staid palmetto trees;

Among the first to cross Long Bridge ; where,—almost terror dumb,—
The gentry cried, " they come ; great guns ! the nutmeg Yankees come ! "

The first "forlorn hope" volunteers to cross Port Hudson's verge,—
Fit honor to your brave THIRTEENTH, and gallant General Birge !—
Nay, first, your own historians say, when Richmond's flag went down,
To leap triumphant o'er its walls, and greet the captured town !

O, noble record of a State, upon whose shield before
Had shone, emblazoned, deathless deeds of patriot men of yore ;
O, Mother of a glorious race, whose loyalty, the same
Through all the years, could only add fresh laurels to thy fame !

And now, a grander spectacle, to all the earth we show,—
As, in the peaceful walks of life, once more we come and go ;

Nay, as, once more, in friendly grasp, fraternal hands
entwine,—
And whilom foemen gladly meet as brothers of lang
syne!

The dream is past; so let it fade;—the hideous,
dreadful dream;—
The night is o'er; so let us hail the morning's roseate gleam.
O'er all the land once more behold the starry flag
unfurled,—
Whose radiant sheen, now all undimmed, shall yet
illume the world!

S. B. S.

POEM,

READ AT SILVER WEDDING OF HON. AND MRS. WM. D. BISHOP, BRIDGEPORT, CONN., OCTOBER 21, 1875.

RING out, ye joyous marriage-bells! ring out your
silvery chimes;
And wake, this hour, the memories of other days and
times;
Of days and times since first we saw this newly
plighted pair
Set forth together, all the joys and ills of life to share.

I see them now; he, freshly forth from academic
bowers,
Aglow with hope, alert with zeal, assured of ripening powers;
She, foreordained a heart like his to captivate and
win,
By charms that could but half reveal the lovelier
soul within.

It was a gladsome spectacle; the future seemed so
fair,
And life was all rose-color then unto the youthful
pair;

Yet not so glad, so picturesque, so eloquent a sight,
As, 'neath the fav'ring smiles of Heaven, we witness here to-night!

For time, each year's development so kindly did unfold,
That all, and more, is realized, than early hope foretold;
And bride and groom, we dare to say, as swift years have flown o'er,
Have learned to honor and to love each other more and more.

We know the charm of youthful hope—I mean, we "old folks" do,
Who, five and twenty years ago, had found it "sweet to woo;"
But Hope stands always at the prow, and holds more sure command,
When brave Fruition sits astern, and lends a helping hand.

The youth and maid could promise fair;—of course, they always do;—
But time alone can tell if they shall keep their promise true.

Ah! many a wedding day has dawned with bright auroral glow,
And been the prelude of a life of bitterness and woe.

And therefore, with enhanced delight, and with peculiar pride,
As five-and-twenty years have sped, we greet this groom and bride;
And as we note how pleasantly their wedded lives have run,
Pronounce with hearty joy the benedictive words, "well done!"

No doubt they've had their small disputes; no doubt, in their dominion,
They each may now and then have had a "contrary opinion."
Mayhap, as somewhat tardily, some night he did come in,
He had to hear those dreadful words:—"My dear! where have you been?"

Perhaps, sometimes, he thought he felt a spasm of distress,
At figures, for what seemed to him a quite superfluous dress;

But when the fabric was made up, the sum grew less
alarming,
And he was ready to agree "she never looked so
charming!"

Such conjugal asperities as these two may have had,
Have evidently left no trace or record that is sad.
Each one the heart's desire has seemed so nicely to
fulfill,
That while he seemed to have his way, she always
had her "Will!"

Ten years ago, the compliment methought exceeding clever,
That she, a fifteen-summers bride, was "handsomer
than ever;"
And now, she is so very old, it cannot make her vain,
As, challenging dispute, I pay the compliment
again.

Ten years ago,—ye may recall, whose memories are
not dim,—
Our muse embodied in her song, some pleasant
things of him.
He keeps on growing, and revolves in more ex-
panded ring,
And quondam Railroad President is now a Railroad
King.

Ten years! what mighty grief they brought for
some of us to bear,—
But they have left at this hearth-stone,—thank Heaven,—no vacant chair!
O, sire and dame! with us this hour recall with
pious joy,
How through your ministrations fond, God spared
your darling boy!

And now it but remains to add, in some befitting
phrase,
Kind wishes that a favoring sun illume the coming
days;
That peacefully and prosperously the stream of life
may flow,
And—in the self same strain we sang, so many
years ago—

That—rarest chance to mortal lot; still let the wish
be spoken—
The silver cord be loosened not, nor the golden
bowl be broken,
Ere at life's even you shall stand, inspired by memories olden,
To join each faithful hand with hand, in nuptials
that are golden.

And when the promised Bridegroom comes, O may
we all behold
The crystal stream, the silver thrones, the City of
pure gold;
And join that august shining throng, before the
Great I AM,
To celebrate, eternally, the Marriage of the Lamb!

S. B. S.

TO A LADY,

ON BEING ASKED FOR ANOTHER OLD-TIME VALENTINE.

WHAT! ask a Benedict like me,
  At such a dreadful lapse of time,—
A quarter of a century,—
  To string the olden beads of rhyme?
Indeed, it were a fruitless task,
You know not, lady, what you ask.

For I am older, staider grown;
  My face betrays the weight of care;
And close beside each temporal bone,
  Behold the streaks of silver hair!
I'm sorry,—but it must be told,—
The dismal truth;—I'm growing old!

And yet, not cold;—for now, indeed,
  As on thy blithesome face I gaze,—
As on some luminous page, I read
  The memories of those halcyon days.
Old flames rekindle, and in sooth
I feel the glorious thrill of youth.

And, oh! how gently hath the hand
  Of time upon thy brow been laid;

Bespeaking, as with fairy wand,
  Days more of sunshine than of shade.
Thou same bright, sparkling, *saucy* "Joe"
Of five-and-twenty years ago!

Health, wealth, and love, and every weal,
  Through years and years to come, be thine;
With mellow softness o'er thee steal
  Anon the rays of life's decline;
Till,—this thine earthly season past—
Thou shalt o'erlook the stars at last.

S. B. S.

LOVE'S BIOGRAPHY.

JOHN PRESCOTT was a comely youth;
The type of health, the soul of truth.
His widowed mother often sighed
With thoughts of woe and hopes of pride,
As sire in son she more descried.
And oft the gossips' chatter ran,
That John could choose when once a man.

A hearty, gleeful, hoyden girl,
Was John's pet playmate, Catharine Earl.
Next neighbors; and alike in age;
Taught from the self-same primer page
By Catharine's father,—saint and sage.
And each, in memory's earliest year,
Had followed at a parent's bier.

And every tie which childhood knows—
Which dearer through our lifetime grows—
Wove friendship for this lad and maid.
As children they had often played
In garden, grove, and brookside glade;
Where now, beneath the moon they told
The never-new and never-old,—
The nonsense lovers will repeat,
And think it quite as true as sweet.

C. A. S.

POEM,

READ AT THE OPENING OF THE NEW TOWN HALL, AT GREAT BARRINGTON, MASS., JANUARY 5, 1876.

DEAR, gentle friends; dear native scenes; O, how I love ye all,
Who come this hour, a truant son, responsive to your call;
Not, as in words, just fitly said, the future to forecast,
But, haply, here and there to catch some glimpses of the past.

For that is all that's left to me; indeed, this night I seem,
While gazing down the retrospect, as wakened from a dream;
Songs of a dear and cherished past repeat their olden strain,
And I'm a Barringtonian,—a Berkshire boy again!

And now—I tell you plainly—if you wish to hear from "Sam,"
One thing I do insist on:—you shall take me as I am.
My song will be so personal,—so egotistic, too,
Outside reporters, all avaunt! there's no place here for you!

Among the first scenes I recall—oh! forty years ago—
My home was in the Chatfield house, within a half stone's throw;
Where, as I came the primal facts of life to realize,
The General Whiting premises allured my infant eyes.

'T was quite a manor in those days; around, for many a mile,
The General was sovereign, and lived in fitting style.
The mansion was historical, and grand; but, to my gaze,
More splendid seemed the carriage-house, which held the coach and chaise.

The office on the corner stood, where, once or twice a week,
Came suitors, hot for justice, at "'Squire Kellogg's" hands to seek;
And there, the General, oft in wrath magnificent to see,
Taught Increase Sumner how to grow imperious as he.

No railroad separated then the Chatfield grounds from these,
But high board fences tried to keep us boys from off the trees,

Of whose seductive "golden sweets" we all were very fond,
And now I just recall that juicy melon-patch beyond.

But to explore so far as that, required exceeding care;
Not all possessed the hardihood the venturous deed to dare;
But boys are made up variously, and thus 'twas understood,
That what Bob Girling wouldn't do, "your uncle" surely would!

Just north, with Castle street between, a building used to stand,
Where, it was said that all the needs of life were at command.
You could be born there, go to school, keep store, learn all the trades,
Nay, spend your evenings, if inclined, with lots of pretty maids.

"J. C. & A. C. Russell" kept the store; and overhead,
The Berkshire Courier first began its influence to shed.

Miss Steward kept the school, and culled me out from all the boys,
To make me sit amongst the girls. (She thought I'd make less noise!)

Next north, was "Major Billy's;"—the old red house and the well;
How, in my mind, and most of yours, their vivid pictures dwell!
And next, the stone church, in whose rear the meadow lilies grew,
And from the "Rock-House," leaping forth, the brook meandered through.

Across the street,—I see it now—the ancient tavern stood;—
A long, broad, low, incongruous, unsightly hulk of wood.
I've seen some architecture since, but let me here declare,
For just downright magnificence, my *boy* ideal was there!

I wonder now, how many times, how much I've longed to pay,
To put that structure back again, for just a single day;

To wander through its quaint old rooms, its corridors and halls,
Run up and down its creaking stairs, and gaze upon its walls.

An old sign, in the garret stowed, the information bore,
That "Captain Walter Pynchon" kept the tavern years before;
And numerous are the legends yet, the fancy to inspire,
Of scrapes, and jokes, and mugs of "flip," around that bar-room fire.

The timbers proved exceeding staunch, and when George Ives appeared,
And on the spot with statelier walls, the Berkshire House was reared,
Dismembered, rudely quartered first, 'twas piecemeal drawn away,
And here and there, and extant still, that tavern stands to-day.

The town-house, in those earlier days, stood up street, o'er the bridge,—
A decent structure in its time, its white front crowned the ridge.

There "Locofocos" met defeat, and "Whigs" went
in to win,
And then all hands shook hands again at L. L. Gor-
ham's inn.

When news of Polk's election came, the "Locos"
to inspire,
They jollified so strong that night, the town-house
caught afire;
It made a brilliant, brief display, and went up in a
flame,
So, down town,—through the "Locos'" act,—the
hustings *locus* came.

And then, above the Berkshire store, we ope'd the
new town hall,
And had our semi-annual vote, and famous annual
ball,
Where all South Berkshire's "chivalry," and "flower," "*elite*" and "ton,"
Were wont to throng, to celebrate the birth of Washington.

Next, when a noble Christian zeal and pride would
raise to God
A worthier structure, where the old-time meeting-
house had stood;

Become the town house, then and since, the venerable fane
Was scarce vouchsafed a semblance of its old self to retain.

Somewhat, I know, of fond regret, in each breast woke its fire,
That morning, when the old church bowed to earth its battered spire;
The upturned faces of that throng my mind is picturing yet,
For each bespoke a sudden pang, and every eye was wet!

Green be its memory, old town hall, old temple of the Lord!
Where, in my first years, Parson Burt proclaimed the living Word;
Where, all your days, ye natives born, ye have been wont to find
So much to feed the hungry soul, and mould and grace the mind.

So all things flourish and decay; yet, all along the past,
Mark how each structure, each emprise was better than the last.

Take birdseye view of all this vale; compare its now
and then;—
On every hand, what monuments to dead and living
men!

The church, the school, the library, the factory, the
store,
The telegraph, the railway train, the bridge, the
teeming shore;
The very water that you drink, the very gas you
burn,
Improved highways, new miles of streets, bright
homes at every turn;

Your model Exhibition grounds, the products at
each fair;—
How each and all, and more unsaid, would make
our grandsires stare;
And now, this last, not least, but fitly crowning work
of all—
This Town House, builded for all time; this spacious, beauteous hall!

* * * * *

Here let it stand; and in its front, upon the graceful slope,
The statued angel point aloft to realms of radiant
hope;

And with benignant hand the while, extend the laurel crown,
As tribute to heroic sons of this "Great," loyal town.

Oh, I am proud that I was born within this lovely vale!
Some roses here caught early bloom, that never shall grow pale;
Yet every elm-tree bough seems like the willow, as it waves;—
The town, so full of life for you, for me is full of graves!

Go back with me the dozen years since I had place with you;
Where, where are vanished all those olden faces which we knew?
Long roll! it sadly, sweetly ends with name of her so dear,
Who bade the world her soft "good-bye" with the expiring year! *

How might I dwell! No,—you shall see, a moment's space beyond,
CAMILLA† flash her glorious orbs, and wave her glorious wand.

---

* Mrs. Bigelow, just before deceased,—a very benevolent lady.

† Camilla Urso, who followed the opening exercises with a concert.

For me, almost the sweetest task of all my life is done;
Now, let us all uplift the prayer: "God bless us, every one!"

S. B. S.

LINES,

READ AT BURNS FESTIVAL, BRIDGEPORT, CONN., 1876.

How leaped my heart within my breast; what sudden thrill was there,
That moment, when the guard cried out the railway station, "Ayr!"
Bright day in memory's calendar, in that refulgent June,
As through the flowery meads we rode, to reach the banks of Doon.

'T was all alive—the broad highway—with vehicles which bore
Their pilgrims to that cherished shrine from many a distant shore.
So, all the summer days, they said,—and so the record told,—
Came multitudes from near and far, that valley to behold.

You shall find valleys just as fair, and flowers as bright of hue,
Amidst familiar scenes you take your daily rambles through.

The Doon is not so proud a flood, nor can its "banks and braes"
Outrival Housatonic's shores, or claim a juster praise.

There's no strange beauty in the bridge that spans the rolling stream,
Nor in Kirk Alloway, rent by Time with many an envious seam,
Nor in the cottage more remote, within whose humble door
The eye but notes the circumstance of this world's veriest poor.

What magic spell pervades the scene? pray tell, why gather here
The lords and ladies of the earth, with each recurring year?
Did some great conqueror drive herethro' his chariots of war,
And pierce the air and rend the vale with thunderbolts of Thor?

Did some proud queen awhile sojourn, with royal retinue,
Here, by some castle, knightly tilt and pageant to review?

Did some grand martyr here resign his body to the stake,
And make oblation of himself for truth and conscience sake?

Ah, no! a simple peasant boy, who looked with modest eye
To see grand folk—now all forgot—in stately pomp roll by,
At sixteen years, enamored fell, with that poor peasant maid,
So, wrote her rhymes, and so, thenceforth, his being's law obeyed.

At once, a new inhabitant of the Parnassian grove;
At once a genius fully fledged; as from the brow of Jove
Leaped armed Minerva;—so uprose to heights of instant fame
That rural bard;—and ROBERT BURNS became a deathless name!

"Wild boy" was he? 't is true, and yet 't is idle to ignore it—
That bridge is now a famous bridge. because Burns staggered o'er it.

That hut belittles palaces, as all the world confesses,
Since Burns had there his babyhood, and wore his swaddling dresses.

Ah, well! the crowns earth's true kings wear, are not cheap crowns of gold;
But coronets, bedecked with gems and jewels manifold,
From regions of the infinite, no vulgar minds explore,—
Those vast, illimitable heights that sparkle evermore!

O, give me once again, this life, those halcyon hours to spend,
Where waters of the Bonnie Doon, with Ayr and Ocean blend,
And on that simple rustic bridge, to linger and to dream,
And watch the tide, and lazily throw pebbles in the stream;

And think how, century agone, those precincts, then so dull,
Became so classic all at once, of memories so full,

Because one simple, truthful soul shed glory all around,
And made of unpretentious soil, a very hallowed ground!

Then look upon the bridges twain, which span the dying river,
And spake in words the poet heard, and shall be heard forever;
Then look to find the mystery far down into the well,
Where, as the poet told us, "Mingo's mither hanged hersel';"

And then ascend the monument, and view the landscape there,
And gaze within, on "Bobbie's" face, and Highland Mary's hair;
Then to "the Grotto" turn aside, to see how "Sauter Johnnie,"
With "Tam O'Shanter" held carouse, as nightly chum and crony.

Then once again remark the walls, which long ago resounded
With roystering Scotch hilarity—"confusion worse confounded;"

And quaff the cup of "mountain dew" for many
glad returns
Of glad birthdays and memories, to glorious ROBERT
BURNS!

S. B. S.

POEM,

READ AT THE ANNUAL BANQUET OF WILLIAMS COLLEGE ALUMNI, PARKER HOUSE, BOSTON, JANUARY 18, 1876.

Now, this is rather comforting, ourselves to settle down
Round Parker's famed mahogany, in famous Boston town;
Admire each other mutually, and keep away the chills,
While thinking of the dear old home far up on Berkshire hills!

O, how it must be blust'ring there, around those classic rocks
Between West College and the place where dwelt Professor Cox;
Where,—even now the very mouth of smiling memory waters,—
Those buckwheat cakes were handed round by those three buxom daughters!

We used to take the meeting-house upon the leeward side,
And re-adjust our coat-tails, and a breathing space abide;

Then face again the elements, that seemed, with wild
uproar,
From "Snow-Hole," by Æolus sent, their fury to
outpour.

It may seem strange; but ne'ertheless, I'd rather
nestle here,
My time of life; and feel this warmth, and share
this generous cheer,
Than, e'en for once, that most tempestuous prome-
nade to take,—
That tri-diurnal exercise, for health's and stomach's
sake!

But that was in the wintry days; for, when the vernal gale,
With perfumed breath, brought newer life to mountain and to vale;
And Pisgah answered Greylock's smile, across the
gorgeous scene,
As each unto the other waved his bannerets of
green;

O, never, o'er the globe's expanse—I dare this hour
declare,—
Ye brothers, who meanwhile have breathed Italia's
fragrant air,

And roamed through every land, in quest of regions
of delight,
Have ye beheld a spot more fit to ravish sense and
sight!

But truce to this;—for I am warned to leave this
theme alone;
So many sweeter bards have sung strains sweeter
than my own,
About each precious hill and dale, which to those
parts belong;—
I leave them all; they're not the regnant purpose of
my song.

I sing of WILLIAMS, now and then, as she to me appears,
While gazing down my retrospect of almost thirty
years.
A drive of forty miles "o'er land"—no railroad in
those days,—
And old "West College" first loomed up to my admiring gaze.

Hard by, "East College" stood, and "South," and
embryo "Lawrence Hall;"
Observatories twain beyond; the "Chapel;" that
was all;

But no, not all; some "Domes of thought" sent forth their kindly gleam,
And in their midst—how I recall—MARK HOPKINS towered supreme!

And there we had our daily tasks, our daily sports, and there
Professor Albert's "conference room" echoed the daily prayer;
And we were taught in gracious ways, that we can ne'er forget,
The lessons, come whatever may, will leave their influence yet.

New halls and towers have risen since, their lovely sites to crown,
And Williams is no more, as erst, an isolated town.
New streets, new parks, new monuments to heroes old and new,
On every hand to-day confront the old-time student's view.

And, better, all the fleeting years have but enlarged the roll
Of men, whose mental, moral force is felt from pole to pole;

And Alma Mater wears a bright'ning halo round her head,
While multiply her honored names—her living and her dead!

Search all the records of the land; scan fame's immortal scroll,—
The list, unfading through all time, of men of brain and soul—
List to the Forum's clarion voice; the Pulpit's thundering tone,
And strains poetic,—household words, in every clime and zone;—

Go through the halls where Science waits, where Justice holds her seat;
Where Senates think; where scholars sit at their Gamaliel's feet;
Explore each field of Enterprise, of Valor; Everywhere
Behold, in goodly multitude, the sons of WILLIAMS there!

O, surely, Heaven's blest favorite is each ingenuous youth,
Who seeks within these classic shades the treasuries of truth!

Praise to her Sisters! yet we know he shall not elsewhere find
A Mater aught more cherishing, more bountiful, more kind.

From out her gates, he can but go with manlier resolve,
To mingle in life's conflict, and its mighty problem solve;
And Memory, as the years expire, wherever he may roam,
Shall cherish, with a fond delight, his sweet scholastic home.

And, by that token, we are met, with greeting to each one
As brother, and our Alma Mater's true and loyal son.
So may we meet, in days to come; and always to discover
New jewels in her radiant crown, and evermore to love her!

And when the next Centennial year, for this our glorious land,
Shall roll its round, may we have left some footprints on time's strand;

And sons of WILLIAMS, yet unborn, recall, and haply save
Our death-starred names upon her roll, from Lethe's envious wave!

And be it hers to gather in increasing stores of truth,
And flourish in enlarged estate, and everlasting youth;
And scatter seeds of wisdom forth from farthest shore to shore,
Till Earth itself shall pass away, and Time shall be no more!

S. B. S.

POEM,

DELIVERED AT THE DEDICATION OF THE SOLDIERS' MONUMENT, BRIDGEPORT, CONN., AUGUST 17, 1876.

OUR hearts are full; Goddess of song! one favoring glance bestow,
And re-awake the slumbering lyre, and set the verse aglow,
So we may voice the sentiments which to the hour belong,
And make these all-pervading thoughts articulate in song.

How seeming strange! what tongue of seer or prophet had foretold,
A simple score of years agone, the scene we here behold.
So, like huge giants, grand events do ever stalk sublime,
New mile-stones to uprear along the vast highway of time.

So, ever on the world's broad stage, the heroes come and go,
To speak betimes the needed word; to strike the needed blow;

So monuments have risen, and shall rise, while ages roll,
Until the very heaven itself shall vanish as a scroll.

So history instructs us all, and still repeats the story,—
No age unto itself shall claim monopoly of glory.
The stern, ambitious centuries shall with each other vie,
And virtue shall not cease to live, and valor shall not die.

So, these our own experiences, our minds do but enable
To rescue all the storied past from the domain of fable.
Who doubts to-day what courage nerved the men of elder Rome,
Whose very eyes have seen its very counterpart at home!

A hundred years—a breath of time—have passed away since when
Our fathers sought to 'stablish here a nursery of men.

Prolific years! O, how events within their circle crowd,
To make their children trebly glad; nay, jubilant and proud.

For, under God, to all earth's states and empires, we have shown
How every man may be a man, and each possess a throne;
And just proclaimed to all the waiting world in tones sublime,—
"This Union, indestructible, shall last as long as Time!"

And round the world, to make those tones so resonant to-day,
How well we know what noble forms are mould'ring into clay.
So, to their memories we come this cenotaph to rear,
And once more shed above their dust the reverential tear.

And, after all, 't was timely done; not ingrate be it said,
Hath this our loyal city proved unto her bravely dead.

O, better thus, that after lapse of these reflecting
years,
So fresh at last, so grand, so fair, our monument appears.

Hereby the dead, and e'en our living selves, we do
assure
Of gratitude unspoiled of time—potential to endure,
And grow as an undying cypress o'er each hero's
grave,
While grows to vaster bounds and ends, the State
he died to save!

And unforgotten be the thought, that—most divinely human—
This gratitude found surest place within the breast
of woman.
Why not! pray tell, by whom each death-inviting
deed was done?
Some maid's fond lover; wife's fond spouse; some
mother's cherished son!

O, when the everlasting Book, in syllables of
gold,
The unrevealed biographies of angels shall unfold;

How then, on every dazzling page, in each resplendent line,
Eternally the records of true womanhood shall shine!

"What lives she for?"—exclaimed a youth, with supercilious air,
As at her cottage door a dame sat knitting in her chair;
"What lives she for?"—the auswer came;—"Her husband and three sons
In one brave charge at Gettysburg, fell dead before the guns!

A fourth son holds judicial seat; while yet another stands
A famed Apostle of the Word in yet unchristian lands.
She only waits in God's good time, His rich rewards to share,
So there she sits, serenely sad, and knitting in her chair."

Throughout the years since waged the war, some hearts, with impulse tender,
Have throbbed, a tribute to our brave in fitting form to render;

To-day—the work consummated—to each and every
one,
In each breast wells the sentiment—"Ye faithful
souls, well done!"

And now, outlooking on the sea that clasps the
smiling strand,
Defiant of the shocks of time, that glorious form
shall stand,
With outstretched arm, magnificent, the laurel to
bestow
On heroes whose bright names adorn the lettered
plinth below.

Our soldier boy, with form erect, shall greet each
rising sun;
Our sailor watch the gorgeous west, as every day is
done;
While Liberty, now all white-robed, displays the
sword that gave
To her true life, the while it broke the shackles of
the slave!

They tell us, in the not remote, nor doubtful by-
and-by,
Along these shores, the most majestic argosies shall
ply.

This placid inland sea those mammoth shuttles shall pass through,
Forever weaving webs between the Old World and the New.

Then, from their decks, the emigrant alike, and titled guest,
As, gazing from the starboard side, their curious eyes shall rest
On fair Columbia's shore, among its crowning roofs and towers,
Shall single out, with pleased surprise, this Sentinel of ours;

And learn, ere yet their feet have pressed the hospitable earth,
What tribute our New England pays to valor and to worth;
And feel impatient haste to touch the soil of Yankee land,
And hear a hearty Yankee voice, and grasp a Yankee hand!

Here shall the beauteous fabric stand, as seasons come and go;
Reflect the summer's sun, and wear its wintry robes of snow;

And, in their time, the autumn leaves; and, every joyous spring,
Allure the birds to gather round, and build their nests and sing.

The boys, in mimic soldier-garb, shall here make holiday;
The yachts do glad obeisance as they toss within the bay,
And children hold their festivals close by, within the grove,
And plighted ones stroll here at eve to whisper words of love.

Here shall the stately equipage, and unpretentious wain
Bring oft their groups to view these forms, and read these names again;
And music, chiming with the waves, shall wake melodious air,
And twilight offer respite here to daily toil and care.

And so the sure years shall revolve; and when, amidst the dead,
On humbler tablets, here and there, our own names shall be read,

Enough for us, in coming time, in memory of these
days,
If lips unborn shall bid us share the tribute of their
praise.

Meanwhile, O, fair instructress! teach the lesson
from above,
How better than material good is the sweet wealth
of love;
Inciting, as we gaze on thee, such converse and be-
haviour,
As makes us more akin to God, and to the gentle
Saviour.

S. B. S.

LINES,

READ BEFORE I. O. O. F., VIRGINIA CITY, NEV., APRIL 26, 1868.

In these emphatic and tumultuous days,
When sins are to the lowest scale deplored,
Or favor strained in every term of praise—
As ladies' notes are largely underscored;

When argument seems but a needless speech,
Unless it bear, for force, some deadly threats,
And riot is assumed the mode to teach
That Charity which pardons and forgets!

When all is last, and everything is first,
When good is best, and bad 's denounced the worst,
And men and actions either kicked or cursed;

When simple positives of human thought
To fierce superlatives are raised and wrought,
And old poetic types of joys and woes
Are dwarfed by new hyperboles of prose;—

In short, when modern heat of temper and of tone
Has, in the moral and the lettered sense,

Destroyed the climate of a tempered zone,
  To substitute the torrid and intense :

How can we hope our set and sober theme
  Will marked attention and respect invite,
When in imperfect phrase we tell a scheme
  That needs no plea, that seeks no proselyte ?

Yet may we sing, though our admonished muse
  Itself proclaim the critic's chosen wrong,
And seem, at first, to question and accuse
  For faults which title all the following song.

Hail, mighty Sun ! that gladdens into morn
  The hours that date the instituting birth
Of this Grand Order, whose design was born
  Beneath the Angel's good-will chant to Earth !

Hail ! men in bonds to fellowship and truth !
  United by the dying, o'er the dead ;
Or, having passed the discipline of youth,
  The rocky road, without a guide, can tread !

Hail ! blessed memories, which the day invest !
  Not heard in story, nor explained by creeds :
Though hidden. yet the Ciphers which suggest
  Form choral alphabets of friendly deeds.

Welcome the year! for which ye now, anew,
  Repeat your vows to sacred toil and strife,
And pledge the glory of the Past's review
  In ample token of a higher life.

What summons bid these goodly men repair,
  With obvious pleasure and enlightened zeal,
To upper chambers which with ritual care,
  Are ope'd by signs, and closed with secret seal.

No public heralding the stated hour,
  No printed words the usual objects tell;
No sect seductions wield attractive power:—
  The finest chapel and the sweetest bell;

The loveliest shepherd of the wealthiest flock;
  The largest gathering of the worldly great;
The church, where simple purchasers of stock
  In weekly mourning humbly congregate;

None such as these appeal or motive lend
  To fill these courts, or propagate our plan;
For he who enters must be vouched a friend;
  Who gains the grasp need only be a Man.

Though doubly sentineled and barred the gates
  Of Temples which our Order rears and rules,

Lo! not in vain the weeping widow waits
Without the portals of the Vestibules.

O, Ministry to suffering, sublime!
O, shrine of Mercy, quick to Heaven's assail!
Where, through the babble of this heartless time,
With helpful grief is heard the Orphan's wail!

The trophies of great battle triumphs bring
And fill the museums for a nation's pride;
As they are gathered let the welkin ring
With songs which desperate threatenings defied.

Raise high the pedestals, in park and town,
Whereon the Hero's marble form may stand,
To mark and to perpetuate renown,
For love and service to a glorious land.

Adorn each capitol's rotunda space
With paintings of bright deeds for Freedom's home.
And crown the champion of an age or race
Upon the summit of the soaring dome!

But where the earthly monuments of those—
Save they have built an alms-house for their fame—
Whose labor to relieve the common woes,
In worldly walks had reaped a mighty name?

And even though the costly Mural gave
  A truthful tale of duty without price,
The stolen hymn that marks each villain's grave,
  Provokes the thought of Virtue mocked by Vice.

And where the prizes Charity has gained
  In Misery's scenes, which her apostles trod?
Intangible *her* trophies—else profaned
  The honor and the husbandry of God!

There is no history for the mortal eye,
  There is no shaft that smites the distant cloud,
Graven or raised with grace to testify
  Of kindred acts which Heaven's blest vaults enshroud.

In this new land, where each man has his creed;
Where meanest delvers often strike a lead;
Where bloody tragedy, audacious theft,
And homes of peace connubial bereft,
Whatever verdict partial juries take,
By natural laws are bound a book to make,
Where well-born subjects early leave their nurse
But to relieve the parent's plethoric purse;
Where little girls to debauchees are tied,
Until the Judge declares tho Priest has lied;

Where married women, of reproachless fame,
With each new bonnet change their wedded name,
And, pitying, view those left by them in lurch—
Their poorer sisters of the self-same church—
Who, it would seem quite rational to fear,
Will never marry—-more than once a year!
Where politicians sneer at moral worth
As not related to official birth;
Where candidates long hanker on the shelves;
Where snobs and loafers satirize themselves;
Where wretches known to be in guilt so deep
That angels vainly for their souls might weep;
To tenderest passions mournfully appeal,
And picture love and truths they never feel;—
Out from their pits of sensual blackness run
Their fiery cars of rhetoric to the sun!
Where brainless vagrants, filled with dirty spite,
Affect the courage of an Ishmaelite;
Where money-sharks relentless prey, and then
Are epitheted, "First-rate business men!"
Where sordid self is potentate and rule;
Who gives for friendship is an arrant fool!

Where scarce relieved frivolity prevails;
  Where Mercenaries crawl to honored place;
Where Legal License actually avails;
  To *consecrate* the world's supreme disgrace;—

How can you think to organize a plan
  That shall retain its working skill and power
To cheer the heart and meet the wants of man;
  Without a startling tocsin for each hour?

Thy neighbors' dangers and thine own attend
  On every moment, threatening every breath!
Where is the system that shall wisest lend
  All human aid 'gainst Chance, Disease and Death?

When great catastrophe occurs, and calls
  For special contributions and relief;
When fearful carnage all the land appalls
  And moves the coldest to a generous grief;

Abundant means for succor are obtained;
  Ten thousand hands, gratuitous, extend
To help, till life and peace once more are gained,
  And dreadful memories to the Past descend.

But, in the callous or indifferent world,
  When quiet broods upon the social face;
When all are not in shocks of sorrow whirled,
  How find and soothe the miseries of the race?

This greatest precept must be held in view—
  Given by the Father to the perfect Son:—

Whatever right or duty thou wouldst do,
  In secret service let the work be done!

Strip from the Symphony the vulgar rhyme
  Which blasphemy upon its cords has hung;
How clear the soul lifts with the swelling chime!
  How purely thrills the music, harped or sung!

Music! Th' Etherial, and the Undefiled!
  The heart and utterance of celestial truth;
Revealing in its innocence a child;
  Its beauteons strength portraying sinless youth.

So man: weak, vain, when nurtured with pretense;
  If private hour and fellow mortal's needs
Conspire to drive each earthly impulse hence,
  May execute the unpolluted deeds!

Deeds of redemption; though the Judge devotes
  All other actions to comsuming fire—
Changed by celestial alchemy to notes
  In Time's great anthem, for the Harvest Choir!
    Aye! Deeds that shall be celebrated when
    The Morning Stars, in rapture, sing again!

C. A. S.

THE FUNERAL.

It was a sightly funeral train,
The undertaker man,
With coffin-faced solemnity,
Conspicuous, led the van.
The priest, with comely garb and mien,
Sate, reverent, at his side ;
Then came the hearse, whose stately plumes
Bespoke a solemn pride.

"First carriage":—wherein honest grief
Seemed manifest displayed,
And kerchief'd eyes would fain shut out
Observance and parade.
"Coach Number Two":—a lighter shade
Of sorrow and distress ;
Then "Number Three" :—appearances
Of partial listlessness.

But curious ; the occupants
Of carriage "Number Four,"
Yawned, as to vote the whole affair
A ceremonious bore ;
But, "Five," "Six," "Seven," made amends,
With ever-broadening smile,

As ancedote and joke went round,
  The journey to beguile.

But—vastly worse—our truthful muse
  Would hardly dare to state,—
Were not these verses based on fact—
  The scenes in "Number Eight;"
Where two gay youths and two fair maids
  Were visibly diverting
Their minds from the solemnities,
  By levity, and flirting.

And then behold in "Number Nine,"
  A scene transcending far,
All we have chronicled as yet,—
  Four men, each with cigar;
A robe upon their knees outspread,
  Suspicious flask and cup,
Forecasting resurrection,
  By playing "seven up!"

Then, in the last conveyance, rode
  The female we all know,
Who never lets occasion pass,
  To supplement the show;

And weeps and sobs, until the sight
  Is pitiful to see,
And then inquires, as nears the grave,
  "Whose funeral might this be?"

S. B. S.

A SAILOR'S VISION.

INSCRIBED TO MISS S. M. H.

THE night was beautifully clear,
  High up the full-orbed moon was shining,
As I,—glad that our port was near,—
  Upon the capstan was reclining,

Spying the sea, and backward thinking,—
  Such was my wont when watching nights;—
From future thoughts persistent shrinking,
  As never yielding old delights.

Alone my solace in the past,
  Through all the hours of toil and care:
The morrow's sky was overcast
  With clouds whose depths I could not dare.

The sailor's thoughts of home were sweet;
  Though late in life he learned their truth,
He prayed that he in Heaven might meet
  The first companions of his youth.

How the dear scenes passed in review,—
  Pictures of gold he pondered o'er!
How far beyond all price they grew,
  As he repeated, "nevermore!"

And yet there was no mean repining,
  No sickly yearning for the lost;
Those tender memories interlining
  Life's record, cheat it of its cost.

With pain at times we throw them by,
  But soon return, when 'tis revealed
That in those shades which never die
  The actual substance is concealed.

It was not fear or shame that filled
  My soul, when forward it might look:
An "undefinéd presence" chilled,
  And cursed the prospect I forsook.

But now, why should I try evade—
  So close the Fleet Wing's harbor lay—
Reflections, which before forbade
  The simplest comfort on my way?

Eight bells struck aft; upon relief
  I did not join the crew below;
Their hearts with joy, as mine with grief,
  Unreasonable bounds o'erflow.

Beneath the boats I made my bed,
  Hid from the moon's destructive beams;

Again the earliest pages read,
And gained the quiet boyhood dreams.

What is this strangely following sight?
What blessed Angels walk before;
Repeat the day, dispel the night,
And make me anxious for the shore?

Almost a copy for the time
That I had held in such esteem,
Hope for its likeness seemed a crime,
Was promised in the Sailor's Dream.

With me such unbelief remained,
Against its haunting force I strove;
But constantly it was sustained,—
With every calculation wove.

Four times the Farallones we made;
Three times the lights flashed on the lee;
Four times the winds opposing staid,
And drove us to the open sea.

What curious passions fill my mind!
Now they depress and now elate,
When after five long months we find
An entrance through the Golden Gate.

And here begins the wondrous choice ;
  And here commenced prophetic days :
Familiar was the Pilot's voice ;
  I recognized the city's ways.

With utmost faithfulness, each part
  Of hour and day disclosed the fact
Which I had written on my heart,—
  Foreshadowed, and fulfilled exact.

The old New England home, once more !
  The welcome, and the cheerful fire,
Contrasted suffering, than before
  A keener relish must inspire.

But ah ! the vision failed to tell
  Of her, whose beauty soon destroys
The peace of life, I loved so well ;
  A deeper hope my soul employs.

With unaffected ease she spoke
  Of mutually familiar friends :
The memories her words evoke
  A cherished possible transcends.

I lent to her my favorite books,
  And proved our tastes alike inclined :

Forgetting e'en her charming looks,
 In her enchanting grace of mind.

* * * * *

The story of the Dream 's complete.
 'T was fully true, save nought of *one!*
If a revealing trance repeat,
 And finish what was thus begun—?

C. A. S.

SACRAMENTO, Nov. 25, 1857.

POEM,

DELIVERED AT THE ANNUAL EXHIBITION OF THE HOUSATONIC AGRICULTURAL SOCIETY AT GREAT BARRINGTON, MASS., SEPT. 29, 1876.

I'M no farmer; not a syllable from lips of mine
shall drop,
To accelerate or magnify a solitary crop;
And I only come, with careless rhyme, to greet
these friends of mine,
The acquaintances of years ago, the neighbors of
of "lang syne."

And 'tis singular—I came to sing,—but all things
sing to me.
Olden tunes come wafted to my ear from every rock
and tree;
And I seem but echo, as I stand within this native
vale,
And each object in the landscape round repeats an
olden tale.

But how things have changed! go back with me the
four and thirty years,
To the time when this good enterprise began with
doubts and fears.

'T was a curious coincidence ; the railway train, you know,
First arrived in town that day, and brought its crowds to see the show.

And the "show" was scattered all around,—a little here and there,
Oxen here, sheep over yonder, and confusion everywhere ;
Butter, cheese, and patch-work counterpanes, and what not, stored in halls,
While along the street were improvised seductive oyster stalls.

O, let modern cookery essay its best exploits in vain,
For those oysters, and that gingerbread we'll never taste again,—
So delicious, and so toothsome, and done up so very "brown,"
Titillating the olfactories of all the boys in town!

How we used to hoard our shillings up, for weeks and months ahead,
To invest in those bivalvous plants, and buy that gingerbread!

And how some have made their fortunes since, who, all those years ago,
Peddled sweets and peanuts to the folks who came to "cattle show!"

I remember, to the rearward of the stone church used to stand
Half a dozen gorgeous wagons, with their fancy goods on hand,
And some very flippant orators their merchandise would cry,
O'er-persuading by their eloquence, the rustic passers by.

One I think of in particular,—most charming auctioneer—
Whom I knew I might anticipate with each returning year;
Whose financial sacrifices, if the half he said was true,
Must have made him bankrupt, if alive; I'd like to 'put him through!'

Then, the man who showed the learnéd pig, and donkey with three legs,
And the cripple, who displayed the ball that knocked away his pegs;

And the everlasting soap man, nevermore to be forgot,
Who could cleanse your coat or conscience from a microscopic spot!

'Twas in those days, Major Rosseter—methinks I see him now—
Something over seventy years of age, walked proud behind the plow
While before, at least a hundred stalwart oxen were aligned,
And His Excellency, Governor Briggs, and magnates marched behind!

And in front of all, surrounded by enthusiastic boys,
That new village brass band vexed the air with complicated noise,
And escorted all the people, to the semblances of tunes,
To the meeting where should be dispensed the speeches, songs, and—spoons!

From beginnings such as these, the institution thrived and grew,—
For its founders, as the sequel proved, built wiser than they knew;

I might tell you all the history in lengthy diatribe,
As, through many a year, as I recall, I played the role of scribe.

What intense debates we used to have, when first awoke desire
Some distinctive habitation for our purpose to acquire;
And how many croakers shook their heads, and said it wouldn't pay;
Who shall find their sage prognostications all at fault to-day!

And now what an educator this emprise hath proved to be!
Looking back a generation, what results we come to see.
Better farms and better mansions, better harvests now than then;
Better quadrupeds and bipeds,—brighter women, thriftier men!

So, one thing begets another, through our life-work as we go,
And each tributary makes the river grander in its flow;

And unto what vast proportions it shall magnify and swell,
In the century that's coming, who shall venture to foretell?

In that wondrous exhibition, now surprising all the earth,
How we witness with amazement, to what Art hath given birth,
Unto patient Labor wedded, as together, hand in hand,
They have cultured all the planet and embellished every land!

See how Russia vies with Turkey, and Australia with Japan,
In the onward march of progress, all contesting for the van.
Side by side see China, Germany and Austria advance,
With the Netherlands, Spain, Norway, Sweden, Italy, and France!

Then the Argentine Republic, Chili, Mexico, Brazil,—
In the world's confederation, each a mission to fulfill;—

While old England, on whose vast domains there
looks no setting sun,
With a pride we all forgive her, shows the trophies
she has won!

Unto all of these according, as we do, the meed of
praise,
How our own beloved Columbia evokes our own
amaze,
As in each field of endeavor, each proud rival she
defies,—
In the tournament of nations, bearing off the highest
prize!

And for all her sudden glory, I assert that unto
you,
Men and women of New England, much of all the
praise is due.
Take the purple wings of morning, girdle all the
globe in vain,
Nowhere else shall you discover more of sinew, heart
and brain.

And from out these rural valleys, and from off these
mountain slopes,
Have gone many brave evangelists of this young
nation's hopes.

'Tis the country makes the city, and your country
boys are they,
Who control your grand metropolis and capital, to-
day.

Now, the lesson I would leave you, friends and
neighbors, as we part,—
Cultivate not matter only, but the vineyard of the
heart.
Give the plow its meed of honor, but no less the
brain and pen,
And, whatever else, keep raising your true women
and good men!

S. B. S.

LINES,

PRESENTED AS A SILVER WEDDING GIFT.

Full five and twenty years ago,—
Ah, me! what recollections swarm,—
Louisa changed her maiden name,
To please her Francis Mandlebaum.*

And if for me, whose diary page
In single blessedness descends,
The century quarter seems an age,
How must it look to these dear friends?

For they have had such cause for joy,—
Red-letter hours of festal mirth,—
In anniversary employ,
For wedding day and children's birth;

And they have had such scenes of woe,
As death of children must decree,
Since five-and-twenty years ago
They married 'neath the almond-tree.

To them, indeed, the span of years
With tenderest incidents is set;

---

* Signifies almond-tree.

Not one of which, mid smiles and tears,
  Could they consent to quite forget.

Now when they round this arc of time,
  I hope they will not spurn from me
The gift I'd lay with friendship's thyme,
  Upon their silver almond-tree.

C. A. S.

LINES,

READ AT BURNS FESTIVAL, BRIDGEPORT, CONN., JANUARY 25, 1877, IN RESPONSE TO A TOAST—THE LASSIES.

WHAT wonder Scotia's lyric bard
  All lyric bards surpasses,
Whose inspiration was the glance
  Of Scotia's bonnie lassies.
In Edinboro',—on the Clyde,
  In Ayr—delicious creatures!—
How I have worshipped, (as I sighed,)
  The glory of their features.

Perhaps it is ozonic air,
  Off those gigantic mountains;
Perhaps the waters, as they flow
  From Afton's sparkling fountains:
Perhaps, more like, the genial light
  Of wholesome hearths, and cozy,
That makes those eyes so clear and bright,
  Those lips and cheeks so rosy.

There's many a Highland Mary yet,
  That land can reproduce,
And many a maid walks there as proud
  As in the days of Bruce;

And many a Queen of Scots still lives,
  And Vernons and Mac Ivors,
In fact, if not in fiction, leave
  A host of sweet survivors!

O, when shall I forget the morn,
  On which the Judge and I,
At Melrose Abbey's guarded gates,
  For guidance did apply.
Soft eyes from out the lattice peeped,—
  A welcome voice, but shy,
Said, "I'll encase my feet from dew,
  The lawn is scarcely dry."

Then, in a trice, from out the door,
  A vision, I'll declare,
Burst, such as never seemed before
  Transcendently so fair.
That tabernacle of all grace
  I see in day-dreams now:
That figure, and that radiant face,
  And that Madonna brow!

Sir Walter tells us, as we know,
  To see Melrose aright,
We should behold its ruined walls
  Beneath the soft moonlight.

The dear old soul! he could but say
  'Twere more delightful Aidenn,
To gather its traditions up
  From lips of such a maiden!

I know not of her name or place,
  Nor can conjecture even
Whether on earth still beams her face,
  Or one new star decks heaven.
But, living yet, a health this night!
  There's not a flower that blows
More fragrant on the banks of Tweed,—
  Fair rose of fair Melrose!

O, Scotland! ever bright'ning page
  In my memorial volume;
For all thou hast, and art, we'd raise
  The laudatory column!
Thy scenery, thy history,
  The scrolls thou hast unfurled,—
The lanterns thou hast set ablaze
  To lumine all the world;

Let others speak to-night of these,—
  As fittingly they will.—
Be mine my pretty text to keep—
  My sweet task to fulfill;

To sing a simple heartfelt strain,
  In honor of dear woman,
Who everywhere, but nowhere more,
Than upon Caledonia's shore,
  Allies divine with human!

O, I am growing old apace,
  And yet—I know not why—
Not unneglected of my glance,
  The lassies pass me by.
I love them all;—fair flowers they are
  By our kind Author given,
Vouchsafing here some little share
  And foretaste of that Heaven.,—

Where, let us hope, we all shall meet,
  And on the blooming heather,—
The other side of Jordan's stream,—
  Roam lovingly together.
So I conclude with sermon, what
  Was meant to be a song,
And, in a word—God bless us all!—
  The sermon wasn't long.

S. B. S.

SHAKESPEARE.

LINES READ AT THE ANNUAL BANQUET OF ST. GEORGE'S SOCIETY, BRIDGEPORT CONN., 1877.

THREE centuries ago there trod
The banks of Avon, up and down,
One, who upbore no earthly crown,
But crowned magnificent of God.

Imperial soul! so vastly stored
From out the treasuries of thought;
What empyrean realms it sought;
What undiscovered heights explored!

Shakespeare! Arch Poet, bard sublime;
Seer, autocratic sage profound;
How shall thy crescent fame resound
Through all the corridors of time!

Earth's sceptred kings may come at will,
And each abide his little day;
And strut his while, and pass away
And other kings their places fill;

But THOU shalt still assert thy throne,
Whose grandeur shall attempt in vain

All lords of earth ; and thou shalt reign
Majestical, supreme, alone!

For thou hast caught from out the spheres
Of upper air, Promethean fire.
Proud Hermit, where none dare aspire,
Thou scornest the retreat of years ;—

Years which shall pass us laughing by,
And leave us wrecked on Lethean shore ;
Whilst thou shalt live forever more
In thoughts and words that cannot die!

S. B. S.

THE FATHER AND THREE SONS.

From the German.

As old in years, and rich in goods,
And flocks, and teeming soil,
A sire apportioned to his sons
The product of his toil.

"One diamond ring," the old man said,
"Is here, which I withhold;
It shall be his, who can to me
The noblest act unfold."

Thereat the brothers separate,
And go their several ways;
And to their aged sire return,
At lapse of many days.

Then spake the eldest brother: "Hear!
A stranger all his hoard
Entrusted me; the which I held,
And faithfully restored;

"Say, Father, may I not presume
To claim the glittering prize?
How looks a noble deed like that,
In the parental eyes?"

"You did, my son,"—the old man said—
"What duty bade you do.
The deed was good,—not noble though,
'T was simply, to be true."

The other spake: "As journeyed I
Along in careless way,
I heard a fearful wild outcry
From out a storm-tossed bay.

"I plunged into the angry wave,
The drowning child upbore;
And saved it from the watery grave,—
Could noble man do more?"

"My boy," the sire replied,—"You did
What mortals here below
In kindly offices of love
Unto each other owe."

"The youngest spake: "Upon the brink
Of a stupendous steep—
Unconscious of his peril—lay
My enemy, asleep.

"Within my hand I held his life,—
One thrust had hurled him o'er,—

I drew him back; we slew our strife.
  And we are foes no more."

"O!" said the sire, with loving glance—
"Hither my noble boy, advance!
The ring is thine! *Welch edler Muth!
Wenn Man dem Feinde Gutes thut.*"

S. B. S.

THE TRAMP'S SOLILOQUY.

Last night, within the Station House,
I was distinctly floored.
I noticed, while I had my bed,
Therewith I had my board.
But now it 's morn, and breakfast time;
I'll sally forth and beg.
I'd like a cup of old Bohea,
A biscuit and an egg.

Well, here's a place seems promising;
I'll ring the kitchen bell.
There's something luscious broiling there,—
O, what delicious smell!
Ah! here comes Bridget;—Pray, my dear,—
Your cooking I admire,—
Would you a gracious morsel give
To quell my stomach's ire?

What's this she says?—"Begone, you wretch!
Your blarney is all stuff;
And your profession 's overdone,—
We've seen and heard enough!
Begone, I say! and mind you this,—
Don't show your face here more."

With that, she tosses up her nose,
  And, spiteful, slams the door.

Well, well, I'll go across the street,
  And see what better luck ;—
A saucier girl, in all my rounds,
  I'm sure I never struck.
O, ho! what's here!—a boarding house :—
  I'll make another dash ;
I see the breakfast bill of fare,—
  Fish-balls and mutton-hash.

* * * * *

Now, if that matron had but thought
  To serve those viands warmer,
And not from off that baby's plate,
  I wouldn't wish to storm her.
Here, pup ; here kit! come, try your teeth
  And talented digestion ;—
I pass—pass out, on this queer game,
  Take, eat; don't ask a question!

But now, 'tis getting serious,
  And whither shall I wend?
A lively notion strikes my mind,—
  The labor-search pretend.

Here's just the place; I see a face
  Benevolent, all over;—
O, lady! for the love of God,
  Some work for me discover!

I'm travelling by night and day
  The wide, wide country through,
To find some steady place to stay,—
  Some useful thing to do.
And even now I'm famishing,
  And oh! were I but fed,
How gladly would I scrub that walk,
  And rake that flower-bed!

* * * * *

I had her there; that tea was fine,—
  How nice the ham and eggs!
The pancakes came right in my line;
  Once more I'm on my pegs!
This spoon I'll pawn somewhere away—
  When many days have sped;
O, lady! here's your health; good day!
  O, slighted flower-bed!

S. B. S.

LINES,

READ AT F. W. PARROTT'S GOLDEN WEDDING, BRIDGEPORT, CONN., MAY 10, 1877.

THE golden wedding! O, reluctant Muse!
Once more be wooed from out thy coy retreat;
Smile on thy humble suppliant: nor refuse
This brilliant throng, this honored pair, to greet.

Semi-Centennial! what a lapse of years,
Since these good friends in wedlock clasped the hand,
And forth, with alternating hopes and fears—
Adventured the long stroll upon Time's strand.

I learn to honor, as I older grow,—
As I would fain be honored, were it mine
So long to live; the "gude folk" whom I know,
Whose history reaches to the far "lang syne."

Half century ago;—Exceeding queer!—
This couple strayed beneath the soft moonlight.
How many forms, like mine, which were not here,
Are gathered to congratulate, this night!

For we were dead;—out in the void somewhere;—
As dead we shortly hence again shall be;—

The world moved on without us; while this pair
  Were living, breathing, loving souls as we.

The same hills here reflected the same sun;
  The same fields spread their carpeture of green;
The same bright river sought its course to run;
  The same sweet stars looked out from Heaven serene;

And most of us were, where,—O strange! we dread
  Once more in course of nature to withdraw;
In realms, where kindred souls each other wed,
  And Love, we trust, is universal law.

O, what poetic sermon would we sing,—
  So the kind muse, would breathe into the strain;—
But ah! she flitteth with uncertain wing;
  I strive to grasp a feather, but in vain!

Half century ago, my friends, is something of a while.
It means a toilsome journey, friends, and many a weary mile.
And when we greet the man and wife, who all that length of time
Have clung together; prose is dull, and thought should dress in rhyme.

For what a theme it opens up to the poetic pen!
And what perspective stretches out betwixt the "Now" and "Then."
What memories it congregates in overwhelming throng,
To challenge all the force of speech, and melody of song!

I see in distant retrospect, the sturdy, striving boy,
Ambitious, all his energy in life-work to employ;
To give the world endeavors best; and, in return demand
Some recognition of his worth, at this world's jealous hand.

Here was he to the manor born;—a native of the soil;—
Here, spent his childhood and his youth; and here his manly toil.
Courageous and laborious, these many years along;—
O, what career more fit to be enwoven into song!

Life's real heroes don't wear star and garter all the time;
Your quiet, unassuming men are fittest theme for rhyme.

I know some steeds upon parade evoke a loud applause,
But in the long run give to me the faithful one that DRAWS!

Some men produce, while more consume;—this friend, his whole life o'er,
Has added, not subtracted, in the count of earthly store;
Grown rich, perhaps;—within a home where luxuries surround it,—
He'll leave at last his neighborhood much richer than he found it.

So, as the soft approaches come, of life's late afternoon,
Fain would we summon the fond muse, in lightly sandaled shoon
Hither approach; and for the nonce, with smiling face, look down,
And deck this septuagenary brow with fitting crown.

But hush! we can but apprehend, there'll be domestic strife,
Unless, right here,—the muse pays some attention to the wife!

O, what a pretty girl was she! with glance so bright
yet tender,
Which brought the boy upon his knee, and bade his
heart surrender.

We'll not narrate the courtship scenes enacted by
this pair,—
As intimated heretofore, we were engaged elsewhere.—
Had we been here, officious aid had hardly been allowed.
Two—then as now—was company; but three, too
big a crowd.

Tradition has it, that the girl had many a sighing
beau;
And, for a time, not wholly smooth, Love's rivulet
did flow;
And yet our hero broke the ice, and did not yield
nor falter,
But persevered until he led his lady to the altar.

Though his has been a good success, the world's affairs amid,
His marriage was the smartest thing, we think he
ever did.

A faithful helpmeet he acquired; a loving wife and
mother;—
So he could say through all these years;—"there
never lived such other."

She helped him toil and calculate; fond babes to
him she bore;
She aided to accumulate in basket and in store;
And sometimes—barely possible—her sceptre was
the ladle,
To make "creation's lord" sit down, and rock that
boisterous cradle!

Yet she was a true heroine; how often have I heard,
She'd let him come home late o' nights, and never
say a word!
I state this for the benefit of other ladies here—
One, in particular, I see, I think is "on her ear."

O, I might sing the livelong night, to coax a cry or
laugh;
You notice, what I'm dealing out, is something
"half and half;"—
But these old people, you can see at superficial
glance,
Are growing dreadful frisky, and impatient for the
dance!

So, let the hearty bugler blow his most arousing
horn!
Ring, bells! Attune the jocund hours! don't let's go
home till morn!
But, when we go;—both glad and sad,—how must
we all agree—
What we have seen this nuptial tide, we never
more may see!

S. B. S.

MORS.

I DREAMED there was a luxury in death.
  Fond friends and kindred round the couch were sighing,
While there in state, quiescent, I was lying,
  Awaiting calmly the expiring breath.

It seemed. as on a throne I was uplifted,
  So all surrounding faces gazed on me ;—
O, had I been with tongue of angel gifted,
  How had I half disclosed what I could see!

I saw, with rapt and beatific vision,
  Worlds far beyond, and O, so far above!
Where, midst the empyrean spheres elysian,
  The seraphs love to live, and live to love.

Then, all at once, at beck of some supernal
  And glorious being—radiance o'er her head—
I seemed to soar into the realms eternal,
  And earth's poor grovellers pronounced me " dead."

S. B. S.

SPRING.

SHE comes! I know her footsteps as they fall
  On this glad earth, so gloriously drest,
Once more in all her bowers to install
  This new-born goddess, this delightful guest.

She comes! I scent, in violet and rose,
  Her perfumed garments as she trips along;
How every apple-blossomed ringlet flows,
  As she moves on—a personated song!

She comes! the forest trees are all awake;
  The cataract exults; the warm sun shines;
The birds their southern fastnesses forsake,
  To build once more their nests in northern pines.

She comes! the boys and girls are all aglee;
  The coasting and the skating days are past.
"Good-bye, decrepid Winter! here comes she!
  We love her after all, the first and last!"

She comes! best season of the rolling years,—
  Most welcome; would we doubt the reason why?
She tells us every time she re-appears:
  "The dead shall rise again; ye cannot die!"

S. B. S.

ALBERT.*

Not wrapped in memory's spell,
But in some other self enshrined;
Absorbed, yet free to dwell
Within the frescoed chambers of the mind.

Unnumbered scenes are set,
Distinct, but incomplete they seem;
As when a heart regret
Swells to the anguished outcry of a dream.

Mid twilight views of years,—
Serene—exulting—yet oppressed;—
Wherein the boy appears
I've rocked a thousand times upon my breast.

'Tis but a flashing look,
I wish and wish not to prolong!
'Tis caught, then quick forsook:
The wild, weird witchery of his infant song!

And then consummate skill
On harps of most melodious strings,

---

* Albert was returning, when drowned at Halifax, from a two years' residence in Europe. He was a fine musician, and musical composer. His musical works have been collected and published in an elegant volume, by O. Ditson & Co., Boston.

Bequeaths the ecstatic thrill,—
The sorcery Genius summons, weaves and flings.

Again those pictures come
Of peaceful sail; of wrecking shocks!
The captain steeped in rum,
Tossing his vessel on the jagged rocks!

O God! amid the roar
Of waves and winds; 'mid women's cries;
Did that sweet spirit soar,
Bathed in symphonious echoes from the skies!

Child of last hope and fears!
Youth, with seraphic rhythm endowed!
Comrade of choicest years,
A brother's soul above thy grave is bowed!

C. A. S.

THE PRODIGAL SON.

Since I heard Doctor Chapin a certain Lord's day,
His Sabbath evangel from Heaven convey,
I remember the service—how fitly begun,—
As he read the old parable—"Prodigal Son."

As that voice, so magnificent,—rendered the text,
A stranger enraptured, whose seat was just next,
Accosted me thus: "How the God-man in Glory,—
I speak reverential;—could tell a sweet story!"

The prodigal son! I would touchingly bid
Every prodigal son to do just as he did.
You're a prodigal now; you need only return,
To discover what hearts for your welcoming yearn.

No matter what goods and what hours you have squandered.
No matter how far from life's duty you've wandered.
There's a sun,—aye, a Son!—on your pathway to shine,
Through a lens that's all human, but O, how divine!

The good brother was jealous; he stayed on the farm,
And faithfully wrought with laborious arm;

No matter ;—reserved with a fatherly care,
In the old man's heart's chambers, a place was still there!

And the boy ;—we'll acknowledge his courses were wild,
But he learned the sad lessons; and, once more a child,
From the dreadful deceits of the world would fain come
Penitential to beg for the old home, at home!

Did the fond sire reject him? The Gospel shall sing,—
"Bring forth fatted calf; the best robe; the bright ring!
With the echoes of merriment, household, resound!
For our dead is alive, and our lost one is found!"

O, THIS is Religion! we're prodigals all,
Who inhabit and tread this terrestrial ball;
But, for sinner, transgressor, for every one—
There is hope ;—read the story; the prodigal son.

S. B. S.

GEORGIANNA.

O, BOSOM friend of many years!
Partaker of my hopes and fears;—
Rejoicing when I did rejoice,
And, when I wept, with gentle voice,
And sympathetic words, assuaging
The agony within me raging;—
Fond mother of fond babes of mine;
Priestess, at our domestic shrine;
Sunlight of our domestic hearth;—
This benizon, of little worth,
Take from thine ardent swain of yore,
Whose love hath ripened more and more;—
Georgianna!

Strange! how as people come and go,
I chanced that sparkling lass to know.
From out her eye there flashed one dart,
Which quite transfixed, and won my heart.
I yielded all I was, and had;
Too fortunate, too proud, too glad
To clasp as mine that faithful hand,
And kneel beneath the silken band,
Which bound us happily in one,
As was our wedded life begun;
Georgianna!

What treasure in my chosen mate,
No chosen words can fitly state.
All our experiences through,
Thou hast been constant, loving, true.
In all vicissitudes of life
Thou stand'st approved,—a model wife!
Mayhap our grandchildren may read
These words, and give them reverent heed;
Georgianna!

The years roll on;—'tis growing late,—
And we anon must separate;
But somewhere, on some shining shore,—
Where amaranth blooms evermore,—
Let's hope, the good God will permit,
That, re-united, we may sit,
And hear sweet strains of music sounding,
Where Heaven's grand minstrelsy resounding
Shall welcome to the scenes above
The earth-born souls most meet for love;
Georgianna!

Meanwhile, be thou,—as thou hast been,—
Within this home enthroned as queen.
Still give, from thy resources ample,
Our children, precept and example;

Be my first critic as thou hast,—
Mentor unknown through all the past;
And where or how our lines may be,
Beam on my pathway; cleave to me;
Georgianna!

S. B. S.

OUR FATHER.

BROTHER! we cannot close these waifs of ours,
Until upon that honored grave we place,—
With filial and with reverential grace,—
A simple garland of memorial flowers.

A man not only good and true, but great,—
To us, indeed, almost a demi-god;
His smile was bliss; his frown was gloom; his nod
Oracular; his lightest speech was weight.

Whoe'er would meet his logic, must prepare;
Whoe'er impugn his honor, must take heed;
Whoe'er his learning would attempt, must read;
Whoe'er would tell him falsehood, must beware.

Imperious oft, and with his thoughts astray,
How would he sometimes overawe us boys.
How well admonished then to hush our noise,
And shift elsewhere our racket, and our play.

Yet we remember, in his leisure hour,—
The golden moments of his care's surcease,—
How would he, giving else a brief release,
Abundant floods of warm affection shower.

What fund of wisdom, wit and anecdote
From that prolific intellect outpoured!
How apt, how lavish, from his memory stored,
Could he the royal bards and sages quote!

How Judges hearkened; and the learnéd Shaw
Exclaimed, as he, our father, argued oft
With rivals of that day, on themes aloft,
"He came to Berkshire county to learn law."

But oh! before the "august twelve," how vast,
How irresistible, o'erwhelming powers
Our sire displayed; as through unheeded hours,
Spellbound he held his willing captives fast!

We know some littler men had larger sphere,—
And we have lived the why to understand;—
But when and where he spake, was to command;
He feared no anakim,—he was their peer!

How oft, in afternoon of Sabbath day,
Would he the psalmist and the seer intone;
Voicing the sacred text, as he alone
Could render words earth's saints were born to say.

(And there our mother and our sister sat,—
What specimens of glorious womanhood!—
Both gone;—O God! I would not, if I could,
Re-break my heart upon a theme like that!)

Brother! whate'er we fail of, or acquire;
Whate'er we lose in future, or secure;
One fixed, irrevocable boon is sure,—
The certain sonship of a noble sire.

S. B. S.

THE END.

THE AUTHORS' PUBLISHING COMPANY'S

NEW BOOKS.

☞ The Authors' Publishing Company *will send any of the following books by mail, postage prepaid, to any part of the United States, on receipt of the price.*

HIGHER THOUGHT.

Evolution and Progress:

An Exposition and Defence. The Foundation of Evolution Philosophically Expounded, and its Arguments (divested of insignificant and distracting physical details) succinctly stated; together with a review of leading opponents, as Dawson and Winchell, and quasi-opponents, as Le Conte and Carpenter. By Rev. William I. Gill, A. M., of Newark Conference, N. J. *The first volume of the International Prize Series.* Third Edition. Cloth extra, imitation morocco, fine paper, 295 pp., 12mo., Price . $1 50

Each volume in this series was awarded a prize of *Two Hundred Dollars* in addition to copyright, in a competition which was open one year to the world, and where over three hundred manuscripts were submitted and read.

DESCRIPTIVE OPINIONS OF EVOLUTION AND PROGRESS.

One of our most candid and thoughtful writers.—*Dr. Crane.*
He is a clear and strong reasoner.—*Cincinnati Christian Standard.*
A particularly strong argument.—*Evansville (Ind.) Daily Journal.*
It is ably written. Builds on philosophical principles.—*Brooklyn Union.*
The attitude of Mr. Gill, and his courage in maintaining it, are worthy of note.—*New York World.*
I rejoice in all attempts of this kind, made in a spirit like that which prompts your work.—*Herbert Spencer.*
His writings are marked by strong common sense, sound logic, and clear demonstration.—*Methodist Home Journal.*
It is a book of original thinking on one of the greatest themes.......A keen, thoughtful, vigorous volume.—*Golden Age.*
He strikes with no velvet glove, but with a steel-clad hand, dealing his blows with equal profusion and impartiality.—*New York Tribune.*
His effort is earnest, able and bold...... It presents, in all their naked strength, thoughts and arguments which will have to be met and answered.—*The Methodist, New York.*

Analytical Processes;

Or, The Primary Principle of Philosophy. By Rev. William I. Gill, A. M., author of "Evolution and Progress." *The Third Volume of the International Prize Series.* Cloth extra, fine paper, uniform with "Evolution and Progress," 450 pp., 12mo. Price $2 00.

A work which the committee cannot describe without seeming to exaggerate. It is marked by extraordinary depth and originality, and yet it is so clear and convincing as to make its novel conclusions appear like familiar common sense.—*From Report of Committee of Prize Award.*

It contains a vast amount of able and conscientious thought and acute criticism.—*Dr. McCosh, Prest. Princeton College.*

A specimen of robust thinking. I am very much gratified with its thoroughness, acuteness and logical coherence.—*Dr. Anderson, Pres't Rochester University.*

Ecclesiology:

A Fresh Inquiry as to the Fundamental Idea and Constitution of the New Testament Church; with a Supplement on Ordination. By Rev. E. J. Fish, D. D. Cloth extra, fine paper, 400 pp., 12mo. . Price $2 00.

Doctor Fish disposes this volume into four parts.—I. The Fundamental Idea of the Church; II. The New Testament Church Constitution; III. Application of Principles; IV. A Supplement on Ordinaton—and addresses himself to his themes with the full earnestness of ability, clearness of logic, and conscientiousness of spirit which comprehensive treatment requires. As a "building fitly framed together," it is a fair-minded and standard contribution to the best religious literature of the Christian age.

The Beauty of the King:

By Rev. A. H. Holloway, A. M., author of "Good Words for S. S. Teachers," "Teachers' Meetings," etc. Cloth extra, 174 pp. 12mo, $1.00; full gilt, beveled edges, $1.25.

A remarkably clear, comprehensive and intelligible exposition of the natural and spiritual causes, processes and effects of the birth, life and death of Jesus—a subject much discussed, yet not generally understood now-a-days.

Life for a Look:

By Rev. A. H. Holloway, A. M. Paper covers, 32mo.
Price, 15 cts.

Earnest, cogent words, marrowy with the spirit of honest, old-fashioned Religion.

Is Our Republic a Failure?

A discussion of the Rights and the Wrongs of the North and the South. By E. H. WATSON, author of "United States and their Origin," etc. English cloth, ink and gold, 12mo, 436 pp. . . . . Price, $1.50

In a spirit of genuine candor and unswerving impartiality.—*N. Y. Sun.*

It is fair, candid, impartial, the whole subject well treated.—HON. J. H. BLAKE, *of Boston.*

I like the spirit of the book, its comprehensive patriotism, its liberal spirit, and its healing counsels.—HON. GEO. S. HILLARD, *author of "Franklin Readers," "Six Months in Italy," etc.*

I read the manuscript with much interest—an interest belonging to the arguments themselves, but now increased by the perfection given to the form and style.—HON. MARTIN BRIMMER, *Boston.*

Lucid and just. The method of the argument, the facts on which it proceeds, and the conciliatory spirit which invests them, contribute to the book a value which cannot be too highly estimated.—GEN. JOHN COCHRANE.

The principles of American statesmanship which it asserts, must essentially prevail, unless we are so soon to fall from our original high plane of constitutional republicanism. I shall spare no exertion to promote the knowledge of such an able and impartial and statesmanlike compendium of our present political philosophy.—HON. JOHN QUINCY ADAMS, *Mass.*

Clearly expressed, and the argument is closely and ably maintained. The tone and the temper of the writer are beyond praise. They are as valuable as they are rare. They are those of a patriotic and philosophical observer of men. The like spirit everywhere diffused among our people would make fraternal union as certain as desirable; and if brought to the discussion of public affairs, would secure the adoption of wise and beneficent counsels.—HON. GEO. H. PENDLETON, *Ohio.*

Universe of Language:

Its Nature and Structure, with Uniform Notation and Classification of Vowels, adapted to all Languages. By the late GEORGE WATSON, Esq., of Boston. Edited with preliminary Essays, by his daughter, E. H. WATSON, author of "Is Our Republic a Failure," etc. Introduction by WM. W. GOODWIN, A. M., Eliot Professor of Greek Literature in Harvard University. 12mo, cloth extra, ... $1.00

Life and Lectures of John Moffat, of Tenn:

Edited by the REV. R. L. ABERNETHY, President of Rutherford College, North Carolina. 12mo, paper covers, 50 cents.

A work of thrilling interest, especially to young men. It presents the outline of a life of one who came up through great struggles, and whose name has, over many States, become a household word as the advocate of Temperance, Education and Social Reform.

PRACTICAL THOUGHT.

Mercantile Prices and Profits;

Or the Valuation of Commodities for a Fair Trade. By M. R. PILON. Handsomely printed, 8vo., paper, 100 pp., ... In Press.

The author has brought broad experience and comprehensive research to bear upon his subjects. His style is terse and perspicuous. He uses the easy and concise language of an educated business man; and, with wonderful art, invests every chapter with the grace and charm of a well-told story.

Monetary Feasts and Famines;

Labor, Values, Prices, Foreign and Fair Trade, Scarcity of Money and the Causes of Inflation. By M. R. PILON, author of "The Grangers." Uniform with "The Grangers,"—(*In Press.*) . .

Gold and Free Banks:

Ways to arrive at the Demonetization of Gold and Silver, and the establishment of Private Banks under control of the National Government. By. M. R. PILON, author of "The Grangers." FIFTH EDITION. 8vo., 186 pp., paper cover, . . Price 75 cents.

The work is interesting, and especially valuable to financiers.—*Jersey City Daily Journal.*

He gives expression to a good deal of sound financial principle.—*Louisville Daily Commercial.*

It is full of common sense......Valuable for its facts, its thoughts and its suggestions.—*Troy Daily Whig.*

Is written in an interesting and popular style and contains much useful information.—*Oakland, Cal., Daily News.*

The subject of the high valuation of gold and silver currency is fully discussed, and offers some new ideas worthy the attention of those interested in monetary affairs.—*Toledo Commercial.*

The author is a merchant who has extensively studied the currency problem. His hits are often sharp and incisive........Mr. Pilon would provide ample banking facilities for every city, town and village, with both stock and land security.—*Cincinnati Daily Star.*

........Discussing the currency question in an original, forcible and entertaining style. The author has brought together a great amount of varied information upon the whole subject of money......Those interested will find unquestioned ability in the author's handling of it.—*Baltimore Methodist Protestant.*

The Manuscript Manual:

How to Prepare Manuscripts for the Press—practical and to the point. Paper, 26 pp., 8vo. Price 10 cents.

A most useful little companion to the young writer and editor.—*The South, New York.*

Gives excellent hints to intending writers.—*Cleveland Evan. Messenger*

ÆSTHETIC THOUGHT.

Irene; or, Beach-Broken Billows:

A Story. By MRS. B. F. BAER, author of "Lena's Marriage," "The Match-Girl of New York," "Little Bare-Foot," etc., etc. *The second volume of the International Prize Series.* SECOND EDITION. Cloth extra, fine thick paper. 12mo. . . . Price $1 00.

Natural, honest and delicate.—*New York Herald.*
Charming and thoughtful.—*Poughkeepsie Eagle.*
Depicted in strong terms.—*Baptist Union, New York.*
Eminently pleasing and profitable.—*Christian Era, Boston.*
A fascinating volume.—*Georgia Musical Eclectic Magazine.*
Characters and plot fresh and original.—*Bridgeport News.*
With freshness, clearness, and vigor.—*Neb. Watchman.*
Delightful book.—*Saturday Review, Louisville, Ky.*
Lays open a whole network of the tender and emotional.—*Williamsport (Pa.) Daily Register.*

The unity is well preserved, the characters maintaining that probability so essential in the higher forms of fiction.—*Baltimore Methodist Protestant.*

There is a peculiar charm in the reading of this book, which every one who peruses it must feel. It is very like to that which is inspired in reading any of Hawthorne's romances.—*Hartford Religious Herald.*

Wild Flowers:

Poems. By CHARLES W. HUBNER, author of "Souvenirs of Luther." Elegantly printed on fine tinted paper, with portrait of the Author, imitation morocco and beveled edges, 196 pp., 12mo. *Just ready,*

Price $1.00. The same, gilt top, beveled edges, $1.25

As a poet MR. HUBNER is conservative—always tender and delicate, never turbid or erratic. He evinces a strong love of nature and high spirituality, and brings us, from the humblest places and in the humblest guises, beauties of the heart, the life, the universe, and, while placing them before our vision, has glorified them and shown that within them of whose existence we had never dreamed.

Her Waiting Heart:

A Novel. By LOU CAPSADELL, author of "Hallow E'en." Cloth extra, 192 pp., 12mo. *Just ready.* $1 00.

A story of New York—drawn from the familiar phases of life, which, under the calmest surfaces, cover the greatest depths. Charming skill is shown in the naturalness of characterization, development of plot and narrative, strength of action and delicacy of thought.

Shadowed Perils:

A Novel. By M. A. AVERY, author of "The Loyal Bride," etc. English cloth, 260 pp., 12mo, . . . $1 25

The story is bold and dramatic in action, graceful in narrative, strong in characterization, intense in interest, sweet and pure in tone, and is marked by keen sympathy with the lowly and oppressed.

Egypt Ennis; or, Prisons Without Walls:

A Novel. By KELSIC ETHERIDGE. Paper, 97 pp., 8vo., ... Price, 35 cents.

Has the curiosity-exciting tendency.—*Boston Beacon.*

The interest grows and retains attention to the end.—*N. O. Picayune.*

Short, sententious, marrowy, and spiced with episodes. Has a warm southern aroma of orange and magnolia blossoms.—*Baltimore Meth. Prot.*

Of rare beauty and power in its vivid, life-like picturing of men and places. . . . . . Through such artistic touches of skill and strength we are wafted in thought as we follow the hero and heroine through the mazes of the old, old story.—*Ladies' Pearl, St. Louis.*

The Travelers' Grab-Bag; or, the Heart of a Quiet Hour:

A Hand-book for utilizing fragments of leisure in railroad trains, steamboats, way stations and easy chairs. Edited by AN OLD TRAVELER. . . . Paper, 100 pp., 8vo. . . . . Price, 35 cents.

Full of spice and fun.—*Baltimore Meth. Prot.*

No traveler should be without it.—*N. Y. Forest and Stream.*

Teeming with rollicking humor and a kind of satire that will be enjoyable.—*Pittsburgh Commercial.*

The Anti-Biled Shirt Club:

Clear type, heavy tinted paper, 12mo, . . 25 cents.

The curious and ludicrous experiences of a party of gentlemen who sought happiness in the forests of Maine; graphically told with a naive humor and delicate satire; fresh and spicy.

Women's Secrets; or, How to be Beautiful:

Translated and Edited from the Persian and French, with additions from the best English authorities. By LOU. CAPSADELL, author of "Her Waiting Heart," "Hallow E'en," etc. Pp. 100, 12mo.

Saratoga Edition, in Scotch granite paper covers, 25 cents.

Boudoir Edition, French grey and blue cloths, . 75 cents.

The systems, directions and recipes for promoting Personal Beauty, as practiced for thousands of years by the renowned beauties of the Orient, and for securing the grace and charm for which the French Toilette and Boudoir are distinguished, together with suggestions from the best authorities, comprising History and Uses of Beauty; The Best Standards; Beautiful Children; Beauty Food, Sleep, Exercise, Health, Emotions· How to be Fat; How to be Lean; How to be Beautiful and to remain so, etc., etc.

Sumners' Poems:

By SAMUEL B. SUMNER and CHARLES A. SUMNER. On heavy tinted paper, with three engravings, comprising plate portraits of the authors on steel. 12mo, 500 pp., imitation morocco. $2.50

The Buccaneers:

A stirring Historical Novel. By RANDOLPH JONES, Esq. Large 12mo, cloth extra, ink and gold, . . $1.50

Is drawn from the most daring deeds of the Buccaneers and the sharpest events in the early settlement of Maryland and Virginia. It is so full of thrilling action, so piquant in sentiment, and so thoroughly alive with the animation of the bold and ambitious spirits whose acts it records with extraordinary power, that the publishers confidently bespeak "THE BUCCANEERS" as the most strongly marked and the best of all American novels issued during the year.

☞ Inclose three-cent stamp for pamphlet, comprising descriptive catalogue and the plan of organization and working of The Authors' Publishing Company. Address,

THE AUTHORS' PUBLISHING CO.,

27 Bond Street New York.

www.ingramcontent.com/pod-product-compliance
Lightning Source LLC
LaVergne TN
LVHW011257110826
845149LV00001B/161

* 9 7 8 1 4 1 8 1 8 8 7 3 3 *